Deep Dixie

Deep Dixie

◆

Annie Jones

Multnomah®Publishers *Sisters, Oregon*

DEEP DIXIE
Published by Alabaster Books
a division of Multnomah Publishers, Inc.
© 1999 by Annie Jones

International Standard Book Number: 1-59052-525-6
Previously 1-57673-411-0
Cover images by Photodisc
Cover design by Brenda McGee

All Scripture quotations, unless otherwise indicated, are taken from
The Holy Bible, New International Version (NIV) © 1973, 1984 by International Bible Society, used by permission of Zondervan Publishing House

Also quoted:
The Holy Bible, King James Version (KJV)

New American Standard Bible (NASB) © 1960, 1977 by the
Lockman Foundation

For information:
Multnomah Publishers, Inc.
P.O. Box 1720
Sisters, OR 97759

Library of Congress Cataloging–in–Publication Data
Jones, Annie, 1957–   Deep Dixie/by Annie Jones.   p.cm.
ISBN 1-59052-525-6
ISBN 1-57673-411-0 (alk. paper)   I. Title
PS3560.045744D43 1999   99-22247   813'.54–dc21   CIP

05 06 07 08 09— 10 9 8 7 6 5 4 3 2

To Elizabeth Jones Gibson,

Sylvia Jones Mudd, and

Margaret Jones McGuffey,

three true Southern belles

whose hearts are always open and

houses are so tidy it makes me want…to just give up on mine!

(What? You thought I'd say grab a broom and start cleaning my house?)

Thank you to Deanna and Janella who did not let me get lazy in my writing.

To Wordsmiths group, which is filled with such talented writers that just being allowed to share in their work inspired me to work harder at my craft.

To Susan Richardson for sharing her memories of Jackson, Mississippi, I only wish I could have used more of them, she painted such a lovely picture of it for me.

And to the Southern belles of the Southern Belle Board on America Online for talk of so many things Southern, from gardens to grits.

One

$\blacklozenge$

Even so faith, if it hath not works, is dead, being alone.

JAMES 2:17 (KJV)

THE FIRST TIME HE LAID EYES ON HER, RILEY WALKER SHOULD have known he was in over his head.

He'd been taking a sort of self-guided inspection tour of the town of Fulton's Dominion in the company pickup. He'd driven over from Deepwoods using the most beat-up of the available trucks because even as the sole owner and boss, he did not believe in taking the best for himself and leaving the people who were putting in a hard day's work with the hand-me-downs and leftovers. Besides, he had a soft spot for the fifteen-year-old truck he'd inherited from his late father, a faded blue junker with white and gray lettering on the door: Walker and Son Sawmill.

At least that's how the logo should have read. However, mud from the miles of Mississippi back roads he'd taken had caked on the grill and spattered over the door so that the most anyone could hope to make out at this point was "Walker... w...ill."

Not that the mess or the masked letters bothered him. Both he and his truck had looked a lot worse at the end of a work-day. He opened his collar another button and rubbed his neck where the unaccustomed tie had half-strangled him all morn-ing. It and his sport coat lay in a heap on the seat now, along with a file of information he needed to go over tonight. He shifted in his seat, reminding himself to tell his mother to either quit feeding him so well or to start buying jeans a size larger. Riley hated all things constricting, which was probably why he'd never married and always busted his backside to stay in business by himself. Until now.

He pulled up to one of only four stop signs marking off the corners of the placid-looking town square, then gave the sleepy scene the once-over. Lawyer's office, antique shop, women's dress shop featuring everything from sweatshirts to a bridal gown in the windows...Riley made mental note of the store-fronts he'd passed on this block. A sporting goods store, drug-store, and a doctor's office lined the street to his right; across the square, with its park benches, covered picnic area, and req-uisite monument to the heroes of the Great War of Northern Aggression, stood a furniture outlet shop, library, and town hall.

All in all, a fine little Southern town. Just the kind of place he'd like to be a part of, the kind of place that seemed far better suited as a home than a town reliant on his mill and the lum-ber industry for its livelihood. This, Riley thought, was the kind of place a man came to raise his family, grow old, and retire in peace. And, in his case, in prosperity.

He glanced again at the file, grinned, then rolled down the window to prop his elbow outside and take in the nearly spring-like February weather.

Riley liked what he saw of Fulton's Dominion. More to the point, he liked what he had found here, and what this serene place now represented to him. And it was important that he like it. He was going to become partners with the town's founding family in the community's primary source of industry and employment.

A silent partner, that was the deal. He was to have no significant duties beyond reading the monthly reports, signing the occasional piece of paperwork, and attending the quarterly meetings. For now, anyway. Riley drew in a deep breath and all but belly laughed as he exhaled. This was the opportunity of a lifetime, and it had been extended to him by none other than John Frederick Fulton-Leigh himself.

Riley still wanted to look over the records and reports on the status of the company and have his lawyer go over the contract before he signed anything. But he had little doubt that, barring anything drastic happening in the next few days, he'd sign those papers.

He couldn't afford not to. It was too smart a business move and absolutely imperative for the sake of his family. This deal was the very thing he needed to secure his daughter's future, in more ways than one. With this unexpected invitation, Fulton-Leigh—a notoriously shrewd, but big-hearted business man—had just handed Riley the answer to his prayers.

The old truck shuddered, but the engine growled in readiness to surge forward. It was Riley who hesitated. Two empty parking spots in front of the doctor's office had caught his eye. He wasn't expected back home anytime soon. Why cut this visit short when he could use the time to walk around, see things up close, maybe even shoot the breeze with a local or two? Just that quick, he made up his mind to do it, to stop and poke around town awhile to see what kind of welcome he could stir up.

He flicked on his blinker, turned the wheel in a hard right, and stomped on the gas.

The angry blare of a car horn tore through the stillness of the almost idyllic small-town scene.

The truck's brakes squealed as Riley rammed his foot down on the pedal. His entire body tensed in one hard movement, every muscle stretching, flexing, straining. He gripped the wheel and gnashed down his teeth so hard they ached, as if all that could keep his half-ton heap of metal and machinery from slamming into anyone or anything.

The truck skidded to a halt, its back end fishtailing just enough to one side to have taken the door off another car had one been in the next lane. For two or three heavy, pounding heartbeats, Riley shut his eyes and whispered some of the most sincere words of thanks to God he had ever uttered. Then he opened his eyes.

The honking culprit—a sleek, red luxury car—went gliding through the intersection, pretty as you please. Had she even paused for the stop sign? He was sure she hadn't. As for the dark-haired beauty in the driver's seat, she never so much as turned her head to see what kind of havoc her recklessness had caused. She just sailed on past, clutching the steering wheel like a championship-mad NASCAR driver with the finish line in her sights.

Riley's blood pressure rose and he leaned out the window. "Hey! There are other people using these streets lady!"

As zingers went, it stunk. Had absolutely no effect, either.

Didn't make the woman stop and realize the kind of problem her thoughtless, selfish actions might have caused. Nor did it make Riley feel any better about almost having crashed his truck or about having, for all intents and purposes, wrecked his positive impression of the town he needed to think so highly of.

He gritted his teeth. When he became a part of this community that lady had better look out. He was not going to put up with that kind of behavior in a town where he was raising his little girl. No way. No how.

He had half a mind to chase that crazed woman down and tell her as much to her face. Not because he sought out conflict so readily, but because he saw her as a danger and thought she needed to be made aware of the possible consequences of her idiotic behavior. When Riley saw something that needed tending to, he tended to it. Period.

Years ago in a high school youth group lesson, he'd been asked to find a verse that best described his outlook, a motto for living, as it were, that he could apply to all aspects of his life. Even back then Riley had no trouble singling one out. From that day forward he could quote James 2:17 word for word, and he often did just that to remind himself of who he was and what he felt God expected him to be.

"So faith by itself, if it has no works, is dead," Riley whispered, almost without being conscious of having spoken aloud.

The sentiment still summed him up pretty succinctly. He relied on his faith in God without hesitation, and from that found the confidence to carry out his faith in himself and others, and to work hard to keep that faith alive and growing in every way. In business life, family life, spiritual life, everyday life—in every way—Riley made it a point to act on his beliefs.

Right now he believed someone ought to teach the careless woman a lesson.

Her brake lights flared.

Well, maybe that someone could be him.

The red car came to a halt, right there in the middle of the street. It just sat there for a full minute, not moving forward or backward. In contrast, the three or four people inside the car had erupted in a commotion of hands waving, fingers pointing, and arms flailing. Riley even thought he heard a yappy little dog barking.

He heaved out a sigh that disguised the kind of word he usually worked hard to keep out of his vocabulary. He glanced up at the stop sign, then at another car pulling up to his left. He wondered if it mattered if he just went on or not, since three-fourths of his truck was thrust at an odd angle into the intersection. It mattered. He couldn't very well storm up and lecture that woman for running the sign if he did the same thing getting to her. He stayed put, his eyes on the car stopped in the street.

Suddenly the red car lunged forward, stopped again, then lurched into one of the empty parking spots in front of a building with a brass sign listing the names of two doctors and a physician's assistant.

"Perfect." Riley had her now.

The car to his left drove away and he took off, determined to slide into the space before him and out of his truck and nab that negligent nut before she got away from him. He slowed to pull his truck into the slot on the driver's side of the gleaming red automobile.

"What on earth?" Riley hit the brakes again.

With the flawless timing of a two-man saw operation—an exacting dance of give and take—the driver's door flung open just as Riley made the turn into the spot.

He came to a full stop.

The driver leapt out, her shoulder bag flying and bouncing against her dark purple businesslike suit. She tossed her long, black hair back over her shoulders, and used one hand to hold her skirt down. She never so much as wobbled on her high heels as she stepped, dead on, into his truck's path.

Her eyes, the set of her chin, the very way she carried herself spoke a mix of fire and fine breeding that set off warning sirens in Riley's head. Yet there remained a vulnerability about her that made him lean forward to study her a moment. Maybe it was because her reaction seemed almost like a mother bear protecting a cub. Or because beneath the polish of the clothes, the look and the bravado, she had the face of an angel and the kind of figure that never showed up in women's magazines unless it was as a "before" picture. She wasn't fat, far from it, she looked healthy and strong. She was—

"Oh, no you don't!" She planted her feet firm and threw up her hands in a move he suspected she'd perfected as a kid, lip-synching to the song "Stop in the Name of Love."

She was *amazing*. Riley couldn't hold in his grin. His one-time anger now reduced itself into a mishmash of feelings that took on the chiseled clarity of a glob of cold grits.

"Hold it right there, Bubba!" She had an accent rich as Mississippi top soil, with a full, cultivated quality that told anybody listening this lady was not somebody to be fooled with.

His grin broadened. He leaned out the truck window. "Name isn't Bubba, ma'am, it's—"

"Forgive my manners, but I don't have time for introductions. Suffice it to say, sir, that unless your name is painted on this place along with a big ol' 'Reserved for' sign, it doesn't really matter who you are. You *can't* park here." She stabbed her finger downward with a defiant flair worthy of one of her foremother's protecting the homeland from marauding Yankees.

"So just back up the Bubba-mobile and find another spot."

"Bubba-mobile?" Suddenly she didn't seem quite so charming.

A white-haired man in a rumpled business suit popped out of the front seat on the passenger side. He raised his hand in the air, one finger pointing heavenward like an old-time politician making a campaign promise, and announced, "I've got to get that wheelchair. Don't nobody go nowhere 'til I'm back."

"Wheelchair?" Riley watched the poor old fellow toddle off and disappear into the doctor's office. What kind of unthinking imbecile careens through town and runs a stop sign with an elderly gentleman in need of a wheelchair in tow?

Riley turned his attention back to the woman who had almost collided with his truck, his mind clear once again. "Listen, lady—"

"I thought I made it clear to you. I do not have time to listen. I apologize profusely for this little inconvenience, but I do think it's the least you can do for me, considering you almost came hurtling through a stop sign back there and could have done who knows what kind of damage to me and my passengers."

"I almost—? Hurtling? *Me?* Ran a stop sign?"

"No need for a confession of guilt, sir. I won't take down your license plate and turn you in." She'd been fiddling with her pocketbook and all of a sudden she whipped out a shiny black pen with gold fittings. She pulled off the cap to reveal the gold nib that looked more like a piece of art than a writing tool. She brandished the elegant thing with a flourish. "That is, I won't take down your license and such unless it becomes absolutely necessary."

"Don't threaten me, lady, threats don't impress me. Besides if anyone here needs to be taking names and kicking up a fuss with the law, it's me." He held his hand toward her. "In fact, if you'd loan me your pen a moment, I think I might do just that."

She looked at his hand as though he'd stuck out a three-day-old dead fish.

Though he had cleaned up for his business meeting, there was no hiding the calluses and scars.

She recapped the pen with a sharp click and gripped it in her fist. "I'd rather not."

He curled his fingers into a loose fist himself. "Yeah, well, maybe I shouldn't have—"

"Apology accepted." She dipped her head in a most gracious bow but kept her eyes riveted on him in an unmistakable warning not to confuse gentility with weakness.

Having been raised by a woman who could host luncheons for Ladies Bible Aid Society—complete with fingerbowls and fresh flowers, excuse herself to take him to the woodshed and tan his hide for acting up, then return in time to pour the tea— Riley was not likely to make that miscalculation. He clenched his teeth. He would never direct pure, unvarnished anger toward a woman unless she threatened the things he held most dear, but frustration? That he had no problem showing. "I wasn't apologizing. I was—"

"Just leaving?"

Frustration? He had the feeling this little gal handed it out by the bucketful. "Is this how you treat people in your town, lady? Almost run them down, pretend the near-death experience was their own doing, then deny them access to public property on a high-handed whim?"

"High-handed? I have never been called high-handed in my life!" She apparently had no reservations about showing anger when she felt justified. "I will have you know that I was raised on the principles of fairness and kindness in a family that values things like honor and morality. High-handedness is *not* the kind of thing we aspire to. I assure you, I strive to respect all God's creatures."

Had she just likened him to a *creature?* He did his best not to smile too much over how much he was genuinely enjoying her huffy display. "That's mighty decent of you, Princess Snooty-Patootie. Yes, indeed, that you would *strive* so to respect the likes of even me. Shame you don't have the same respect for the laws of the road and the rights of others using them."

"What did you call me?" Her cheeks went red. Her eyes grew wide.

On her, it looked good—but it didn't change Riley's mind. And though he couldn't believe he'd used the phrase that proved he had to find a way to communicate that neither included lumbermill swearing nor six-year-old teasing, he felt compelled to say it again. "Princess Snooty-Patootie."

"How *dare* you!" If she'd been closer, Riley had no doubt he'd have felt the sting of an old-fashioned Southern belle slap in the face. "How dare you almost plow into my car, then try to blame me, then without so much as knowing who I am or anything about me, start calling me names than imply I'm some kind of...of...spoiled princess type."

He let his expression tell her he called them as he saw them.

"Ohhh." She wrung the single syllable out between her teeth.

If she was going to say more, he didn't know because just then that red car of hers jiggled a bit.

Riley narrowed his eyes, trying to assess what was happening. But the back side of the car had one of those detachable, tinted plastic window shades pulled down, which blocked his view into the backseat.

From the far side, the back passenger door opened. A puff of hair that looked like orange-tinted cotton candy stuck out first, getting a good two or three seconds lead on the head that sported it. The woman, dressed in varying shades of clashing pink from head to toe, didn't say a thing. She seemed oblivious to Riley's huge truck or the driver's flamboyant act of putting her body in its path.

The woman just turned, stuck her head back in the car, and began making cooing sounds…as though she were coaxing someone else to get out.

That figured. This lady's car was probably like one of those cars at the circus where clown after clown after clown climbs out, and just when you think there can't possible be any more…

The woman pulled out the smallest, surliest looking bundle of fur—dressed, no less, in one of those froufrou doggie sweaters with big red hearts on it—that Riley had ever seen.

Making kissing sounds that only seemed to egg on the tiny poodle's hostilities, Cotton Candy Hair shut the car door with her hip. Hurrying off down the sidewalk, she called out, "Don't you tell your grandfather I've gone to the drugstore, you hear me? You know he's only allowed in there for lunches anymore, straight to the counter, straight out again. I won't have that ornery old sticky-fingered nincompoop wandering in there and getting us both ejected before I can pick out all the magazines I want this week."

Riley tilted his head and raised his eyebrow a bit. "Raised in a family that values honor and morality, huh?"

"So, my grandfather has a…" She shut her eyes. Something that was neither a twitch nor a wince passed over her features, she waved her hand, and just that quickly the expression disappeared. She took her pen in both hands, held it in front of her, waist level and looked him straight in the eye. "My grandfather has a problem, but at least he understands the concept of there being some places he must not go. And he heeds those boundaries like the gentleman that he is."

"And that I am not? Is that what you're saying, Princess?"

She did not reply. But then a true lady wouldn't have, would she? Riley snorted to show his opinion of her superior attitude and her imaginary "boundaries." He flexed his hands against the steering wheel. For one utterly decadent moment, he imagined gunning the engine—with the brake on, of course. One good rev that would make the old truck shake and sputter, maybe even backfire, combined with the no-nonsense look he usually saved for rowdy mill workers might just put her in her place.

Or at least move her out of his.

She glared at him, as though she knew what he was thinking and daring him to try it.

"Why am I even bothering with this?" He shook his head and forced himself to let go of the notion of parking his truck, of making his point, and most of all of reaching this woman's conscience and showing her how destructive her actions might have been. "Women like you never learn anyway. You don't take responsibility for your actions or care how your selfishness affects others. It's all about you and demanding that the world revolve around your wants and desires."

Her lips parted. The flush on her cheeks went pale.

He almost felt sorry for her, almost questioned his snap judgement. But he, of all people, understood the level of manipulation and personal denial this type of woman used. He knew firsthand the kind of devastation a woman like this, intent on having her own way, could leave in her wake. Nothing he could say or do would make one bit of difference.

He sighed. "Keep the parking space lady."

She tipped her chin up. If it was in triumph, it seemed a sad one. She mouthed a thank you.

Riley gave her a nod, his lips pressed shut. He backed the truck up just as the white-haired gentleman appeared at the door of the doctor's office pushing a wheelchair.

She stuck her pen in her jacket pocket then rushed to her grandfather. She took control of the chair but did not allow the old gent to climb on board. Instead, she took off with the thing at such a clipped pace the man did not even try to keep up.

Riley drove by slowly, wanting to make sure she knew that somebody saw her for what she really was.

She never so much as looked up at him. She just hurried to the car with the chair, set its brake, then opened the back door on the driver's side.

Figures. She wanted the spot so she could more easily load the chair she wouldn't even let her grandfather use. Of course, that was a shortsighted jump to an uncertain conclusion, but Riley did not feel particularly generous right now. He turned his attention to the road, took a moment to size up how best to get out of town and head home, then took off.

Despite his ill feelings, something in him would not let him go without one backward glance. What he saw made him feel like a world-class heel and called into question every ugly thing he'd imagined about the woman he'd just decided was beyond redemption.

At the next stop sign, he twisted his head to get a better view over his shoulder, to make sure he hadn't imagined it.

There, making use of the extra space provided by the vacant spot, the woman who seemed all flash and self-importance, helped the littlest sprite of an old, black woman out of the back-seat of the big red car and into the wheelchair. With a tenderness and patience reserved by most for their greatest treasures on earth, the younger woman settled the gnarled figure into the seat. His nemesis fussed here and there to get things situated, stood back, then stepped forward to go at it again. This time she fixed her charge's dress, making sure it covered the stick-thin legs, then set the woman's sparkling white tennis shoes on the footrests with the most delicate of care.

One trembling, bony hand touched the younger woman's arm, then reached up to tug at her jacket. The woman who had refused to let Riley use her luxurious pen, slipped it out of her pocket, handed it to the old woman, then whispered something that made her companion grin like a jack-o-lantern, missing teeth and all.

Riley exhaled slowly. He should have asked why she wanted that space, not just assumed the woman's motivation was self-ish. She might not have told him, of course. Even today in Mississippi, there were some whites who would not give up even a parking spot for the sake of a woman of color, no matter how frail or old she might be. That this fiery woman of gentle breeding stood up to some stranger in a beat-up truck—a man that she, right or wrong, thought had almost run her down—on behalf of this small, dark-skinned woman said more about her than all the assumptions Riley could concoct in a month of Sundays.

The young woman smoothed her hand over her charge's thin matte of gray and silver hair, gentle as a mother caressing a child's downy head, then leaned down and placed the sweetest of kisses on that gaunt, dark cheek. She moved around to take hold of the wheelchair and, with one flip of her hair and shake of her shoulders, put her suit and her bearing in order.

As she wheeled her charge forward, like a lady-in-waiting bearing the queen of the land, Riley couldn't help smiling to himself again. Fulton's Dominion was going to be the right place for him to raise his daughter after all. He just knew it.

Two

Consider it all joy, my brethren,
when you encounter various trials, knowing that the
testing of your faith produces endurance.

JAMES 1:2 (NASB)

DIXIE'S WHOLE BODY ACHED. HER HEAD, HER NECK, HER STOMACH, her calves...everything right down to her toes resonated with dull, throbbing weariness. *That* she could handle, of course. A hot bath, a couple of aspirin, and those discomforts would pass. What she could not so easily rid herself of was the building sense of worry and dread that gnawed at her already frayed nerves. Those amplified her grief and left her feeling more alone than she had ever felt in her entire life.

She missed her daddy. Plain and simple. She mourned him as much today as she had just over a week ago when a heart attack had taken him away.

Dixie clutched an overstuffed cushion from the display sofa, which sat with its back to a big plate-glass window in the showroom of Fulton's Fine Furniture Outlet Store. She closed her eyes and curled forward over her tightly crossed legs. Still, even in her melancholy, she was careful not to let her simple black dress hike up too much or to do anything that could be called unladylike.

She was, after all, Dixie Prescott Fulton-Leigh, daughter of John Frederick Fulton-Leigh, great-granddaughter of Samuel Prescott Fulton. Her great-grandfather had founded this town where even now every family had at least one person working for, retired from, or hoping to get on at Fulton's Fine Furniture Manufacturing or one of its connected businesses. She had a heritage to live up to, an expectation both past and present to think of. It was only that very old, Southern school of thinking—that notion of propriety, duty, and comportment drilled into her since childhood—that kept her from curling into a ball right now and crying her heart out.

Her daddy's death may have made her feel like a lost little girl, but that did not mean she had the luxury of wallowing in self-pity or grief. Dixie knew, little-girl-lost feelings notwithstanding, that she was a grown woman with very grown-up responsibilities pressing down on her. And if she didn't get back to work now, those responsibilities could well push her under. And take the better part of Fulton's Dominion, Mississippi, with her.

"Are you all right, Miss Fulton-Leigh?" Mavis Hornby, who last month would have addressed Dixie by her first name or by some generic endearment like *Sugar,* hovered nearby. "Is there something I can get for you?"

Dixie thought of the coffee—black-as-crude-oil and almost as thick—that Mavis always kept warming on the crusty coffeemaker in the back of the showroom. She stopped herself from making a face and managed to just shake her head. "No, thank you. I really need to get back to work. That seems to be the only thing that helps me much, staying busy."

"I know what you mean. If it's any comfort to you, I hope you know that everyone who worked for your father is deeply saddened by his passing." Mavis's voice cracked, she paused for a moment, visibly composing herself, then went on. "Everyone here at the outlet store, over at the manufacturing plant, even everyone out at the transportation and delivery station, they weren't just workers to your daddy, they were…they were real people that mattered to him."

Dixie noted how Mavis had stopped short of the obvious, saying their employees were like family to her father. She supposed she could think of it as a show of respect. More than likely, though, it was because no one really wanted to be counted as kin, even in sentiment, to the people who lived in the huge old mansion on South Dominion Avenue.

She set aside the oatmeal-colored throw pillow she'd been hugging, not quite able to meet Mavis's gaze. "Thank you. It is nice to hear how much Daddy meant to people."

"We…we'll all miss him very much."

"Yes, I know that his hands-on approach made this business very special to this town." And made the pressure on her all the more intense. She stroked her hand down the woven pattern on the pillow, gave it a pat, then finally looked up to the other woman. "You may have thought that because I spent most of my time on the road doing sales and marketing for the company, that I didn't realize what a special bond Daddy had with everyone here. But I want you to know—" she reached out and gave Mavis's hand a quick, heartfelt squeeze—"I do."

Mavis nodded. She tightened her grip for an instant, then

let her fingers slip from Dixie's. It would have been a fine cue for the older woman to make her excuses and get out of there. Instead, she lingered, wringing her hands together as if there were something more she still needed to cull from this conversation.

Dixie uncrossed her legs. Maybe giving the appearance that she was about to get up and go might spur Mavis to say whatever it was she was holding in.

Apparently it worked. "Miss Fulton-Leigh?"

"Yes?"

"Are you sure..."

She left it dangling there in a way that made Dixie's bone-weary body tense. If there was one thing Dixie wasn't right now, it was *sure*...of anything.

"Are you sure there isn't something I can get for you?" The words rushed out like a kid trying to run a weak fib past a parent.

"No, thank you, Mavis. I'm fine. I just stopped to rest a minute and that gave me time to let my emotions get the better of me, I think."

"Yes, I can understand how that could happen." Mavis moved closer. She sniffled, turning to look out the window as if seized by a sudden fascination for the main street of the tiny town where nothing truly interesting had happened since the much ballyhooed bottle rocket incident that ruined the Fourth of July parade two years ago come summer. "Today I ran into your grandfather at the drugstore lunch counter. He gave me one of his business cards, like he does, you know?"

Dixie nodded.

"And durned if I didn't tuck that card in my pocket to bring back to give to your father." Mavis withdrew the crisp, rectangular card from her shirt pocket. She sniffled again, her eyes brimming with tears. "I was halfway up the stairs to his office before I remembered your daddy wouldn't be there to take the thing, laugh, and file it in the box he keeps to give to your grandfather whenever the Judge says he needs a new batch of business cards."

Dixie smiled. "You'd have thought Grandpa would have caught onto that trick, wouldn't you? Everyone giving those cards back to Daddy? He's been recycling the same box for years now, I think."

"Well, your grandfather never had cause to question it because he had a lot of faith in anything your daddy did. And no one ever told the Judge about the cards because there was no harm in it, far as I can see." Mavis held the business card gingerly, probably being cautious not to smudge or bend it. Her voice held a certain air of caution, too, a quiet kind of testing-the-waters quality that put Dixie's own emotions on alert as the woman continued. "You know, your father had a way of inspiring fierce loyalty and an almost unquestioning trust in everyone he dealt with. Everyone knew they could count on your father, for sure."

Dixie swallowed hard, trying to force down her apprehensions about the implications of Mavis's remark—and what she suspected lay behind it.

"A lot of people are wondering if things would still be the same, Miss Fulton-Leigh." Mavis extended her hand with the card between two fingers. "With the Judge's business cards, I mean."

That wasn't what she meant at all. Dixie could tell from the woman's wary expression. Her eyes said what not a one of her employees would tell Dixie to her face: they were just as scared as she was about this unforeseen, drastic change of command. Probably more so, because even if she ran this business into the ground, Dixie would still have a home, a means to keep dinner on the table, and a future.

Too many of the folks who took home a paycheck that now bore her signature could not say the same thing.

What would she tell those people if she failed? How would she ever make it up to them if she simply could not do what was required of her? Self-doubt gripped her. Who was she to think that she could do this at all?

The plea for reassurances shone in Mavis's eyes.

Dixie's mouth went dry. Who was *she,* that so many people would dare depend on her?

"Who are you?"

Dixie could practically hear the voice of Miss Lettie, the woman who had raised three generations of her family including Dixie herself, ringing in her ears. The gruff but stalwart, long-retired maid with wisdom of nearly one hundred years of living on God's earth would not abide this feeling sorry for one's self. She'd shake her gnarled fist and admonish Dixie, *"You are a vessel of the living Lord, an heir to the kingdom of glory, a princess…"*

Dixie tensed at the title. Another voice that she had been trying to keep out of her thoughts these last two weeks sprang from her memory: *"Is that what you're saying, Princess Snooty-Patootie?"*

With vivid detail she recalled her run-in with that… that…that…stubborn yahoo. That belligerent, wild driver who thought being a strong woman who knew how to stand her ground meant she was putting on airs and acting high-handed. That…that *man* with the unruly waves of black hair that all but begged for a woman's touch. She flexed her fingers. And the eyes that sparked with mischief even as they hinted at something much more dangerous.

She smoothed down her collar. The man who had made up

his mind about Dixie without even knowing her and who had not been any too kind in doing it. She let her hand fall to her side. The creep.

Miss Lettie had quoted from James that day to quiet Dixie's frazzled nerves: *"Count in all joy, my brethren, when you meet various trials for you know that the testing of your faith produces steadfastness."*

Dixie had joked then that she ought to be downright steadfast out of her mind with joy after dealing with that arrogant jerk. Then she'd added that she counted herself tested enough for quite a while, thank you. Lettie had giggled. Little did they know what was to come just two short days later...

Dixie blinked and realized Mavis was still standing there, waiting. She glanced down at the card held out before her, and noticed the slight tremble in the older woman's hand.

Who was she that so many people would dare depend on her? Dixie straightened her shoulders. She was the last best hope for her town, her family, and her business. Her parents were both gone, her aunt and grandfather were worse than no help at all. She was the only one left to do what needed to be done. She was a vessel of the living Lord, whose faith would prove steadfast. She had the strength of her upbringing, the aid of her education, the drive to do the right thing, and the tenacity to see this through. *That's* who she was. That's who she had no other choice but to be.

And sitting here feeling sorry for herself was simply not an option. Dixie stood slowly. She smiled with genuine affection and gratitude as she reached out to accept the white card with the neatly embossed black lettering. "You tell everyone who's wondering that I will do everything within my power to see that things stay the same, Mavis. Starting with recycling Grandpa's business cards."

"Thank you, Miss Fulton-Leigh." Mavis reached out and caught Dixie up in a brief, impromptu hug, which Dixie happily returned.

A shrill beep signaled that someone had just come in the showroom door.

Mavis pulled away. "I'd better see to that."

"Sure. I've got to get on upstairs to the office myself. I have a meeting with Daddy's attorney—*my* attorney—this afternoon. I'd like to see what I can get sorted out on my own before he gets here. Don't worry, Mavis, everything will work out just fine." Dixie gave a little salute with the business card. Chin up, she headed for Daddy's office and her first real taste of those trials she would have to face and overcome in order to keep her promise.

Riley sat with his elbow sticking out the open window of one of the newer company trucks. He and Red Braden, the man who would take over most of the running of the mill now that Riley had sold it, had made a long day of it, and they still weren't back at the office a good hour after quitting time. When the phone rang in the truck's luxury cab, and Riley heard who it was, he pulled over to the side of the dirt road to take the call from Mr. Fulton-Leigh's attorney.

"Yes, hello. We didn't meet the day I came to Fulton's Dominion, but, of course, I am aware of your firm's involvement. Thank you for returning my calls." *Finally.* Riley knew enough proper business etiquette not to say it out loud. He had pushed open the truck door and turned sideways, to give himself both light and leg room. "I was a little concerned, Mr. Greenhow. You see, Mr. Fulton-Leigh and I last spoke the day after our first negotiations. We'd made a verbal agreement to go ahead with the deal, and he promised that papers reflecting the minor changes I specified were to be drawn up. It's been ten days now and—"

The attorney, Howard Greenhow, jumped in, speaking in harsh, clipped words as he spilled out a blunt, unemotional explanation that ended with a curt "good-bye" and the unequivocal *click* of an abrupt hang-up.

"Yeah, well, good-bye to you, too." Riley swung his legs back inside the cab and slumped in the seat, leaving the door open despite the late February evening's chill.

"What?" Red's round face scrunched up into more lines and furrows than a fancy wrinkled pup. "Something go haywire?"

Riley shook his head in disbelief. "I don't know whether to cuss or cry."

"It'd have to be something pretty awful to make *you* do either one, I guarantee. So I take it this is something big."

Riley managed a dispirited smile at that. "If you count having most of what you've based your future on suddenly all take a nosedive as big, then yes, it's something big."

"The old man check out of the deal?"

"The old man checked out of everything, my friend." Riley exhaled in a hard, quick huff but that didn't relieve the heaviness sitting high in his chest. "He died, the day after I last spoke to him."

"Sorry to hear it." Red removed his hard hat and held it to his chest, bowing his head. Riley noted the gesture with a shake of his head. Of all the traditions and rituals prominent among long-time Southerners, a respect for those who'd passed on, even strangers, remained unflinching. When the other man lifted his head and replaced the hat over his blazing red hair, he shrugged. "So it sort of threw a monkey wrench into your business deal, huh?"

"Yeah." Riley nodded. "I'm heartsick about that, too. I won't deny it. But I also feel bad about the man himself. I *liked* that guy, Red. I honestly looked forward to being in business with him, not just with his company but with *him.*"

Red didn't seem to know what to do with his hands.

Riley understood his uneasiness. Good-ol'-boy heart-to-heart talks seldom occurred in these parts without the aid of at least one six-pack, or a hunting trip, or a really good story about your favorite hound dog. But Riley had just had his whole world turned wrong-side-up and he felt like talking, so he pressed on.

"You know, I saw a little bit of myself in John Frederick, in the way he wanted to make sure the company he owned stood for something more than the bottom line. The way he didn't tolerate a bunch of pretense or any insincerity." Riley gave a little laugh. "Did I tell you about how right after I met with John Frederick I came across this woman who—"

"You told me. You told everyone, boss. Twice."

Riley nodded, smiling still at the memory of his last sight of her.

"I guess I feel bad that I misjudged her like that, probably in part because I was all worked up about the things Fulton-Leigh had just told me. You know, how he'd gone on about how much he loved his daughter and how he had to do what was best for her future by bringing fresh blood into the organization. It got to me because that's just how I feel about my Wendy. I was thinking all about how I was going to move to Fulton's Dominion and how much better a place it would be to raise my girl than a mill town. Then that woman sort of upset my little apple cart and I wasn't very nice to her."

"Yeah, you told me. *Twice.*"

"What does that all matter now anyway?" Riley rubbed one

hand back over his hair. "The deal isn't going through. None of those things I'd hoped and planned for are going to happen now at all."

"What are you saying, boss?"

"The deal. It's as dead as the man who offered it to me." The minute Riley heard the hardness of his own words, he hastened to add, "God rest his soul."

Red mumbled a sympathetic agreement then scratched at the back of his thick neck. "But you'd reached some kind of agreement with Fulton-Leigh. Ain't his family obliged to honor that?"

"Nothing was signed." Riley pulled the truck door shut with enough force to communicate his animosity over the whole mess to anyone within hearing distance.

"The man shook your hand on it." Red frowned. "He gave you his word. Don't that count for nothing?"

"According to this attorney, it doesn't. Seems this fellow pretty much has taken control of the whole works for now. He told me he has power of attorney for the older pair of Fulton-Leigh's survivors, so even if the family wanted to honor any deal the old man had cooking, this man could veto it without breaking a sweat."

"Veto it, change it, or push it through against the family's wishes, it sounds like. Lawyers!" Red set his jaw and squinted out the windshield like a man spoiling for a fight. "They go and ruin everything."

"Not all of 'em, Red. Not all of 'em."

"Oh, sorry, forgot that you're dating one, boss." Red ducked his head.

Am not, he wanted to say, but everyone in town thought different and the lady lawyer in his life had done nothing to set the record straight. *We're good friends,* he wanted to tell Red, *that's all.*

Companions for dinner on Friday nights, someone to sit by in church…that was it. There was no future there. That's what he wanted to tell Red, but he didn't. He'd never let Carol believe that he would ever return her feelings. Still, as a gentleman—and he was one despite what certain princess-types with their Bubba-mobile cracks might think—he wouldn't humiliate Carol.

"This lawyer, Greenhow, let me know right off that the deal had not been finalized and therefore was not valid." Riley hooked his thumb in the steering wheel. "Called himself the 'go-to guy' on all that family's business from now on out. Said there would be no need to bring in another partner as long as he maintained control. Said it kind of snotty, too. Like he didn't think my money was good enough for them now that he was in charge of everything."

"Your money has always been good enough for me, boss. I've been mighty proud to work for you and your father before he passed on all these years."

"You sound like you're making a farewell speech, Red, ol' buddy." Riley chuckled.

"Well, ain't I?" Red took his hat off again, this time turning it so as to give the impression he'd become absorbed in adjusting the band inside as he spoke from the heart. "You sold the mill already, boss. That deal *is* signed, all legal-like. Done and done. The new company has moved me up to take things over and come Monday we'll have a new logo and letterhead on all our transactions. I don't think there's a thing you can do about that, can you?"

"I still have an obligation to Wendy. I said I'd cut back my hours and move her to a better home and I will. I've just got to find another investment that's as good as the one I just lost."

"I wish you all the best, boss." Red's handshake spoke so eloquently of gratitude and respect that it humbled Riley a little to be on the receiving end of it.

"Thanks." Riley released Red's hand and started up the truck. "We'd better head back to the mill. Wendy's got some kind of ballet recital practice tonight, and I said I'd pick her up at 8:30 because my mother hates to drive after dark. If I'm late, Momma's bound to volunteer me to work at the real recital, so I can't make the same mistake on the big night."

"Maybe you ought to call her now to let her know you're on your way then. I know I always get extra points for doing that kind of thing around my place."

"Good thinking, Red." Riley grabbed up his cellular phone and began punching in the number, more to show his confidence in the new mill manager's advice than because he felt the need to check in at home. Momma had everything under control. She always did. That was one thing Riley never had to worry about. He pressed the send button then lowered the mouthpiece to talk to Red. "One thing I'll miss at whatever new venture I take, having you around to help keep me in line."

"Don't care about keeping you in line as much as I want to keep you out of one of them frilly tutu thingies," Red grumbled.

"Huh?" The phone began to ring on the other end.

"You said if she got mad your Momma was going to make you be in the show..." Red let his voice trail off. He looked so tickled with himself that you'd have thought he swallowed a feather.

Riley rolled his eyes. The phone kept ringing. "She'd volunteer me to work the concession stand or take tickets or something, not dance around in a tutu."

"Bet they'd make more money having you prance around on stage than having you dish up cheese nachos and pour warm, flat beer."

"Red, it's a little girls' dance recital, they don't serve—" Riley stopped mid-sentence to click off the power on the phone. He didn't understand why he hadn't gotten an answer, and suddenly that took precedence over this silly conversation. He stared out at the darkness and the desolate road ahead. "That's weird. Momma didn't pick up the phone. That's not like her at all, she just can't stand to let a phone ring."

"Maybe she went out—"

"She doesn't drive after dark."

"Maybe some friend came and got her and took her out."

"Yeah, maybe." Riley reached for the phone again. "Maybe I'd better try calling once more. Maybe I made a mistake in dialing or—"

With his hand just inches above the phone, it let out its shrill mechanical ring.

Riley snatched it up. "Walker here."

"Mr. Walker, good," the voice on the other end said in a solemn monotone. "You don't know me. I'm with the county ambulance service and we're in your home. We heard the phone ringing just as we got here and so I checked the caller ID and called back, hoping I'd get you or at least a trustworthy friend we could notify."

"Notify?" Riley tried to make sense of it all but the man might as well have been speaking another language. "Notify of what? You say you're in my home? Is my mother there? What's going on? Has something happened to my daughter? To my mother? What?"

"Mr. Walker, please. I can't stop and go over it all with you now but your mother has had a bad fall. She's conscious, but dazed and in pain. There's no way of telling for sure, but I'd wager she's broken a bone, maybe even banged her head a little. We're on our way to County General Medical Center, now. Can you meet us there?"

Riley checked his watch. His mother needed him, but Wendy would be waiting for him soon. He'd never been in a position like this before. In every other emergency situation he'd encountered since he'd taken Wendy in to raise as a baby almost seven years ago, his mother had been the person he relied on, his safety net. He had to make a choice now and he did not like it, not one bit. Still, he knew what he had to do. "I have to pick my daughter up first."

"Well, get there when you can. County General. Do you know where it is?"

"Yes. I'm on my way." Riley tossed the phone to Red for the other man to turn off and hang up. He pulled his truck onto the quiet road and drove—drove and prayed with all his heart that everything would be all right.

It had to be all right. It just had to be.

Three

---◆---

The prayer of a righteous man is powerful and effective.
JAMES 5:16B

"I AM SO MAD AT DADDY FOR DYING AND LEAVING ME IN THIS awful mess that I could just…strangle him!"

Dixie pushed aside a bulging green and brown ledger held together with a succession of faded red rubber bands, each more stretched to its limit than the next, and every one threatening to snap at the slightest provocation. The movement sent a shower of pink and yellow receipts and bills of lading cascading off her father's huge antique desk. "This is just so unlike him, to have things in such disorder. I know he was trying to put some deal together because he mentioned it when we last spoke, but the only evidence I can find of that is the way everything else was left unattended."

"I've told you and I've told you, Miss Fulton-Leigh, you do

not have to tackle this all at once." Howard, the junior Greenhow of Greenhow, Greenhow, Byson, and Pryor, Attorneys at Law, bent to collect the papers she'd spilled onto the deep blue and green, handloomed rug. "Settling your father's estate, getting up to speed on his records, learning about his business, plus tax information, and payroll and personal accounting practices—it's a huge undertaking, Miss Fulton-Leigh."

He snatched up a pink receipt then placed it quite precisely on the desk.

Dixie watched as three more papers slid off to take that bill's place.

"Tremendous, one might say." He gathered together a handful of pages in both pastel pink and yellow then added them to the lurching pile with a firm pat as if to warn them to stay put.

Dixie stared at the haphazard reminder of her own struggle to sort out her father's usually well-organized records. Greenhow was some kind of fool if he thought he could hold back the inevitable. Just as Dixie would be some kind of fool to think her drive and determination alone could bring order to the turmoil her father had left behind. She trusted in aid from the highest source, that God held her life and well-being in his loving and capable hands, but she also knew that she needed earthly assistance and she needed it soon. Otherwise...

The tower of paperwork representing her newly acquired and ever-mounting responsibilities wobbled, then seemed to settle.

Greenhow sighed.

A single page rustled.

The lawyer sucked in his breath, thrusting his hand out, stiff-armed.

Too late.

Without any further warning, the whole, deranged heap

surged off the side of the desk, swishing and hissing and flapping as the papers poured downward like rain gushing down a gully.

It did not surprise Dixie how much it soothed her to sit and watch the chaos empty itself onto the floor of Daddy's meticulously appointed office. How she longed to just let go like that. To let everything come swooshing out until there was no more care or worry or grief left. Just imagining herself doing that very thing eased her pinched and knotted muscles a little.

Greenhow started to bend again to begin retrieving the papers.

Dixie coughed.

The three pages remaining sloughed off the edge of the desk to cover his oxblood, wingtip shoes. He pulled up short, snorted, and let the papers be. "As I was saying, this is really too much to take on, especially for…" He drew the last word out, making a gesture with his hand like someone playing a game of charades. But instead of seeming to coax her to finish the statement, he gave more the impression of someone trying to avoid saying something vulgar in mixed company.

She gave him a blank look.

It did not encourage him to elaborate. He just churned his hand in the air with more embellishment and said, "Especially for…"

"For…" She mimicked the man's inflection flawlessly, letting her voice trail off just as he had, though she did forego his weak, wincing expression. It was a business trick she'd learned from her daddy, throwing someone's words back at them, then nailing them with an icy glare. It often nudged a conscience toward the truth or, lacking that, embarrassed a person into blurting out what they really meant just to fill the awkward silence.

Her father never did cotton to innuendo or coy implications. Anyone who did business with or on behalf of John Frederick Fulton-Leigh spoke their mind right out. Either that or they kept their mouths shut. If she ever hoped to fill her father's shoes—she glanced down at her size 7 sling-back heels and corrected herself—if she ever hoped to step into her father's position in work and in the community, she could accept no less from her associates than he would.

She propped her elbows up and laced her fingers together. At thirty-two, with a good fifteen pounds extra padding on her and the kind of air-brushed complexion only a stacked genetic deck could provide, she knew she wasn't as scary as Daddy had been. But she had caught a glimpse of herself in the powder room mirror just before this meeting began. With pale, blue-purple bags under her eyes and her hair pulled back in a low, tightly coiled bun that could hardly be distinguished from the collar of her black silk dress, she looked frightful enough. She set her jaw and pierced Mr. Greenhow with a hard look, goading him to finish what he had started.

The lawyer coughed. Of course, it was a fake cough. He didn't even hold Dixie in high enough regard to pretend it was anything else by covering his mouth when he did it. Other than that, he made not one sound to attempt to excuse or explain himself.

Daddy would have thrown the man out the door for less— if the lawyer were lucky. She glanced heavenward, not seeking divine guidance but to steal a quick peek at the familiar bullet hole her father had left unpatched in the office ceiling. Daddy had his ways of dealing with people, mostly relying on his reputation, power, and persona. When they didn't work he found more creative approaches to get what he wanted.

Dixie, however, did not have her father's large frame, cold

eyes, booming voice, or personality—one so big it projected out from his physical form like an aura of electricity that could be either benevolent or dangerous. No, she did not have her father's presence to call upon. Or his skill with firearms. What she *did* have was his absolute refusal to put up with snobbery, arrogance, or nonsense from someone hired to provide professional input.

She dropped her palms to the desk and leaned forward. "It's too much to take on for what, Mr. Greenhow? A woman?"

She refrained from saying "a little woman" or "a pretty, fickle, frivolously rich woman," even though those were the words she suspected had run through the middle-aged lawyer's balding head. Dixie eyed him over the mound of file folders still scattered before her.

This man, with all his paper rattling, negativity, and now foggy innuendo had just gotten on her very last nerve. Not an easy thing to do, by most people's account. She knew all too well that talk around town painted her as some kind of saint capable of putting up with things far beyond the reach of most human endurance—most notably, her family.

That bump in her train of thought made her tilt her head to one side and hone her gaze even more keenly on the man standing possessively in the dead center of Daddy's office. "Or perhaps you were alluding to some failing in the Fulton, Cunningham, and/or Fulton-Leigh gene pool?"

She rattled off all the variations of her family's surnames, though folks in town still tended to refer to them all succinctly as *The Fultons*. There had been no actual *Fulton* in town since her great-grandfather died in 1950. It had been a smart business move on her father's part to hyphenate his family name, Leigh, with the old family name—just a gentle reminder of who his family was and how they were connected to the town's founder and the town's only factory.

"Were you going to say this job is too much to take on for someone from my family, Mr. Greenhow?"

"No, now, I did not say any such a thing." He raised his hand.

She noted that he sported a bona fide manicure. He had to have gone a far piece away from tiny Fulton's Dominion, Mississippi, to have gotten that without causing tongues to wag. "What extravagance," folks would say, shaking their heads. "Who does that Howard Greenhow think he is? Some movie star? Some TV lawyer? Certainly throws his money away like one."

"Mr. Greenhow, it appears to me that my family's business has provided a very nice lifestyle for the members of your law firm." It wasn't as blatant as accusing him of squandering cash like a TV lawyer but it got the point across.

"We worked for every penny we've earned, I assure you."

She nodded, managing an amicable smile. "And you stand to earn even more should you convince me I am unequal to taking on my father's obligations, because you will then do it for me. With due compensation, of course."

"Are you making some kind of accusation, Miss Fulton-Leigh?"

"No, but I have the feeling *you* are, Mr. Greenhow." Her pulse fluttered like a scared rabbit's but she dared not back down now. Fear and uncertainty would not win out today; she would be strong and sure. She would be her father's daughter and starting now she would not let anyone ever doubt that. "Why don't you just come out and say what you mean? I can tell you want to leave me with the impression that I should not even try to deal with my daddy's business and I want to hear why you think that."

A thin veil of sweat beaded up on the man's now-flushed forehead. "Well, there have been some questions...some speculations...some..."

"Down and dirty, mealy-mouthed, too-good-to-be-true and too-juicy-to-be-kept-to-yourself gossip?" She was just trying to help the man get to the meat of things.

"Some *conjectural* discourse." He ignored her help, mopped his brow with a white handkerchief he'd produced from his pocket, and went on without missing a beat. "Myself, I have nothing but respect for the way your father has conducted himself professionally."

"But?"

"*But...*" He bobbed his head as he spoke, his gestures close to his body. "You can see for yourself that your father had begun to let things slip these last few months. Now, you weren't around to notice it like others might have been, seeing as your...work—" he ground out the word like he felt her contribution to the company had been anything but work—"took you out of town for often weeks at a time. Still and all you can certainly see the evidence now of how things have begun to deteriorate around here."

She couldn't deny that. Daddy's office had always been immaculate. He'd always promptly overseen every piece of business that went on in the company he had started in 1965 with the Fulton family's financial backing. She scanned the disarray, the bills and invoices left scattered and stacked everywhere.

She wet her lips, unsure she really wanted an answer to the question she was about to ask. "So, does all this—" she slung her arm out to indicate the confusion of paper everywhere— "mean the company is in some kind of serious trouble?"

"No, No!" He paced a few steps, tentatively, as if he were

stalking something ellusive.

She sighed in relief. "I thought not."

He pivoted on his heel and went in for the kill. "I'd have never allowed that to happen!"

"My *father* would never have allowed that to happen." She would not allow this little man to trod on Daddy's memory to put himself and his firm in a better position to move in and take things over. "And let me assure you, Mr. Greenhow, neither will I."

"Of course." He tugged at his tie. "Of course. It's just that things are currently a bit disorganized and there are a few problems that need immediate attention before they get out of hand."

"Such as?"

He narrowed one eye at her and frowned. Or maybe the growing irritation with her that affected his stance and the tightness in his voice now had him squinting and grimacing involuntarily. "Frankly, Miss Fulton-Leigh, your payroll is too big and your benefits package too generous, for starters."

"And it's your advice that this company should cut back on those?" She'd heard Daddy rail against Greenhow's ideas before. They had been the family attorneys since the senior Greenhow, a childhood friend of her father's, had drawn up the incorporation papers over thirty years ago. He'd kept them on because they were hometown folks, an old friend, he'd said. But Dixie thought her daddy probably actually liked locking horns with stubby old Howard now and then, especially since Daddy never had any doubt over who would win out in those contests of will and opinion.

Dixie, on the other hand, found it all distasteful and a waste of precious time. So she played Greenhow's part for him to hurry things along. "While we're at it, maybe we should think about using a lower grade of materials in our furniture? The customers won't know they're sitting on inferior padding, fabric, frames. Who's going to tell them? The workers we haven't laid off will be too afraid for their jobs to speak up. Meanwhile, the company will be able to lay back and rest easy on the nice, fat cushion of a larger bottom line."

"You say it like I'm suggesting you should steal milk money from grade-schoolers and rob little old ladies of their life-savings tucked away in the sugar jar."

"Well, aren't you?"

He clenched his jaw so tightly his lips turned practically white.

She supposed that was the only answer she would get from him on that.

"Actually, those are just some ideas of mine, some areas that need to be addressed." He smiled. It was the kind of smile that made her feel like brushing off unseen cobwebs and other creepy things. "There are other issues here, at the plant. The trucking department must be seen to right away. Someone has to step in and oversee that, and you know your grandfather won't—"

"Let's leave my grandfather out of this, please."

"Then that leads us right to another concern, your...personal domain? That might prove very distracting if someone really needed to focus all her energy on business."

She knew exactly what he was getting at, but she wanted to hear him say it. "Go on."

Greenhow raised his chin, or at least one of them. "We have, many of us who worked so closely with your father, found ourselves...more than a little concerned...over the ways in which your father, for want of a better word, *indulged* his family members..."

"Indulged." She drew the word out in a rich, hushed tone, like someone savoring the first taste of fine chocolate. "Ahhh. Now we're getting to it, aren't we?"

A look of studied deliberation clouded Greenhow's face. He rocked back and forth, sizing her up, clearly calculating just how much of his thinly concealed contempt she would stand for.

A pity he didn't know he'd passed that mile marker a long time ago. Dixie rose slowly from the worn leather chair where her daddy had commanded his empire for the last thirty-odd years. She strained to maintain control over every aching muscle and managed, out of sheer determination, not to let this man see any weakness in her.

Greenhow drew a breath and cocked his head. He opened his mouth as if preparing to say something big, or maybe he planned to try to cut her down to size.

She never gave him the chance. Grit and grace were her God-given gifts, and she utilized them both. Straightening her back and folding her arms over her chest, she pinned him with a look. "You are trying to say, as tactfully as you know how, I'm sure, that this is too taxing a job for a spoiled Southern belle whose only training comes from a few years in a cushy job marketing the family business. That it is far beyond the grasp of someone so woefully unprepared to tackle the real, day-to-day trials of running the Fultons' businesses, much less handle the delicate financial conundrums of managing my great-grandfather's fortune."

"It's a big job for anyone," he muttered, his pudgy fingers clawing at the small knot in his silk tie. "I was only trying to suggest—"

"Oh, I know what you want to suggest, Mr. Greenhow. I know what you'd tell me to my face, were you not so impressed with yourself and your pitiful game of cat and mouse. You'd tell me that the world of business and money is no place for a woman like me. That I should let you handle everything."

"We are more familiar with the…situation here, Miss Fulton-Leigh, and able to take the reins immediately." The deep, garbled tone of his words belied the heart-attack-red color in his face.

"So, I should just let you get on with the real work? Don't ask questions? Don't get involved? You'll take care of every little thing on the business front? And me? I can go home and attend to the kind of thing I am far better suited for—" she lowered her voice to a quiet rumble—"playing warden over the family nuthouse."

His eyes widened.

"Is that what you're trying to say, Mr. Greenhow?"

He pulled himself up to his full five-feet-two-inches and puffed out his chest. "I would never describe you or your family that way, Miss Fulton-Leigh."

"Well, not to my face, you wouldn't." Her sarcasm was borne more of exhaustion than of ill manners.

And she *was* tired. More tired than she had ever thought it humanly possible to be. She plopped back in her chair and put her hand to her forehead, relishing the coolness of her fingertips against her throbbing temple.

"I hope you don't take this the wrong way, Miss Fulton-Leigh, but it's not a bad thing for you to realize that you may not be able to tend to everything you've just been handed all by yourself. You need some help."

"You mean a *man's* help?"

"I mean *help*. I won't pretend that I don't think a man's help—a *husband's* help, perhaps—wouldn't be in order long about now."

"A husband." The whispered word created a gentle buzz on

Dixie's lips. Greenhow wasn't the first person to remind her that in this hour of need a husband might have come in pretty handy.

Dixie herself had thought it off and on many times since she got the call that her daddy was being rushed to the hospital. She touched her fingertips to her hairline then stopped herself from trying to run them through the triple layer of styling spritz that kept her hair tightly to her head.

A husband. Someone that she could lean on and trust, someone she could depend on for support and safekeeping. A person who would always be there for her, listen to her. Someone who would give as much to the relationship as Dixie did, who would cherish and appreciate her, even if he did not always agree with her. Someone she could completely trust as a partner—in business and in life. Did such a creature exist?

If he did, Dixie had not happened upon him yet. She'd thought she had a couple of times but, sadly, the men she had believed capable of that depth of commitment had proved her terribly wrong. Relationships of all kinds, according to Dixie's experience, equaled one-sided responsibility. Who needed more of that in their lives? Certainly not she.

Despite the sorrowful pang of loneliness that welled up inside her, she lifted her chin, sniffled, and echoed the sentiment again in her mind. *Who needed a husband? Certainly not Dixie Fulton-Leigh.*

"Thank you, for your frankness, Mr. Greenhow. I will give your suggestion all the consideration it's due." She folded her hands and watched a vile smugness creep over his entire disposition. When the attitude had consumed him from his ruddy face to his practically dancing toes, she swallowed back a bitter taste in her mouth and squared her shoulders. "That'll just about do it, I think. Good-bye, Mr. Greenhow."

"You mean you're taking my advice and leaving all this for another time?" *Greed-inspired glee.* No other words could describe the lilt in his tone.

"No." She leaned back. The seat groaned and sighed under her weight. Over the years the supple leather of that old chair had conformed itself to her father's frame so that though it had sat empty for nearly two weeks now, it still held the outline of his broad shoulders. For only a fleeting instant it felt like Daddy was wrapping her up in one of his big hugs, the kind that drove away her every fear and doubt and made her feel she could be loved and safe forever.

Then the feeling passed and she looked up into Greenhow's disdainful face. "No, Mr. Greenhow, I mean you're fired."

"But you can't…" The redness flushed from his face and he blinked, his jaw slack. Then he drew in a deep breath and glowered at her. "You don't fully understand what's involved here, what's at stake…Your father—"

"My father is gone and I will not do business with someone who holds my workers, my customers, me, my father, and my surviving family in the kind of shallow, mean-spirited contempt you've shown today. Now get out of my office, or I will have you escorted out."

"This is not finished." He wagged a finger at her even as he moved to make his exit.

"It is for you and your firm, I assure you." She feigned an intense interest in the ledger she'd shoved aside earlier.

"Just because you are a member of this town's founding family, does not mean you can run roughshod over reality, Miss Fulton-Leigh." He stood with one foot in the office and one in the hall, his lips pale and tight, his eyes bulging. "And the reality is that you will regret this move—sooner rather than later. There are problems here at Fulton's Fine Furniture that you are not taking into consideration. Problems I sincerely doubt you have any hope of knowing how to handle."

She supposed she might have taken the threat more seriously had it not come out of someone who looked like a snapping turtle in a chokehold. As it was, she waved her hand, hummed an acknowledgment, and said, "My new lawyer will be equal to that task, Mr. Greenhow. He or she will be in touch, I'm sure."

"Oh, *we'll* be in touch, Miss, you can be sure. You can bet the family fortune on it." The office door slammed shut.

Dixie rubbed the back of her neck, but it didn't undo any of the stiffness there.

She didn't know any other lawyers and she doubted if the other two local attorneys were capable of taking on the company that was the basis of the whole town's economy. From what she knew, those men dealt mainly in wills, real estate, divorce, and adoption—the kind of legal requirements of the average citizen of Fulton's Dominion.

Her needs, the needs of Fulton's Fine Furniture Manufacturing, and those of her family were anything but average. And now she had gone and fired the only hope of help she had in managing them.

"Dear Lord." She laid her head on Daddy's desk. "You have just got to keep your loving hand on me and all those I care about, now more than ever. Because you are the only thing holding me, my family, this business, and by extension, this town, together."

She took a long, shuddering breath, shut her eyes, and let the tears begin to flow. Her fingers clung to the ledger that she now pressed against her chest while she let her heart let go just enough to ask for the thing she needed most. "Guide me, Father, show me the way. And if it's not too much to ask, send just the right person to help me sort this through. Because, for better or worse, I have, in one fell swoop, just stepped out of Daddy's formidable shadow and into—"

Well, Dixie did not want to think about what she'd just stepped into, but whatever it was, she felt without a doubt that she had just stepped into it deep.

"And if you can, please send that someone really fast."

She opened her eyes to survey the pink and yellow carnage covering the floor of her father's office, and wiped away a tear. "Amen."

Four

◆

For judgement will be merciless to one who has shown no mercy; yet mercy triumphs over judgement.

JAMES 2:13 (NASB)

"RILEY WALKER, YOU ARE IN A WORLD OF HURT."

Carol Foster called the comment out across the still back lot of Walker and Son Sawmill, waving a handful of white papers in one hand and clutching her black leather briefcase with the other.

Riley squinted in her direction, even though there was no blazing Mississippi sun to get in his eyes this time of day on an early March afternoon. He shifted his steel-toed work boots in the woodchip-covered ground and adjusted his yellow hard hat first forward, then back, then forward again. He knew why Carol had come, why she had waited until all but a few of his workers had called it quits on his last day working at the mill. He knew what she wanted to talk to him about and he was not a happy man.

"Wait up." She picked her way through small oil slicks, sawdust, and mud just to get from her car to where he stood. Still, her dark blue suit looked like she'd just stepped out of a designer showcase and her high-heeled shoes remained impossibly spotless.

Riley tugged off one leather and canvas work glove and slapped it against his jeans, as if that could get rid of the filth of a full day's work ground into his clothes. He shifted his hat once more, letting some air circulate over his scalp. He should take the fool thing off, as any gentleman would in the presence of a lady, but the thought of how his dark hair would be matted down in one place, drawn up into waves and annoying little curls in another made him think twice. Besides, taking his hat off for Carol might indicate a social pleasantry that Riley just did not feel right now.

"You didn't need to drive all the way out here, Carol. I was planning to come by your office later in the week so we could discuss—"

Carol cut him off with a flourish of her hand. "Couldn't wait. We have a court date coming up in eight weeks, Riley, and if we are not ready, you are going to find yourself in a world of hurt."

"So you said." He folded his arms over his chest, clenched and unclenched his fists, then heaved out a sigh. "All right, then. Why don't we take this to the office and talk about it?"

"I can talk while we walk." She started toward the sturdy shed-on-stilts creation that he had called his office since he took over for his father many years ago.

"Walking *and* talking, huh? That may be asking far too

much for a poor, uneducated ape like me." Riley fell in step beside her.

"Very funny. Lucky for you I don't require anything complicated like gum-chewing or shoelace tying. A simple signature will do. I know you can scrawl out your name, honey, because I've seen you do it on legal documents, credit card receipts, and even the occasional greeting card." Her eyes flashed, then she lowered her lashes and cocked her head. She gave him just a hint of smile as she reached into her briefcase. A second later, she offered Riley the ridiculously expensive fountain pen he'd given her just two weeks ago on Valentine's Day.

Riley made a quick study of the contrasts as the object passed from Carol's delicate, pale fingers to his rough, blunt ones, brown as leather from days working outdoors. The extravagant pen felt awkward in his hand. Pens of any kind were not his tool of choice, but this thing with its gold accents and engraved nib…

A pen just like the dark-haired woman had given her elderly companion after their ill-fated run-in. What had he thought? That if Carol had some outward trapping similar to the woman who had outraged and intrigued him that he might feel differently toward her? That Carol might, by virtue of having this symbol, suddenly seem more compassionate, more appealing?

Riley stared at the pen. He'd given it to Carol because he'd wanted what it represented for himself. He swallowed hard and started to guiltily put the pen out of sight, but before he could slide it into the pocket of his faded denim work shirt, Carol cleared her throat.

"No stalling. Time's running out on this."

"On what?" *Did she know he'd been thinking about their doomed relationship?*

"On *what*? On these." She took the pen again and tapped

the papers in her hand. "You've *got* to sign these papers right now authorizing an all-out slash-and-burn investigation of your sister so we can prove her an unfit mother, once and for all."

He frowned at the pages bearing the familiar name of a private detective in Jackson, Mississippi. "I thought I told you I didn't want to do things that way—"

"And I told you we have to be prepared for anything." Her clipped, dispassionate words rushed over the top of his own slow, calculated ones.

He narrowed one eye, his lips tight against his clenched teeth, then turned to lead the way up to his office. The sparse wooden stairs swayed and groaned under his weight.

"Be reasonable, Riley." Carol's heels barely made a sound on the rough steps as she followed in his wake. "We have to be at the ready with the most compelling case possible as to why you should be allowed to follow through with adopting your niece."

"I've raised her these last six-and-a-half years without any support or contact from Marcia." He gave the office door a shove, then stood aside to hold it open for Carol. "Isn't that enough?"

"Severing parental rights and then reassigning them to another person, even a loving uncle, is not something the Mississippi courts take lightly." She breezed past him.

"They already gave me legal guardianship and full custody of Wendy years ago." He made the argument through clenched teeth.

"It's *not* the same thing." She spun on her heel, her finger stabbing the air at a spot that would have been his breastbone had he been standing any closer to her. "You are asking the state to eradicate any and all claims of a *mother* to her *child*. You can't expect to accomplish that without some powerful evidence as to why it must be done, why the present situation is no longer adequate for the welfare of the child in question."

Riley tensed.

"If you don't do as I've advised in this, I am warning you, you just could find yourself in a—"

"A world of hurt." Riley paced back and forth and inhaled the smell of grease and diesel fumes mixed with the gratifying earthiness of freshly milled wood. "I know. A world of hurt."

"Mock me all you want, but you have to know I'm right."

He turned his gaze away from Carol, with her perfectly poofed-up hair the color of a golden honeycomb. He shut his eyes, but he could still picture her waiting for a better response from him, arms folded, standing stiff as oak beside his desk.

He saw her, but he wondered if she saw him. Not just the man in jeans and steel-toed boots standing before her, or even the guy who got cleaned up to take her to the movies Friday nights and sat by her side in church on Sunday mornings. Did she see *him*—the real Riley Walker? Her insistence in pushing this issue told him she didn't.

"I *don't* know that you're right about this, Carol." He whisked off his hard hat and flung it down. It hit the seat of his chair, rolled off, and landed with an emphatic thud on the weathered floorboards.

Carol glanced down but otherwise stood her ground.

"And you don't know that you're right about this, either, Carol. You're just hedging your bets, trying to cover all the bases." He spread his arms wide, like an umpire calling a man safe. "That's your job—to point out the options to me, and I understand that."

"Good." She held the papers and pen out to him again. "Then maybe we can—"

"Pressing those option against my wishes, though." He

laced his arms over his chest. "That is *not* your job. Not as I see it. Not as I pay you to do it."

The mention of payment brought a fleeting, flinching response. No matter what their personal relationship was—or more aptly put, *was not*—when they got right down to the marrow of it, Carol worked for Riley. And everyone who worked for Riley knew they did things Riley's way or no way at all.

"When you first brought this idea up, I told you flat out no. I wouldn't go along with it." He dropped into the chair behind his cluttered desk. "That hasn't changed."

She gathered her breath up in one sharp intake, as if readying to launch into another argument.

He pushed both hands back through his damp hair, not caring how much of a mess he made of his appearance. With his palms all but covering his ears, he gritted his teeth and forced out a hoarse whisper, "I don't want to fight with you today, Carol."

"I don't want us to fight today or any day." There was a definite air of one-upmanship to her tone.

That was Carol, always taking things a little further than necessary to ensure she came out on top. He laughed without feeling amused, then pointed to the empty seat across the desk. That was as close as he intended to get to asking her to sit down and stay. "Then let's just drop it, why don't we?"

"Drop the whole case?" She remained standing. "Because if you back away from my plan now, Riley, that's what you may be doing. You're reluctance to pursue every avenue, to make sure we have all the advantages in this petition, could jeopardize everything."

She did not see him...not at all. He lifted his gaze to her and simply shook his head.

Carol exhaled in that way women had of sticking home the

guilt without actually having to nag or needle. That hard, purposeful sigh that made even strong men wince like they'd just sucked a lemon through a split lip.

To be fair, he realized he didn't see Carol, either. Didn't see her point of view in this and didn't see how to make her understand his. Riley relaxed, as much as the situation allowed, then swiveled around to stare out the enormous, dust-and-grime-tinted picture window that framed his battered, paper-strewn desk.

Raw lumber, monstrous saws, burly men with chaws of tobacco in their jaws and words not fit for polite company overflowing their mouths—those were the things he understood. Walker and Son Sawmill had risen from a struggling operation to a top producer, from a handful of workers to nearly one hundred employees over the years. Riley had made it happen mostly with his own two hands and his own muleheaded determination. He'd done it so well that when the international companies began buying up the small operations, his could still stand and compete. And he still could if his personal circumstances didn't dictate he change things. He'd sold his company for the same reason he had worked so hard all those years with that single-minded drive: to provide security for his family.

That was all that mattered. Family. It was all that counted beyond faith and honor. Now Carol was asking him to turn his back on two of those things for the only reason he would ever even consider it.

For his child.

A dull ache gripped his chest, like his heart had clenched up into a paralyzed fist. He took a deep breath and stared out the window. As he exhaled, slowly, the pain subsided. "You know I've worked at this mill since I was old enough to ride my bike over after school."

"Of course. Everyone in town knows that, Riley. Everyone knows how hard you and your daddy worked to keep this place going and how, after your father died, you grew it into one of the finest family-owned—"

"Family." With that one, all-important word, he cut into whatever pretty speech he supposed she expected to make. "That's what it's all about, Carol. My family started this place and it was for them that I kept right on building it. Everything I have today, the big house, the big bank accounts, the Walker name and all it stands for…I owe to my family."

"Understood." She laid the pen and papers on the edge of his desk, where he could still see them from the corner of his eye, then reached out her hand but did not touch him. "But you have to understand, too, that family is what I'm talking about preserving."

"By dredging up every humiliating mistake my sister ever made?" He turned to her. He could actually feel his pulse ticking along the tight cords of his neck as he poured his reigned-in emotions into one more quiet question. "By tearing open old wounds just so you can point them out to everyone in town and show us all how deep and ugly they truly are?"

Carol took a step away.

"We've made every effort to find my sister. We've hired detectives and posted notices in major newspapers, even used the Internet. All we've ever gotten is just enough to know that Marcia is out there, that she holds a job from time to time, that she doesn't stay in one place very long, and that she isn't remotely interested in coming back to Deepwoods."

"Oh, we know one more thing, Riley."

"What's that?"

"We know that she hasn't come forward to renounce her parental rights to Wendy." The kick-in-the-gut reality of that statement hung in the air between them. "Riley, she knows that's why you're looking for her and she isn't cooperating with it. That won't make things any easier in court."

"But when I first talked to you about this, you said—"

"When you first broached the subject of legally adopting Wendy, things were very different than they are now."

"Momma," he said quietly.

"You have to face the fact that when your mother fell and broke her hip last week, it changed the entire dynamic of your home life. Before she fell, your mother's presence in your home was one of your greatest assets in showing a judge you could provide an outstanding home life for Wendy. Now your mother's a liability."

"Are you saying Momma's injury could keep them from letting me adopt Wendy?"

"I'm saying you have to think of how it looks to a judge. A workaholic man who has thus far depended on the help of his mother as primary caregiver for the child. And now his mother is incapacitated, perhaps even in need of as much or more care than the child in question."

"Granted, it doesn't sound good when you put it that way." He dragged his calloused thumb down the length of his bristled jawline. "But I've also made some major changes. I sold the mill, freed up my own time to care for Wendy. I'm still looking to move out of Deepwoods to a better environment for her, still expecting to reinvest in a new company or even to start over. Won't that help my position?"

"Maybe. Yes. If it were a reality. The move, the improved environment, those would help, I'm sure. But starting over? The amount of time, money, and energy that would take, not to mention the potential financial risk, would be three strikes against you, in my opinion." She frowned. "Your priority must be to link up with an established, prospering business, like that Fulton deal provided. When you lost that, you lost out big."

He lifted his head, sharp and quick, wishing he could refute her claim—and knowing there was nothing he could say to deny the truth of it.

"The way I see it, Riley, barring another drastic change in your circumstances that would suddenly provide Wendy a far more stable home environment, you're best hope is to show that, flawed though you may be, you are infinitely better able and willing to care for Wendy than your sister." She put her hand to her temple, the strain of the moment etching worry lines between her plucked eyebrows. "We have to show them that they have no other real choice but to strip Marcia of her rights and grant those rights to you alone."

Riley put his head in his hands. *Flawed though you may be…workaholic man…you don't have anything lined up, lost out big time…mother incapacitated…strip Marcia of her rights.* The phrases went spinning through his mind faster than he could grasp their deeper implications.

"Your sister is the one who walked out on Wendy while that child was still in the hospital bassinet." Carol did not let him take the time to sort through his jumbled thoughts. "You and your mother have raised that little girl, provided her sole support, financially, spiritually, emotionally and…and…"

Impolite as it was not to listen, she wasn't saying a thing he didn't already know. He narrowed his eyes and jerked his head once, quick, to the right, making his neck pop, resulting in a sound like a couple of muffled firecrackers.

She must have seen her tact failing as she suddenly cut herself off. Her whole attitude softened. She smiled and cast her eyes downward—that fine Southern belle contrivance that implied deference to a man when, in fact, manipulation was the goal.

Riley cocked his head to one side and stifled a cynical grin. No dose of Southern female charm would get to him. He'd brought up a daughter who had been born with the ability to wrap him around her finger from her very first innocent coo. He'd watched his own sister get whatever she wanted from lovesick men with a look, a pout, and—should those fail— other things. Much as he adored the women in his family, he saw straight through their devices. That, he supposed, was one reason why he never married.

He recognized every feminine trick and felt immune to them all.

Let her bring on her worst. He stretched back in his chair. *I will not be affected.* For good measure, he kicked his boots up onto the corner of his desk and crossed one ankle over the other. "I'm not going to drag my sister's name through the mud in hopes it might give us a little more leverage with some judge who doesn't know my family from Adam's."

"But you need that leverage, Riley. Don't you understand? You need it for Wendy's sake."

The breathy, lilting quality of her voice chafed at his taut nerves. He wondered if Carol realized how distasteful he found her predictable pouting, the blend of cheap pretense, and break-the-bank makeup?

He looked away from her, shamed for the pure meanness of that thought. He cared for Carol, maybe not as much as she did for him, but he did care about her feelings and opinions. It wasn't like him to think so unkindly about anyone, least of all someone trying to help him.

All this mess…Momma's fall, the pending adoption hearing, the harshness of Carol's recommendation, they all colored his perception right now, he guessed. Carol's suggestion most of all.

He glanced up to find her watching him. He sighed. "I'd have liked to have thought that you, who have been my lawyer for the last four years and my…"

A glimmer of hope shone for a moment in Carol's eyes.

It hurt Riley that he could not justify that hope with sweet romantic assurances. "You, who have been such a close friend, would have known me well enough to understand that I would never do what you're asking. I'd liked to think you saw me as a man with more integrity, more compassion, and more faith that God can work things out for the good than to stoop to such a level."

"You have to do whatever it takes to ensure that child a stable environment." She planted her palms flat on the desk and honed in on him. "You know you're the only father figure that child has ever had, Riley."

Father *figure*. The expression hit Riley like a slap in the face. He knew she'd only thrown out the term as a tactic, but to him it was so much more.

Wendy was his daughter. She had been his since that first day when he'd lifted the tiny bundle from her cradle and realized that if he did not shelter her, nurture her, discipline her…if he did not love her, nobody on earth would. Though legalities might say otherwise, Wendy was *his* little girl. It always made his blood run cold whenever anyone went to great pains to remind him that she was not.

If he were in-your-face honest with himself, he'd admit that at the core of that ice-in-the-veins response was one overriding, gut-wrenching emotion: fear. What did he know about raising a little girl, after all? What if he made the wrong choices or said or did the wrong things? How easily that delicate spirit could be crushed. The responsibility was awesome some days.

He rubbed his palms together in a slow, circular motion.

How could these clumsy work-hardened hands of his be counted on to tie a hair ribbon, bandage a scraped knee, or wipe away the tears of that first broken heart? With Momma aging and now disabled, his decision to follow through on full, legal adoption, meant that was exactly what he was preparing to do. He would move from *father figure* to full-fledged father in the stroke of a judge's pen.

He looked down at the pen on his desk and he saw in a flash of memory the tenderness the woman in Fulton's Dominion had shown. Like Carol, she was ready to go for the throat to get what she wanted, but she had known when it was time to put aside ruthlessness and to show mercy and kindness.

There was a lesson in that he could not forsake. Scared as he was at the prospect of becoming Wendy's father, Riley would do what he must. But not at all costs.

"No. I won't do it, Carol." He slashed his hand through the air. "I know you don't like to lose, in court or…at anything. I know you would do whatever it took to keep the odds in your favor, to make sure you don't lose. But this is going too far."

"There is no such thing as too far. Not when so much is at stake." The passionate fire she usually reserved for the courtroom flushed in her face and gave a hushed urgency to her words. "*I'd* think you would take some measure of comfort in my unwillingness to lose, seeing as how in this case, I'm fighting for the thing you value most in life."

"It's because of my family, Carol, that I can't do this. You're talking about publicly trashing not just my sister or my aging, injured Momma's only other child, but Wendy's *mother*. Your…what did you call it? Slash and burn? Your slash-and-burn attitude just won't cut it this time." He glanced down at his desk to avoid eye contact with the woman, to avoid more bad blood and hurt feelings between them. Without warning, the glint of a golden frame caught his eye, and he found himself staring straight into the face of the little girl at the heart of this whole twisted matter.

Dark brown hair, pink cheeks, and a pair of sparkling green eyes so full of joy and love that it humbled him every time he looked into them. That was his Wendy. That was his little girl. As much as he loved that child, he understood Momma loved her only daughter every bit as much. And angry as he could feel toward his sister for the things she had put them all through, Riley loved her, too. He loved her for the little girl she had once been and the woman he prayed each night she would someday finally become.

How could he go into a court of law and systematically rip to shreds, degrade, and humiliate her—and in so doing, probably destroy the chance of his prayers for Marcia ever coming true? How could he make it impossible for Marcia to return, to see what a wonderful child Wendy was, to hug and hold their Momma again?

He gripped the arm of his chair until he could feel the roughened grain of the wood in his palm. His lips twitched with barely controlled emotion as he fixed his gaze on Carol. "I suggest you see if you can't come up with a better way to solidify my position in court. Because I will not sacrifice even one person I care for in the hopes of making myself look better by contrast."

"If you aren't going to take my advice, Riley—"

"Yeah, yeah, world of hurt. I got it. Now let it go, would you?" He rubbed his eyelids with his crooked knuckles, giving only a moment's relief to his dry, burning eyes.

"If you are not going to take this seriously—"

Riley stood so quickly he tipped his chair over. He did not

even flinch as it bounced once on the wooden floor then skidded to a crash against the wall. "Don't ever imply again that I am not taking my family's welfare seriously. To my way of thinking it's *you* who aren't taking *me* seriously. If you were, you'd find me other options to shore up my case."

"I'm sorry—" she held her hands up in a show of helplessness that no man who could see the fire in her eyes would believe—"but I just don't see any."

"Then maybe I should find someone who does."

"Maybe you should." She snatched up the private investigator's form, but left her Valentine's Day pen lying on the desk.

Riley recognized that ploy as well. Leaving the pen was a threat, a way of daring him to choose. Pick up the pen and sign the paper or leave it and lose her. With that seemingly innocent gesture, she was calling his bluff. What the lady lawyer obviously still could not understand about him was that where his family's well-being was concerned, he never bluffed.

"Then send me the bill for the work you've already done."

"Wh-what?"

The harsh jangle of the phone seemed to underscore the ragged edge of the tension between them.

"If you can't find a better way to help me make sure I keep Wendy, I'll just have to find someone who will." He spoke softly, in marked contrast to the jarring ring of the phone again.

"But I…we…" Beneath the perfect tones of her makeup, her face went pale.

"I'm through playing your games, Carol. I've never been anything but up-front with you professionally and personally. You're telling me that you only see one way to handle this case. Well, that way won't do. So I guess I have to find another way without you."

He took her by the elbow, walked her across the room,

kissed her lightly on the cheek, then nudged her out of his office. "Good-bye, Carol."

He shut and locked the door before she could so much as squeak in protest, then turned and walked across the room to answer the phone.

Five

We all stumble in many ways.

JAMES 3:2A

"HEARD A RUMOR ABOUT YOU—AND IT HAD BETTER BE A RUMOR, too—that you went plumb out of your head this evening. Up and fired Carol as your lawyer. Just like that."

Momma's wrinkled old fingers gave a quiet snap, like someone stepping on a small twig on a dusty path.

"Now, tell me that ain't true, boy."

"Can't tell you that, Momma." Riley leaned over the hospital bed and brushed a kiss over her cool cheek. "'Cause then you'd have to hop right up off that bed and wallop me for fibbing to you, and I just know your physical therapist would have both our hides for that."

Despite her obvious irritation with him, she granted him a smile that shone clear into the depths of her eyes. "You're a troublement, that's what you are, Riley Aaron Walker. A pure troublement."

"Then I must be a figment of your imagination, dear mother of mine, because there is no such-of-a word." He gripped the handrail just a hair's breath away from where Momma's frail arm rested atop the thin hospital blanket.

"Pshaw." She rolled her eyes, and though she turned her head away for a moment, not a hair of her steel blue-gray permed hairdo moved out of place. "If I was going to make something up out of my own imagination, it'd be a sight prettier to look at than some fret-faced child of mine clomping around a hospital in raggedy work clothes and muddy boots."

He chuckled at her gentle, teasing reprimand. "Sorry, I didn't have time to change. I got a phone call right after...right after Carol and I parted company. At first I was too irritated to put up with the fellow's roundabout way of getting to his point but then...well, he's a lawyer and it looks like I need a new lawyer, so I heard him out."

"So it is true about you and Carol?" Momma fumbled with the buttons on the control beside her pillow. The bed whirred and raised her upper body into a half-sitting slant. She flinched, shut her eyes, then let out a long, slow breath.

Riley curled his fingers around the handrail, helpless to do anything to ease her discomfort.

When she opened her eyes again, she managed a sweet if not entirely convincing smile.

Riley studied her. "I think you knew it was true before you even asked, didn't you? How'd you find out? Did Carol call her sister down in admitting and tell her so that now the whole hospital knows?"

"Something like that. I don't know if the whole hospital knows, of course. There may be someone in isolation or ICU that hasn't been allowed a visitor yet to share all the good gossip."

He pulled his shoulders back, speaking loudly enough for anyone who might be lingering over their duties in the hallway to hear. "Someday, Momma, I am going to move to the biggest city I can stand and start over where not a soul cares about who I see or don't see or any other thing about my personal life."

Momma gave a gentile snort. "Be easier to get yourself a wife and settle down right here or nearby so that nobody would care so much about your personal life anymore." She gave him a nod that he supposed meant she thought this solution was the best for everyone involved.

The clatter of plastic wheels and metal containers carried in from the open door at his back. The distinct aroma of hospital food—if anything so bland as pasty mashed potatoes and green gelatin could be said to have a *distinct* aroma—wafted in from the hallway.

"Mmmm. Smells like it's dinnertime."

Momma's expression soured. "Smells like someone's boiling flour and water to me. When are you going to spring me from this voodoo boardinghouse and get me home so I can whip up a real meal?"

Just the thought of Momma's cooking made Riley's stomach grumble. He put his hand over the flat muscles of his belly and laughed. "You have no idea how much I'd love to do that. Wendy is so sick of my cooking she's wrangled herself invites to dinner with friends every night this week. I'll need to go pick her up pretty soon now."

"Not without giving me more details, you won't." Her eyes twinkled, but the shadow of underlying pain gave her face a gray pallor. She angled her shoulders ever so slightly in his direction and exhaled loudly at the effort. All joking faded from her expression as she brushed her fingers over his. "So, it's a done deal with you and Carol, then? You've broken things off for good?"

The hint of hope in her tone told Riley she wanted to hear a retraction, to have him deny the rumor and reassure her that everything was going ahead without a hitch.

"Look, Mom, I…"

She seemed so small in that long, metal-framed bed in the stark, impersonal room. He'd never seen his mother look so small before, so fragile. She'd always been the fierce one, the go-getter, a woman of unfathomable faith in herself, her family, and her God. Now, lying there waiting for him to answer, she looked like some little old lady pleading with her eyes to hear that everything was going to work out right for her son and granddaughter.

Momma tipped her head forward just enough to urge him to go on and finish what he had begun to say.

"I…I don't know, Mom. It's complicated."

"Because you don't return the feelings she has for you?"

"That and—" He shifted his boots over the flat, almost colorless carpet. How did he explain Carol's one and only strategy for arguing why he should be allowed to adopt Wendy without cutting Momma to the quick? How could he lay it out to her without making it seem as though she would have to choose between her loyalty to him and Wendy and her everfaithful love for his sister?

He couldn't. To base his request for legal adoption on the mess Marcia had made of her life was nothing short of a betrayal of family love and trust. He would not do it. He saw no reason that Momma should even have to consider it as an option.

"The thing is, I should never have let someone that I know is…that has feelings for me…represent me in personal or business affairs, Mom. It's not a good mix."

"And this new one, *that* will be a good mix?"

"New one?"

"Lawyer. The one that called you up on the phone. You know, I had no idea lawyers did that kind of thing, calling folks up out of the blue in hopes they might have a law case they need tending to."

"Momma, he didn't exactly call me out of the—"

"'Course as much as everybody goes to suing everybody else over every little thing these days, it don't surprise me none that some smart legal eagle didn't turn to the telemarketing approach."

"Who said anything about telemarket—"

"You know what I think maybe you ought to do instead, though?" She raised one finger both to keep him from interrupting and to wag at him as she spoke. "Maybe you ought to call up one of those 1-800-lawsuit lawyers that's always advertising on the TV! Can't be any worse picking a lawyer from a blind phone call, now can it?"

"This was not a blind anything, Mom."

"Least with the TV fellows you can get a gander at what they look like, pick one out that looks successful but not flashy. Maybe the one with slick-backed hair and that gold and rhinestone tie tack. He sure does claim to be able to do a lot for his clients, son. They all do, of course." She patted his hand a little too hard. "What's more I'll bet nary a one of them would let their personal feelings for you get in the way of things, no matter how much you turned on that ol' sawmill charm of yours."

"Now you're just being ornery." He pushed his rolled-up sleeves past his elbows. "And not even very subtle about it, either."

"You get my age you don't have much use for *subtle,* honey."

"So what? You resort to sarcasm?" He shook his head, unable to hide his grin. "Whenever I did that to you, you threatened to take me to the woodshed for sass-talking you."

"Well, you go right ahead and take me to the woodshed if you think you can get me there, but that won't change the fact that the devil you know is usually better than the devil you don't."

"By *devil* you mean…?"

"Lawyers."

"Ah, should have figured that one out myself."

"Here, now, I'm not making any comparisons between Lucifer and the law profession, son. I'm just trying to point out to you that you have just taken on the most important thing you will probably ever try your hand at in your hoping to adopt Wendy once and for all. Hiring a new lawyer because he happened to call you on the telephone a few minutes after you had a falling out with Carol just doesn't make any kind of sense at all."

He stared at her. "You don't believe for one minute that I'd do anything to jeopardize Wendy's adoption, do you?"

"No. No. That's just my own fear talking, son. It so hard to be laid up here when I know my family needs me." She twisted her hands together, then let them fall to her sides, then folded them in her lap again. "If I snapped at you, if I got way out of line, that's why."

"I know, Momma. I know." He laid his hand on hers and leaned to kiss her forehead.

She sighed and gave his shoulder a squeeze.

Riley pulled away and stood straight beside the bed. "I didn't hire anyone, by the way. I just talked to the man on the phone. The reason he called was to let me know about a business deal he thought might interest me."

"Business deal? What kind of business deal?"

"Well, you know how I was going to take the money I made from the sale of the mill and invest it in an already thriving concern? That way I could make myself more available to Wendy and now to you?"

"You could have done that before, Riley, if you'd set your mind on it. Making the mill turn a bigger profit, staying competitive, always promising that next year you'd move us to a better place, take more time off, be home for Wendy every night at supper time.... My goodness, we've lived with all that for too long now to go falling for some pie-in-the-sky promise that things will change."

Riley ran one hand back through his thick hair. He wished he had some way of disputing his mother's point, but how did one argue against the truth?

"Get your priorities straight, Riley. That's the way to show you're ready to become Wendy's daddy for real."

"That's just what I can do with this business deal, Momma. Set things up so that I can be the best father to Wendy possible by providing for her future and giving her my time right now."

Momma's mouth set in a firm line. She gave a brisk nod of approval. "Then I'd say you ought to look into this new business venture, Riley."

"I intend to. Going over to Fulton's Dominion tomorrow morning, in fact."

"Fulton's Dominion? I thought that fell through. I thought we'd heard the last of you getting mixed up with that... that...that outrageous Fulton family!"

"What? You got some good gossip on them, too?" Riley laughed. "What do you use to gather your information, Momma? Computers? Satellites? Secret frequency radio waves?"

"You are not too old to be taken to the woodshed for sass-talking me, son."

A tap on the door kept him from giving her any further cause for wanting to take him out to the shed to dust his britches with a switch.

"Dinnertime, Mrs. Walker." A young woman in a brightly colored scrub suit and a hairnet came into the small room. She slid the large tray bearing a covered meal on the bed table while making small talk about the menu and the desert and how the patients might complain about the food but they seemed to eat it all every night then ask for more.

When she left, Momma leaned forward, peering at the steaming plate of portions in various shades of beige and brown. She wrinkled up her nose, then shook her head and stuck her hand out to him. "Well, it ain't the way I make meat-loaf and gravy but it's what I've got. Best say my thanks for it."

Riley gladly took his mother's hand and bowed his head.

"Thank you for this food, oh, Lord. And for my health, such as it is right now. Thank you for giving me two wonderful children and a beautiful grandchild, even if we can't all be together right now. I trust we'll all be a family again in time, even if it's not 'til we're in heaven."

Riley started to murmur a heartfelt *amen,* but Momma wasn't quite done.

"And if you would, gracious Father, please guide my Riley as he considers this new business dealing. Don't let him get drawn into a big, fat mess with those...with your good and faithful...and, um, *interesting* servants, the Fulton family." She gave his hand a squeeze. "Amen."

"Amen." But before he would turn loose of his mother's hand he caught her with a hard gaze. "I think maybe you'd better tell me just what it is you've heard about these folks,

Momma, before I go getting myself involved in anything pertaining to them and their business."

"I've never heard a bad word spoken against their business." She unfurled her napkin and tucked it into the round collar of her hospital gown. "In fact, we owned a sofa made by that company for years and years. You remember that blue and gold one with the tiny floral pattern woven into—"

"What about the family?"

She picked up her fork and plunged it into the glob of mashed potatoes. "I always liked that sofa."

"Mom." He crossed his arms and dipped his head. "What aren't you telling me?"

"Son, the truth is, I don't know for sure what it is about that family." She put her fork down. "They're just peculiar, that's all I've heard. Wealthy, though, and active in the church and in the community. Whether the community likes it or not."

"I see. So it's a rich, eccentric old Southern family that exerts its influence in the town its forebears founded. And you think that's in some way unusual?"

"You're right. You're right. There's probably nothing extraordinary about them at all. They are probably just your everyday, average, millionaire lunatics." She took up her fork and scooped some meatloaf up with the potatoes and took a bite.

"Don't worry, Mom." He grabbed up the plastic pitcher on her tray and filled her water glass, handing it to her just as she made a face to show her dislike of the food. "I think I can handle myself with them. Besides, Mr. Greenhow gave me the impression I wouldn't be dealing with the family anyway. He seems to have the whole thing pretty much under control."

Momma gulped down one swallow, then another. Then she set the glass down with a decisive *thunk* and met his gaze with a shrewd, skeptical look.

"That's good, then, because if ever there truly was one, from what I hear that Fulton family is surely a first-class example of a complete and utter troublement."

"'There is a patina on everything in the South. An oily grittiness that settles itself like skin over the kitchen canisters and car hoods and antique milk glass lampshades. You cannot rub it off nor wash it off, and the longer you stay here, the more it becomes a part of you.'" Dixie pressed flat the brand-new, red velveteen journal until the binding cracked. "How's that for a start, then?"

"That's lovely, dear. Quite nice. Quite." Miss Letticia Gautier patted her gnarled, mocha-colored hand in the air, as though keeping beat to some unheard song. She nodded her head to that same silent rhythm, swaying gently in her high-backed rocker. "What is it, lamb?"

"What *is* it?" Dixie let her shoulders slump just enough to get truly comfortable and toed her white-socked feet inward. "Don't you recognize what I just read?"

The delicate wisp of an old woman sitting beside Dixie blinked her crepe-lidded, owl-like brown eyes in incomprehension.

Dixie watched her, torn between a smile and exasperation. "Remember how I told you we were going to record your words for posterity? How I wanted to collect your thoughts and experiences as a sort of commemoration for your upcoming one hundredth birthday? Remember?" Dixie held open the cream-colored page filled with the swirls of blue ink, knowing full well that dear old Miss Lettie could not see well enough anymore to make out the words. "Well, that's what I've done. I've taken what you told me and written it down here."

"Go on with you." Lettie's dismissive wave was no less than regal.

"It's true."

"Me? That came from me?" She threw back her head, as much as she could, and gave out a crackling laugh like an old hen having its scrawny neck wrung. Then she coughed, and as her rough tongue rasped against the almost invisible line of her lips, she jabbed a finger toward the journal. "Read that again."

"'There is a patina on everything in the South. An oily grittiness that settles itself like skin over the kitchen canisters and car hoods and antique milk glass lampshades.'" Dixie spoke with the dramatic conviction one might use to intone the words of the Scripture or the prose of Miss Margaret Mitchell. "'You cannot rub it off, nor wash it off and the longer you stay here, the more it becomes a part of you.'"

Lettie tipped her rocking chair back, paused, then let the runners fall forward with a definitive creak. "You got all that from what I said?"

"W-well, yes. I admit I did embellish just a tad but it's still the essence of your words." Dixie closed the book, pulling it close to her chest. "You said—"

"I *said*—" Miss Lettie landed a look on Dixie that left no room for doubt that the elderly woman was still as sharp, as strong, and as unwilling to tolerate nonsense as ever—"What I *said*, Miss Dixie Belle Fulton-Leigh, was that since I came to Fulton's Dominion, Mississippi, in nineteen hundred and seventeen, that I can't recall a day when I didn't sweat!"

"Well, I…"

For several seconds the stillness of the old house her family had occupied since the town's founding wrapped itself around the two of them.

Lettie's milky-eyed gaze remained trained on the younger

woman the whole time until she finally broke the silence. "You did hear me all right, didn't you, Dixie Belle?"

Dixie squirmed like a six-year-old in church called upon to recite a memory verse she had not properly prepared. Very few people could humble her like that, and only one got away with calling her by the nickname *Dixie Belle*. This scrappy imp of a woman who had raised one generation after another of her family, including Dixie herself, had always been able to put Dixie in her place with no more than a look or a word.

The rocking chair groaned out a long, nerve-twisting reminder that Lettie was still waiting to hear Dixie's concession.

She stiffened. The mantle clock in the main room where they sat tick-tick-ticked, commanding time itself to slow to its dull, plodding cadence. The house, in its seeming state of perpetual midday, always in the golden light of sun through yellowed window shades, offered little in the way of something to change the subject.

No. Change was not the way of this house or its owners. In fact, Dixie noted as she glanced around, nothing much in this house had changed in the last forty years. Not easily anyhow—with the exception of the peeling of wallpaper and the loss of loved ones.

Daddy. The reminder of her loss made her breath snag high in the back of her throat. Her heart felt like it had clamped up into a cold little lump. She knotted her arms around herself as if that could keep the worries of the world from closing in on her. Daddy's death had changed things here…changed them drastically, dreadfully, and perhaps irreversibly, though no one but Dixie seemed even remotely aware of that fact.

"Are you two done with your foray into the profundity of literary phantasm?" Aunt Sis flounced into the room. The woman was the widow of Dixie's only uncle. Her legal name was June Cunningham though absolutely no one had called her anything but *Sis* or *Aunt Sis* or even *Miss Sis* in years.

She popped through the swinging door that led from the kitchen, bounded through the large dining area, and flounced into the formal receiving room where Dixie and Lettie sat. Aunt Sis pretty much flounced everywhere she went, except on the rare occasion when she skulked about or swooped in on unsuspecting people making what she liked to call her *"entrance."*

"We're just getting to our first writing session, Aunt Sis. I was held up late at work because we have some major—"

"Oh, I know all about getting held up with crucial matters, sugar." She whipped a lace hankie from inside her oversized straw purse and began fanning her neck and face. The action sent a veritable cloud of perfume wafting over Dixie and Lettie. "You would not *believe* the ballyhoo that went on today at the Every-Other-Thursday-Afternoon Arts and Culture Society. Accusations. Faultfinding. Name calling! I tell you, a bigger pack of whining, miserable, mean-spirited, back-stabbing busybodies I *never* saw. I swear, if they weren't all my very best friends in the world, I would resign as the club's patron on the spot."

Dixie bit her lip to keep from snickering.

Lettie did not even try to hide her amusement at Sis's nonexistent dilemma. She snorted out a laugh.

Aunt Sis tipped her nose up at them both, then put her hand to her painted coral lips. "Peachie Too! Where's my little princess puppy-toes? Peachie Too?"

"Grandpa's taking her for a walk." Dixie tried to return her attention to the journal in her lap.

"A walk? Oh, dear!" Sis clutched at her throat and looked toward the nearest window. "Did he put her sweater on? The lamb's wool one with the faux fur collar?"

Dixie shut her eyes, trying to sound light and pleasant as she sighed and answered. "He put something on her, yes. We all know better than to let that...to let Peachie Too outdoors unless she is properly dressed."

Sis let her purse slide down to the floor with such a thud that Dixie had to look up to make sure her aunt hadn't suddenly fainted from the stress of knowing her dog might be wearing the wrong outfit. "Peachie Too will be fine, I'm sure."

Sis heaved a sigh and moved to the window. "I know you think I'm a foolish old woman."

"I don't think you're all that *old.*" Lettie gave Dixie a grin that showed all four of the one-hundred-year-old stinker's missing teeth.

Dixie laughed.

Sis sniffed. "Tease if you will, but I just know the Judge did not put the right thing on my darling doggie." Sis laid a hand along her cheek. "In this weather she really has to have the lamb's wool. Knowing that Smilin' Bob Cunningham, he has dressed her in something totally inappropriate."

"It's a shame she doesn't use the same care dressing herself as she does that rat she calls a toy poodle," Lettie grumbled under her breath. She let the rocker bring her closer as she kept her voice low enough that only Dixie could hear her. "What has she got herself up in today?"

Dixie made a quick survey of the layers of sheer fabric over some kind of polyester knit dress. "It's her own design. She thinks it makes her look like a fairy."

"You mean a boat?"

"No, not a *ferry*—" Dixie glanced at the way the awful creation made her aunt look broad as a barge in some places—"well, maybe that *is* what she meant."

Sis's sigh was full of deep dramatic effect. "I just know your grandfather has my punkin in that black leather jacket and her red beret. Red! It isn't even her color."

"That's because she's *pink*. She's a pink dog is what she is." Lettie went back to rocking.

"The color of her coat is apricot." Sis peered out the window and twisted her hankie in her hands. "And *I* find it a most appealing hue."

"You would, dear." Lettie kept on rocking while she used one crooked, dark-skinned finger to point to her head, then at Sis.

Dixie followed the gesture with interest. A sharp gasp escaped her lips, which she quickly covered with her hand pretending to have something caught in her throat.

She kept her hand over her mouth and shared a silent giggle with Lettie as she realized for the first time that Aunt Sis's latest hair shade was an exact match for her precious apricot toy poodle.

Sis seemed oblivious. "A black jacket and a red beret. Think of it." Sis lifted her head and paused for a moment as if she were doing that very thing. "You know, the Judge favors that outfit because he says it looks jaunty. He doesn't care one bit that the whole style is passe or that it totally conflicts with Peachy Too's personality."

"You want to dress that thing for its personality, Miss Sis? Get her something in alligator skin," Lettie called out, traces of her old New Orleans accent coming out on a word here and there.

Sis ignored the fashion advice and kept right on fluttering her hankie. "Well, now I am going to be distressed until they return."

"Could you please be distressed on the front porch or at

least in Grandpa's office?" Dixie pointed her pen toward the big French doors off the foyer leading to the converted sitting room where her grandfather kept regular "office hours." "We just got started on Miss Lettie's life story, and I'd like to go on with it."

With a wounded sniff, Aunt Sis displayed her agitation at being thrown out in her hour of woe, but she did as she was asked. Dixie was head of the household now, and she was well aware that in this family that carried a great deal of weight. Which only served to bear down on her shoulders at this very moment.

"Now, where were we?" Dixie opened the journal again and lifted her pen.

"*We* were trying to tell *my* life's story. We just hadn't quite decided on whose version we were going to set down on paper." Lettie rocked back and forth.

"Oh, Miss Lettie, I wasn't..." Dixie squared her shoulders. Recanting was the refuge of the under-confident and the unimaginative. Might as well out with the truth and be done with it. "I was just trying to dress it up a bit, you understand, Miss Lettie, so it would read more—"

"Dressing up is what that fool Sis does to that pink ball of jaggedly fangs and eye-pudding she calls Peachie Too." Lettie snorted. "And it don't change the truth of what that critter is, either."

"Peachie Too isn't pink, she's apricot." It galled Dixie to speak a single word in even the hint of defense of that awful dog, but she had to assert her ground where she could. "And she happens to be a registered—"

"Don't you be like them, Dixie Belle! Don't you be like those others in this place."

The starkness of Lettie's admonition pierced straight to the core of Dixie's being. Her cheeks went hot; her fingers fumbled with the simple task of closing the book in her lap. With one hard look and a few clear, unrelenting words, Lettie had cut through every pretense Dixie might have thrown in her path. She'd found the one thing Dixie feared most of all—that she would become like the remaining members of her family, all talk and flutter, with no substance, no purpose in life.

"I thought I'd taught you better." Lettie cocked her head, the hair crowning her old head looking more like the worn-away nap of an ancient plush animal than the thick, silver plaits it had been in Dixie's childhood. "Now, I do love your folks like I'd love my own kin, lamb. I loved your mama and her brother Young Bobby next to as much as I loved my own dear child, Helen Betty. And you know the truth of what I'm saying."

Actually, Dixie could not recall ever having met Miss Lettie's daughter, and her memories of her mother and uncle had faded considerably since the accident that took their lives so many years ago. She did know that Lettie carried her share of grief and regret over that accident, and that it had caused a rift in Lettie's own family that had never been repaired.

"I love Miss Sis and the Judge." Lettie never called Dixie's grandfather by his most common family nickname, Smilin' Bob. "Miss Sis and the Judge and me, we share us a bond that no one else can fathom. But that don't mean I want to see *you* go on and try to be like them."

"No, ma'am."

"I truly believed you wanted to be all that God intended, good and honest and fair. I believed you wanted to be like your mama, and like your great-grandfather, and like your daddy could be when he set his heart on it. I think you can be all those things if you try."

Strong praise coming from someone who had seen this family's foibles and failings as close as any human ever could. Yet Miss Lettie remained, for all intents and purposes, an outsider. That she thought so highly of Dixie after all she had seen and undoubtedly kept secret, touched Dixie deeply. It made her want to try harder, to be the person God, and obviously Miss Lettie, intended her to be.

Dixie dropped her gaze to the page she'd written. She loved those words. She loved the way she had crafted and carefully formed them. She loved the image they presented of the South she loved…a place inextricably intertwined with this house, her family, and Miss Lettie herself.

The slanting shafts of light around them caught specks of dust and made them sparkle. God alone knew what made up those tiny flecks, bits of human skin and animal dander and things far too disgusting to dwell on overlong. Yet in the right light they glistened like diamonds. Dixie traced the perfect script in the open book with her fingertips, then let her teeth sink hard into her lower lip. The crisp paper fought back at first then came tearing free of the binding with a glorious, low ripping sound that actually made Dixie gasp aloud in satisfaction.

As the page slid quietly to the floor, she picked up her pen and began again, reading aloud as she did to make sure she got it right. "'Since I first came to Fulton's Dominion, Mississippi, in nineteen hundred and seventeen, I can't recall a day when I didn't sweat.'"

"Yes, I do believe you have it in you yet." Lettie hummed a few bars of some faraway lullaby, one eye narrowed on Dixie for what seemed an eternity. "Yes, ma'am, I believe it almost enough to trust you with the stone truth of my life's story. Almost."

Six

---◆---

Now listen, you who say,
"Today or tomorrow we will go to this or that city, spend a year
there, carry on business and make money."
Why, you do not even know what will happen tomorrow....
Instead, you ought to say,
"If it is the Lord's will, we will live and do this or that."

JAMES 4:13–15

"A PARTNER? AS IN EQUAL OWNERSHIP?" RILEY RUBBED HIS HAND down his nearly new, neatly pressed jeans. He shifted his shoulders, constrained now in his best sport coat. He hooked his finger inside the collar of his stiff, white shirt, then whisked his hand down the expensive red-and-blue tie. "You can not possibly be telling me you want me to become a full partner in the Fulton family operation."

Howard Greenhow, sitting behind a desk larger than some

Southern voting precincts, smiled in a way so patronizing that when he opened his mouth to speak, Riley immediately cut him off. He had no intention of sitting through whatever sales pitch, flattery, or outright runaround would accompany such a look.

"I don't have the kind of money it takes to become an equal partner in the Fultons' businesses." Riley went straight for the one point he knew would grab this smarmy lawyer's attention. "And even if I did, when I spoke to Mr. Fulton-Leigh, he gave me the impression that he only wanted to sell 20, 25 percent tops. And he was only doing that so he could set his daughter up with a broader-based support system for the distant future. That was something he and I found in common, a single-minded drive and gut-level sense of obligation to do the right thing for our daughters."

"I completely understand." Without taking his eyes off Riley, Greenhow tapped at the corner of a silver picture frame as if to show his total agreement with that fatherly sentiment.

Riley cocked his head and blinked. Either this lawyer had one of the hairiest children in the world or the man had entirely failed to notice that of all the photos of smiling kids and posed family portraits scattered on his expansive desk, he'd just patted one of a golden retriever with its tongue hanging out.

"Anyway—" Riley leaned back in a vain attempt to make himself more comfortable in his straight-backed chair—"the thing is that Mr. Fulton-Leigh never mentioned a partnership. In fact, he clearly stated that he, and I can only assume his daughter after his death, would always maintain controlling interest. What you're saying to me now—"

Greenhow held up his hands. "Let me stop you right there."

The lawyer's hands were soft and white—clearly the man had never done a hard day of blistering manual labor in his life. Riley stuffed his own rough, calloused fingers into his jeans pockets.

"First, let me clear up a little misconception you seem to have, Mr. Walker. The Fulton family descendents basically own three businesses, each separately held." Greenhow flashed three sausage-like fingers, then stood and plopped three file folders down, announcing the name clearly printed on each one as it landed on the side of the desk nearest Riley. "Fulton's Fine Furniture Manufacturing; Fulton's Fine Furniture Outlet Store; and Fulton's Cartage, Delivery, and Transport."

"This is all very interesting, but—"

"That's the gem, there." Greenhow stabbed one finger at the last folder. "Fulton's Cartage. Lucky for you, this is the one I can promise to get you controlling interest in. It's the one you want. The true seat of power in the Fulton empire."

Riley chuckled and raised a questioning eyebrow. "Empire?"

Greenhow chuckled, too. "That's how John Frederick ran his businesses, my friend, and pretty much this little town. Like they made up his own private kingdom. He saw himself as the benevolent, but indisputable, ruler."

Riley leaned forward.

Greenhow took that as a sign to continue. "Wasn't anything new in that, as you can probably guess from the town's name. That one family has dominated our history, social pecking order, and economy for the better part of the last century."

"Nothing wrong with that, I guess." Riley tried to read the lawyer's eyes but couldn't get a fix on the man's point. "It's not the only small town in Mississippi where things worked out that way."

"No, indeed it's not. And as long as things are...working out, as you say, I suppose there's no reason to monkey with success. However, if things begin to go astray, then it's up to those who can to step in and take whatever measures deemed necessary to get things back on the—" he paused to make quotation marks in the air—"right track."

Riley had wasted his time even coming here today. He suspected as much when Greenhow's first suggestions had gone so far afield of the things Riley had discussed with John Frederick before his death. *Partnerships? Empire? Those who can...taking whatever measures necessary...back on the "right track"?* This man was on a power trip or something equally nonproductive or potentially disastrous. Riley wanted no part of that.

With his credibility and judgement about to come under intense scrutiny in Wendy's adoption case, he could not afford to get involved with anything messy or less than circumspect. Not that he would in any case, but right now so much as the hint of duplicity had him on edge, ready to cut bait and run.

"Do you get what I'm saying, Mr. Walker?"

"Sure. You're saying you don't agree with the way John Frederick's heirs are running things." He shifted his classic black cowboy boots over the thick carpet. "You obviously expected to have more input in things when you told me the deal was a no go, but you got edged out of the power position somehow."

Greenhow shifted his gaze away, saying nothing.

Riley snorted a chuckle at that nonverbal confirmation. "So you just thought you'd try to stir things up, bring in an outsider who might have a better chance of doing things to your liking. Or who, because you helped him buy into a very lucrative business opportunity, would be in your debt, feel obliged to use your law firm, or short of that, throw some other business or favors your way somewhere along the line. Is that about right, Mr. Greenhow?"

"What is *about right,* Mr. Walker, is that a big ol' chunk of this town's economy depends on the success of these three concerns." He spread his hand over the file folders. "And Dixie Fulton-Leigh *cannot* manage them all by herself. Her own father knew that. He knew that when the time came she'd need someone like you to be ready to help her. You just said yourself that's what he told you when he first contacted you about making some kind of deal."

"That deal was just a small slice of a big pie." Riley's voice rose but he maintained a controlled quality that suited the surroundings of the plush lawyer's office. One thing he could not afford was to be thrown out of this place for appearing threatening and have it come back to haunt him in Wendy's adoption. "The deal I discussed with your late client never involved partnerships, seats of power, or controlling interests in the gem of the empire. And it certainly did not include rescuing any incompetent maidens in distress."

"Things have changed."

"And not for the better." He stood to leave, his head shaking. "Why on earth would I sink my hard-earned money into a company you're leading me to believe is on a slippery downward slope?"

"Because you have to."

That stopped Riley dead in his tracks. He tried to show more cockiness than concern as he crossed his arms and tipped his head to one side. "I beg your pardon?"

"Because you *have* to."

Riley couldn't decide if the man was that desperate, that sure of his plan, or just completely out of his cotton-picking mind. Or could it be that he knew something about Riley's personal predicament? That thought blindsided him with such force that he dropped back into his seat.

The truth was that if Riley wanted to present himself as a

savvy businessman with diverse interests and the freedom to spend ample time looking after Wendy, he had to act now. It didn't take a slick lawyer to understand that becoming the major stockholder in something like Fulton's Cartage would be a mighty impressive card to have in his hand when he went to court. To stand before a judge as a respected businessman and not just the overworked ex-owner of a sawmill who had never quite gotten all the dirt out from under his fingernails…yes, that would weigh heavily in his favor.

"I'm listening." Riley sat forward on the edge of the chair. "Why do you think I *have* to invest in Fulton's Cartage?"

"To make my point, let me first lay out a little background for you." Greenhow crossed his legs, swiveled his chair to one side, and tented his fingers above his chest.

He looked like a man settling in to weave a long, intricate story. Riley had neither the inclination nor the time for that. He made a show of checking his watch. "What say you give me just the bare basics? Since my daughter's school is closed this week because of that flu bug going around, and I had to bring her along today, I don't want to impose on your secretary to watch her too much longer."

"My secretary doesn't mind, I assure you." He patted his fingertips together. "I suspect that right about now they've finished their walk around the square and are settling in at the drugstore lunch counter for a soda."

"Nevertheless, I'd like to hurry this along so I can get back to my child. If you've got to give some background, just hit the high points, bring me up to speed, then get to the part where I have to make this investment and why."

"Fair enough." He nodded. "In 1965 my father did the legal work that set Fulton's Manufacturing up in business."

"Too far back." Riley shook his head and shuffled his feet

like he was getting ready to go.

"A few years later—" Greenhow spoke more quickly as if he hoped his speed could make up for the length of his back-stroke—"it became clear that using independent trucking companies to deliver the manufactured goods was not cost-effective. John Frederick's money was tied up, so he could not fund a new venture. But his in-laws could."

Riley sat back in his chair and kicked his leg up so that one boot rested atop his knee. "I see."

"So George R. Cunningham and his wife, Samantha Fulton Cunningham, opened the trucking company to service the needs of the furniture manufacturer. Years later, their son pitched in a part of his inheritance to open the outlet store. Three separate businesses, three separate but cooperative owners, one man in charge of them all."

"You mean one *woman* in charge, don't you?"

"Not if I can help it."

"Beg your pardon?" Suddenly without even knowing this Dixie woman, Riley felt like standing up for her. Maybe it was because he had heard the raw power of fatherly love in John Frederick's tone when he'd spoken of his concern for his only child. Maybe it was because Riley had formed an earnest admiration for the late Mr. Fulton-Leigh in their brief but intense conversations. Or maybe he just wanted to send a message to Howard Greenhow that he wasn't impressed or influenced by the lawyer's snide superiority. Whatever the reason, he decided not to let the contemptuous remark pass.

"If you have something to say, Mr. Greenhow..." Riley drew himself up, knowing that years of working at his own sawmill had given him an intimidating build. He'd long ago perfected a look so hard it could make burly men with chainsaws in their hands step back. "I suggest you say it outright and plain."

"I can't say it any plainer than I already have. Dixie cannot run all three operations." He spun his chair around and thumped his fist repeatedly on the desk pad. "She lacks the training, the intuitive skills, the willingness to give 200 percent and then some to make it all work."

"Excuse me for seeming dense here, but why does she have to? Why can't the people who actually own the companies run them? Or why can't someone be hired to run the businesses for them, if they either can't or don't want to do it themselves?"

"Ahh, yes! I knew you were a man with a good head on his shoulders, a man of action—"

"A man who is running out of patience." Riley put his hand to the arm of the chair as if ready to push himself up and hit the door.

Greenhow leapt to his feet. "Someone *can* be brought in to run the trucking division, Mr. Walker." The lawyer's breathing grew quick and shallow and his eyes glittered like a predator moving in for the kill. He rounded the desk and planted himself between Riley and the only exit in the office. "The money is available for that kind of thing, and even more could be found by someone with the wisdom to use his resources creatively and the courage to make hardline decisions."

Riley felt like he should be humming some patriotic anthem to accompany Greenhow's impassioned speech.

"In fact, that very thing should have happened years ago, but one thing stopped it."

The lawyer paused, as if he actually expected Riley to play into his melodramatic presentation by asking "what?" When Riley simply sat and scowled, Greenhow leaned in close and whispered, "Pride."

Riley gave no reaction.

The ruddy-faced man straightened and whirled around,

pacing as he surged on. "Despite the potential harm to their own net worth, the economy of this town, and the quality of life for their friends and neighbors, this one family has always been just too proud to let anyone else come in and help." He stopped, pivoted, and pointed right at Riley. "Until you."

"Me?"

"You are the first outsider John Frederick ever so much as considered bringing on board. It's his vote of confidence that makes you the *only* option I can set before the Judge as a potential partner in Fulton's Cartage."

"Judge?" Riley sat up. "A judge has to rule on this business deal?"

Greenhow blustered out a laugh. "No, no. The Judge is George R. Cunningham, the man who would become the minor partner in Fulton's Cartage once you bought at least 51 percent."

A judge? With this transaction Riley could suddenly become senior shareholder in the established and respected business of a revered old Mississippi family, partnered with nothing less than a judge. It did not get any sweeter than that for showing the world he was the best person to provide and care for the little girl he hoped to adopt as his own. "And he'd do it? Sell, that is?"

"To John Frederick's handpicked predecessor he would, and I can guarantee you that. And I hold his power of attorney, due to his...advanced age. So you and I can make this deal right here, right now."

It took everything Riley had not to stick out his hand and agree to it on the spot. He had come with an open mind to talk about something he'd already concluded he would go ahead with before Mr. Fulton-Leigh died. The stakes had gone up a bit since then, but then his personal stakes had risen decidedly, too. Listening to Howard Greenhow—and taking into account his circumstances regarding Wendy's adoption—Riley felt he'd be a fool not to forge ahead with buying the offered stocks.

Or was he a fool to listen to Howard Greenhow? He cleared his throat. "Mr. Fulton-Leigh quoted me a price per share when we spoke about this."

"That won't have changed, I assure you."

Riley grinned and shook his head. "Then it's a no go, Mr. Greenhow, because the circumstances surrounding the company and the deal *have* changed—and as we've established, not for the better."

The round-faced lawyer broke out in what Riley couldn't help thinking was his first genuine expression of emotion all during the whole meeting—he laughed. "I *knew* you were the man for this job. Shrewd, fearless, and unwilling to throw good money after bad. I like that. Like it a lot, Walker. I can see why John Frederick picked you."

Riley snorted. He was under no pretenses that he and Howard Greenhow would ever form a mutual admiration society.

"What if I say we can take John Frederick's price down by 20 percent?"

"What if we say twenty-five? I am, after all, going to have to invest more time in this now than I was going to before. My time is worth money."

"Does this mean you're seriously interested? With the reduced rate?"

"I'd want to tour the place."

"Of course."

"And I want to meet the family."

"Ahh, the family." The lawyer's smile stretched outward, but not up—he looked positively pained.

"Is there a problem with me meeting the family?" His mother's warning about the Fulton descendants' reputation for being *interesting* rang like a tin bell in his head.

"No. No problem except that..." Greenhow reached into his jacket pocket and yanked free a handkerchief, which he dabbed back and forth over his forehead. "Before we take that step, let me ask you this, Mr. Walker: When you spoke to John Frederick did he strike you as a man who had his family's best interest at heart?"

"Yes."

"The kind of man you could personally trust?"

"Absolutely."

"He felt the same way about you, I'm sure. He would never have sought you out otherwise. It's important for you to understand that fact before you ever meet this family, before you make up your mind about them and the deal."

Riley opened his mouth, determined to guide the conversation back to the question of his meeting the family, but Greenhow cut him off.

"That's why you are sitting here today, Mr. Walker, instead of one of a dozen other men who have the inclination, the insight, and wherewithal to make this happen."

Riley leaned back in his chair. If the hog slop got any deeper in here, he'd need wading boots just to get out the door. "Get to your point, Mr. Greenhow."

"My point, Mr. Walker, is that you are being handed an opportunity that a lot of men struggle all their lives to try to achieve but never can quite get their fingers on."

Including Greenhow himself, Riley's gut feeling told him. Perhaps Greenhow saw him as a means to an end, making himself the go-to guy in the deal-of-the-decade as far as this town was concerned. The lawyer clearly harbored no respect or affection for John Frederick's daughter, and Riley had to wonder if the lawyer meant to use him to get back at her for whatever wrong he thought she'd done. Riley also had no doubt that if he refused this dream deal, this slick attorney would find another way to get to Dixie Fulton-Leigh.

Riley imagined someone trying a back-end sneak like this to take advantage of Wendy, who could one day conceivably be in the same position as Miss Fulton-Leigh. How would he feel if someone had no problem running roughshod over Wendy, or his mother…or his sister, to fulfill his own agenda? His stomach knotted and his muscles tightened. Anger and outrage swelled up in him, just as they had when Carol suggested they trash his sister in order to make him look better. No real man would stand by and let either of these things happen.

John Frederick Fulton-Leigh could not watch out for his only child now, but Riley could. He could do what was best for both Wendy and Dixie in one decisive move. Only he stood between slimy Howard Greenhow and the woman he had never met but who suddenly represented all the women he loved rolled into one.

He stood and stuck out his hand. "Let's go ahead with it, Mr. Greenhow. How quickly can you get me a contract?"

"Could you hurry it along a little, maybe?"

The pharmacist peered down at Dixie from behind the raised wooden counter with a look that could have frozen fire.

"Please?" Dixie folded her hands together and tried to look demure and deferential when what she really felt was crabby and cantankerous. What had begun as a mad dash to run an urgent errand during her fifteen-minute lunch hour had slowed to a dead crawl, with time running out.

"Sorry, but it can't be helped. Since your Aunt Sis didn't drop off Miss Lettie's medicine bottle, I have to look up the prescription, fill it, make a label, pretty much start from scratch. And there's three other folks called in ahead of you. You'll just have to wait your turn."

Dixie gritted her teeth at Noni Philpot's scolding schoolmarm tone. Noni was the sourest-faced woman you'd ever want to catch sight of, with a disposition that made her always-dour expression seem downright pleasant by comparison. And she treated just about everyone who came through the doors of her understocked, overpriced drugstore like she wished they'd just up and take their business elsewhere. Of course, in their tiny town, there was no *elsewhere* to go.

Dixie sighed.

Whap! No telling what Noni had slapped against the counter, but it sure did work for making Dixie want to get out of there, even more than anything the surly woman could have said.

"I'll just be over at the lunch counter." Dixie pointed like maybe Noni had forgotten where that counter was after only owning the place and working here each and every day for the last ten years. "You can just call me when it's ready."

More whacking and rattling sounds answered her.

"Okay, then." Dixie smiled, gave a wave, took a step backward.

Whap, whap, whap, whap.

She made a beeline for the counter, then plopped herself right down on one of the stools. Rushed, worried, and now falling further behind in her schedule—what she wouldn't give to have a sympathetic ear right now.

Too bad there was no one.

For one fleeting instant she thought she'd bust out crying

all over the "Sights to See in Mississippi" paper placemat in front of her. That darned combination of exhaustion and self-pity had crept up on her again.

Exhaustion, self-pity, and grief, not just for losing her father but for so many things she suddenly realized she had missed out on. Everything had changed so fast. A few weeks ago her life consisted of the best hotels in the South, a lavish expense account, closing big deals for the company, and only coming back to Fulton's Dominion for holidays and a few weekends scattered through any given month.

At least she could take comfort that all that nonsense was behind her. She'd finally have a chance to settle down, to make a home for herself—maybe even find someone to love and have a family with. Daddy's passing had brought her need for those things keenly into focus—and deepened the ache inside her for all she had lost, all she'd never had.

"Be back to get your order in a minute, hon." The waitress clunked down a glass of ice water with a paper-covered straw.

Dixie blinked, taking a moment to realize where she was and how she had come to be there. She started to answer the woman in the brown and gold uniform but by the time she tried, the waitress already had her back to the counter and her attention on something else.

From deep inside herself, Dixie pulled up the most congenial disposition she could. She slid a plastic-coated menu from behind one gleaming, silver napkin holder and flicked it open. "Well, since it looks like I'm going to be here awhile, I guess no one could fault me for grabbing a little something to eat."

"I'm not supposed to talk to strangers, ma'am."

"Actually, I wasn't..." She spun 'round on the stool, stopping short when she caught a glimpse of who had spoken to her. "Well, hello there."

The sweetest pair of big brown eyes batted up at her. "Aren't you just a baby doll?"

Instantly enchanted, Dixie laid her menu down and leaned forward over the empty stool next to her. "Hope you don't mind my saying it, but I do believe that accent of yours is bigger than you are."

"I'm not supposed to talk to strangers," the little dark-haired girl drawled out again.

"You're not here all by yourself, are you?" Dixie glanced around. No one at the counter. No one at the register. "That is, there is someone who brought you in here, right? Maybe just went to the rest room or something like that?"

"I'm *not* supposed to—"

"Yes, I know, talk to strangers." Was that the only sentence this child knew? Dixie darted her gaze here and there over every visible place in the small store. Who would leave a young child unattended like this? Even in a small town like Fulton's Dominion, people just didn't *do* that. They watched the national news here just the same as they did in Jackson and larger cities. Things happened to children left alone. Everybody knew that.

The child set her leg to swinging, the untied laces of one of her precious pink tennis shoes flapping back and forth against her white tights.

Dixie touched her mother's pearl necklace, which she always wore, as if trying to draw on some inherent maternal guidance. Someone would come strolling up to claim the child any moment now. She was sure of it.

Her eyes glued to Dixie, the girl took her large paper cup and almost went blue in the face trying to draw one of the fountain's famous extra-thick milkshakes up through a pencil-thin straw.

Dixie had to hold herself back from taking that straw away

from the girl and handing her a spoon. If she wasn't supposed to talk to strangers, she most certainly would not accept better dining suggestions from one, would she?

The girl gulped, but anyone could tell it was mostly air. She paused and looked down into her cup.

Who was she? Obviously, Dixie did not recognize every child in town, but one old enough to be left sitting alone in the drugstore would most likely recognize *her*.

"You know what I think?" She reached toward the child, but did not quite actually touch her arm.

"I'm not supposed—"

"I think you're not a real little girl, are you?"

The brown eyes blinked at her, the cup sort of sagged in her two small hands until it rested on the hammock created in her lap by her corduroy jumper.

"I think you're one of those robot toys I've heard about that says back whatever you say to it." She cocked her head first one way and then the other. "What do people do? Press that bow in your hair to record a message?"

The girl giggled, her adorably pudgy fingers touching the bow in question.

"Or do you come with preprogrammed sayings, like—" Dixie raised the pitch of her voice and tried to copy the child's striking accent—"'Help! This milkshake is so thick it's making my eyes cross to sup it up through this straw!'"

The girl giggled even more, her eyes shining.

Dixie wished she could nab that little bit of a thing and pull her close in a hug and hold her 'til she knew beyond a shadow of doubt that everything was okay. Instead, she kept on at her game, hoping to reach that point where the girl would trust her enough to tell her why such a young thing was sitting in a drugstore all alone. "Of course, I know you can say that one thing about not talking to strangers. But you know, the thing is, in this town, *I* am certainly not a stranger. Everybody here knows me and my whole family. And I'm thinking if you were from here you would, too."

The girl turned and plunked her cup down on the counter. She sat there looking straight ahead, her jaw thrust forward, her arms folded over herself like the locked gates of Fort Knox.

"You done with that, sweetie?" The waitress came by.

The child didn't move or speak.

"I think she might be waiting for it to melt a little so she can drink it better," Dixie volunteered.

She glanced up at the blond waitress and tried to pull the woman's name out of her muddled memory. Noni Philpot was too cheap to spring for nametags because her sunny disposition kept chasing off the workers as fast as she could get the things made up. Dixie drummed her fingers on the counter, trying to think how to ask someone whose name eluded you to tell you what she knew about another person whose name you could not get out of them.

The stocky blonde fished a nub of a pencil out from her apron pocket and tapped it on a fresh, fat order pad. "You made up your mind, Miss Fulton-Leigh?"

"I...um..."

"Fulton-Leigh? Is *that* your name?"

Dixie gasped, so delighted at the unexpected breakthrough that she couldn't help teasing. "You *can* say something else besides 'I'm not supposed to talk to strangers!' Or has the fry cook become a ventriloquist?"

"I can talk to you now," the child announced. "Because I know who you are."

"I thought so." Dixie nodded, feeling just a bit like a minor celebrity. "I told you, everyone in town knows who *I* am—"

"You're the lady who made my grandma's green sofa."

Dixie started to correct that misconception, but didn't have the chance.

"And my daddy is going to start making sofas, too," the child rushed on, her face flushed with excitement.

"He is?" At that, Dixie forgot about the correction and tried to remember if she'd authorized any new hires at the factory.

"Uh-huh." Both her legs began to swing back and forth out of sync and she bounced in place on the lunch counter stool. "That's why we're moving here."

"You are?" Dixie and the waitress exchanged looks. This story did not add up and Dixie had a very bad feeling about it. "And just where is your daddy now?"

"He's at the lawyer's."

"Lawyer's?" She drew in a deep breath, as if she could draw some calming curative from the smell of old grease on the grill and the musty dankness of the old building. "Making sofas and going to lawyers? That doesn't make any sense, sweetheart. Are you sure your daddy didn't leave you here—" she couldn't say what she feared most, so she just tacked on—"for some other reason?"

"My daddy didn't leave me here. The lady from the lawyer's office brung me—"

"Brought me." Dixie hardly realized she'd made the correction.

"Brought me—" the child echoed without so much as a hiccup in the flow of her story—"here to get a treat while Daddy talked to the lawyer."

"Now that is true, Miss Fulton-Leigh. One a them secretaries from Greenhow, Greenhow, whose-it, and what-have-you did come in and pay for this little gal's shake."

"Greenhow?" Dixie stared blankly ahead.

"That's who my daddy is talking to." She nodded with such enthusiasm her hair kept bobbing after she'd tipped her chin up and hurried on with her explanation. "Daddy says he's maybe going to be a chairholder at the furniture building store."

"He does?" What could that Howard Greenhow be up to? He'd warned her that she was not finished dealing with him, but Dixie had imagined it just an idle threat, a parting shot by a powerless antagonist. Now she wasn't so sure. "Did your father tell you anything else about this? Did he say how he planned to buy into my company because last time I checked it wasn't for sale."

"I don't know." Wendy gave an overplayed shrug. "Daddy came over here to visit once and talked to the man who made the sofas—"

"Did he say what that man's name was?"

"Fulton-Leigh, same as yours, ma'am. Is that *your* daddy?"

"Yes, it is. It was." Dixie cast her gaze down. How much more of a mess could her father have left behind for her to clean up?

"And then my daddy said that he was going to be a chairholder we were moving here because he was going to *ver-si-fy* his *vest-a-mints* so he could spend more time taking care of me. He said the lawyer thought he could help Daddy do that and if he did we'd move here and he'd help make the sofas."

"I don't like the sound of this." Dixie put her hand to the back of her neck, surprised by the cold clamminess of her skin under her thick hair. "I don't like the sound of this, at all."

"It's okay." Wendy reached out and patted Dixie's other hand. "He'll make real good sofas, ma'am. My daddy can do *anything.*"

Dixie looked down at that tender face, so filled with pride

and confidence in a hero of a father who would always be there for her. Oh, to be that trusting again. She swallowed hard and pushed aside the lovely notion. "Well, it looks like my daddy could also do anything—anything unexpected. Now I'm left to try to deal with the consequences, starting by paying a little visit to Mr. Greenhow. It was nice talking with you…what did you say your name was?"

"Wendy."

"Wendy." Dixie bowed her head in greeting and took the small hand in hers for one quick shake. "It was nice to meet you, Wendy. But I've got to run." Still holding the girl's hand, Dixie called in the general direction of the pharmacist's counter, "Noni, someone will be in to get Miss Lettie's pills sometime later today."

"Send anyone but that crackpot picaroon grandfather of yours."

"I know. I know." Dixie bent low and touched a finger to Wendy's chin. "You stay put and keep right on not talking to strangers, you hear me? And you'll be all right here until someone comes for—"

"Daddy!"

In a flutter of dark hair and waving hands, Wendy leapt off the stool and scurried toward the drugstore's glass front door.

Dixie set off after her. The clipped cadence of her heels fell in right behind the *swish-swoosh-swish* of Wendy's corduroy jumper and the quiet rhythmic clacking of the tips of her untied shoelace dancing over the dingy floor with her every step.

An electronic *ding* like a doorbell signaled that someone had, indeed, walked into the store.

Dixie's heartbeat thrummed in her ears, which only added to the crush of thoughts, sounds, and emotions closing in on her. If anything the child said held true, Dixie's quarrel would be with Greenhow. But she would still have to deal with Wendy's daddy and that likely would not be pleasant. Best to see to that first.

She stepped forward, giving a shake of her head to toss her hair into place and to give her a moment to fix a smile on her face and—

"Oh, my word, it's *you.*"

A deep masculine voice softened by surprise and Southern intonation met her ears before her eyes adjusted enough to see anything but the glaring sunlight glinting off the glass door.

Dixie dropped her gaze, half-turning her head away. "I beg your pardon? Have we—?"

A pair of black cowboy boots stepped into her downcast line of vision.

She blinked, then moved her gaze slowly upward, wary of the blinding light and the disadvantage it put her at. Boots, jeans, sport coat, pristine white shirt, silk tie…*expensive* silk tie. What kind of man wore a tie like that with jeans and cowboy boots? She had to see for herself.

She raised her eyes. "No! Not you? *You* are the man trying to buy into my family company? *You?*"

"*Your* company? *You* are Dixie Fulton-Leigh?" He laughed and bent to scoop up his daughter. He lifted the petite child effortlessly up until her head lay on his broad shoulder. Cocking his head, he gave Dixie a lazy, knowing grin that would have brought a weaker woman to her knees. "Well, well, Princess Snootie-Patootie, who'd have thought it? Looks like you and I are going to be partners."

Seven

Everyone should be quick to listen,
slow to speak and slow to become angry,
for man's anger does not bring about the righteous life
that God desires.

JAMES 1:19–20

"PARTNERS? IN A PIG'S EYE!"

Riley laughed. He could well afford to see the humor in this. After all, he held the upper hand—and the majority shares in Fulton's Cartage. Besides, how could anyone not get a good chuckle out of the fact that one of the reasons he had pressed ahead so quickly with this deal was his sense of manly duty? His noble aim to charge to the rescue of Fulton-Leigh's poor, beleaguered daughter.

Riley shook his head and smiled at the one woman on the planet he was pretty sure did not need, nor would accept, his help. "Actually, Miss Fulton-Leigh, partners in the family business."

"*My* family's business." To her credit, it came more like a gentle, determined reproach than the hard challenge it might have been.

"My family's, too, now." He cupped his hand over Wendy's head and stroked her soft, fine hair.

With no more than a flash of her green eyes and a tilt of her head Dixie contradicted his claim, but she kept her lips pressed tightly shut.

Riley wished he knew whether it was his calm insistence or the gesture of fatherly affection that had a silencing effect on her. He had the feeling he would have need of that device again before they got things running smoothly with their businesses...not to mention between themselves.

"Listen, Miss Fulton-Leigh, twice now we've gotten off to what seems like a...difficult start. Since we're dealing with something a little more important than a parking space this time, why don't we go over to your office, settle in, and talk this out like two reasonable, mature business people?"

"Oh, of course, that's exactly what we're going to do." She gave him a smile that came too easily to be real, then stepped around him to place her delicate hand on the door. She gave one hard backward glance over her shoulder. "When pigs fly!"

"You have a thing about pigs, don't you, Miss...since we're going to be working together so closely, may I call you Dixie?"

"You may stand here and *whistle* Dixie for all I care, Mr...Wendy's father. Because we are not going to be working together and I am not going to my office to talk to you about anything." She pushed the door partly open. "I am heading straight over to Howard Greenhow's office and put an end to this absurdity right now."

"Go right ahead." The afternoon sunlight bathed her in heavenly brilliance, but Riley had no pretensions—this woman would happily give him the devil if she got the chance. So he just had to make sure he didn't give her that chance. "March yourself over to Greenhow's office, but it won't do you any good."

She huffed out a *ha* then added, "You can't be all that confident that you have an airtight deal or you wouldn't try to manipulate me away from going over to take this up with your lawyer."

"He is not my lawyer." Riley set Wendy down then crossed his arms. "And he's not in his office the rest of the day. That's why I say it won't do you any good to go over there."

"Then I'll just go and *find* him." She gave the door a shove.

Riley stretched his arm out, his hand up, and caught the door by its metal frame, physically cutting her off and undermining any hope for her flamboyant exit. "I hate to be rude—"

"And yet you seem so practiced at it."

The kindness he had seen displayed toward her elderly companion was obviously not indicative of this woman's general nature. If Wendy hadn't been standing by he'd have thrown a laugh right in the woman's beautiful face then showed her an all-new meaning of rude by taking this boondocks belle down a notch or two.

But Wendy *was* there, watching wide-eyed, so he drew a deep breath. "Look, I know we got off on the wrong foot the other day. This little set-to hasn't done anything to foster better relations, either. But the truth is, we *will* be working together so the least we can do is try to be civil to each other."

"No, the least you can do is to get out of my way. That's advice you'd be wise to remember where I and my family's business are concerned, Mr..."

"Walker. Riley Walker." He offered his hand, even though he had to grit his teeth to make himself do it.

The door fell shut, ushering in a cool gust of March wind.

Dixie shivered.

Riley stuck his hand out just a tiny bit further and waited.

She hesitated. She seemed to want to say something, and then again she seemed to want to say nothing at all. Finally, her gaze darted to the side and down.

Riley followed the line of vision and found Wendy staring up at them both, her mouth hanging open…in awe at their exchange, no doubt. Gently, he reached over, put one fingertip under his sweet baby girl's chin and urged her to shut her mouth. He gave her a wink to let her know everything was all right, then extended his hand toward Dixie again. This time, when he looked at the troublesome woman, there was something different about her.

Her perfect white teeth sank into the full center of her lower lip. Her head was angled down just enough to show her shame at acting so badly toward him in front of his little girl, but not bowed so much that he might think she was giving in to him on any of this. She slipped her hand in his.

Her skin felt so soft against his roughened palm that he marveled when she didn't pull away in disgust. Instead, she clamped her hand solidly in his and gave a firm shake that he suspected did both her genteel upbringing and her daddy's uncompromising standards proud.

"I apologize for my abruptness, Mr. Walker. I've been under a strain lately and…"

"Of course, I should have mentioned right off how sorry I was to hear about your father." He placed his other hand over their clasped ones. To lend comfort and show his support, he told himself, despite the fact that he could have done both those things without prolonging their contact at all, much less intensifying it. "I didn't learn of his passing until yesterday, otherwise I'd have at least gone to the visitation to pay my respects. He was a good man."

"You knew my father?" Her big eyes shimmered with unshed tears.

Suddenly Riley felt like a world-class jerk for the assumptions he'd made about the woman. Anyone who would set aside her own powerful pride and wounded feelings to keep from cutting a man down in the eyes of his child could not be the shrew he'd imagined. She'd just lost her own father, for crying out loud, a man whom she obviously loved and depended on. To top it off, she'd inherited a business along with a family not suited to or interested in helping her manage things. If she was short tempered at having his little surprise thrust upon her, who could blame her?

She had no way of knowing yet that many of her problems handling the business were about to be solved—by none other than him. He shifted his weight and gave her hand a reassuring pat. "I met your father once. We had a nice, long talk about... well, just about everything. I left with the feeling that he and I were a lot alike in many ways."

"Oh?"

"Your father sure thought you hung the moon, you know."

Looking into those guileless eyes, Riley could begin to understand why. Of course, any father might be fiercely protective and utterly adoring of his only little girl. But to have that little girl grow up to be a woman like Dixie...a fighter who defended her own against suspected interlopers, yet was sweet enough to have made a connection with a child she had just met. Well, that kind of daughter, that kind of *woman*, was something special. Riley had realized that the very first time he'd clashed with her. He smiled. "The day I met with your father was the day you and I...um, crossed paths, as a matter of fact."

"Really?"

"Yeah." He nodded. "And I spoke with him over the phone a time or two after that. He was the one who laid the groundwork for this new business relationship of yours and mine."

"We don't *have* a business relationship, Mr. Walker." She pulled her hand free of his.

"We will, Miss Fulton-Leigh." He leaned close to her, not to intimidate her but more to insinuate his very real presence in her world. "By the end of the day I'll have the stock papers that confirm it."

"By the end of the day I'll have all this straightened out and the only papers you'll have, I'm sorry to have to tell you, will be your walking papers." No animosity colored her words.

In fact, if forced, Riley might have called the simple statement conciliatory, even sincere, as if she really were sorry it had come to this.

"Oh, no." He stepped back from her. "You're not going to get me again with that softspoken charm of yours. You're not one bit sorry to tell me that or anything else you think might help your cause. Sorry, lady, you've found one man you can't trick or manipulate. Like it or not, you and I will be working together."

"Trick? *Manipulate?*" Fire flashed in those eyes. She threw out her chest and folded her arms over it. Her cool expression remained unchanged as she fixed her gaze on his. "Those are awfully ugly words, not to mention surprising considering they come from a sneak thief who has crept into the business my family has owned since before I was born and tried to grab a piece of it before my daddy is even cold in his grave!"

"Your daddy is the reason I am here, Miss Dixie Fulton-Leigh. He wanted to bring me on board because he feared something might happen to him and that you—"

"That I wouldn't be able to handle it?" The quiet in her tone was like the stillness before the storm. But no storm came. Her chin trembled. Her arms untwined. "I don't believe you. My father had faith in me, Mr. Walker."

"Yes, he did, but he also was a realist and a man who wanted to do everything he could to make sure his daughter's future was secure." Riley put his hand on Wendy's thin shoulder. He swallowed to wash away any telltale traces of raw emotion. "That's something I can certainly understand."

"I'd like to believe you." She smiled down at Wendy, then gave him a skeptical look. "But the mere fact that you've gone through Howard Greenhow to accomplish whatever it is you think you've pulled off—"

"He's the one who contacted me, not the other way around, if that makes any difference." Her posture relaxed just enough to let Riley know it did matter. "Either way, it's a gigantic waste of time for us to stand in the doorway of a drugstore and try to go over the particulars of this."

"You're right, of course."

"Of course."

"I've wasted too much time here already. I have to track down a certain weaselly lawyer of our mutual acquaintance." She gave Wendy an endearing little wave, then brushed past him to open the door again.

"Talk about a waste of time." Riley jerked his thumb in Dixie's direction as he spoke to Wendy—loud enough to ensure the woman stepping over the threshold heard him. "It's a done deal. She'll find out for herself soon enough, I guess."

He took Wendy's hand and twirled her around, smooth as

any practiced swing dancer, to set her facing the door. Pressing his palm to the glass, he held the thing open wide even after Dixie had let go of it.

"Don't think you're going with me, now." Dixie did something of a sashay herself, pivoting just enough to give him a scalding look. "The sheriff is an old high school pal of mine, and I'd hate to have to call him to run you in on a stalking charge."

"That shows how much she knows, doesn't it, Wendy-girl?" He let the door fall shut. "I don't even wear stockings."

Wendy giggled.

"Very funny. Ha. Ha." Her sarcasm could not conceal the twinkle in her eye or the way her lovely lips lifted in a faint smile. "Instead of trying to steal my company away from me, why don't you go and open yourself up one of those comedy clubs?"

"Maybe I'll ask the realtor we're meeting with later today to see if there's anything like that available. As a possible sideline to my other interests here."

"You have a meeting with a realtor?"

"She had some houses lined up for me to see today and more when I come back over in the morning."

"Well, do yourself a favor, won't you?"

"What's that?"

"Don't put down a deposit." She smiled like a cat full of cream, then touched Wendy on the nose, mouthed a good-bye, and headed off across the middle of the street without so much as a glance to see if any cars were coming.

"She's mighty pretty, isn't she, Daddy?" Wendy gave his hand a squeeze, her entire face alight with innocence and excitement.

"She's mighty *something*, Wendy-girl." *Mighty annoying,*

mighty confusing, mighty sure of herself, all sprang to mind. And mighty likely to get past his defenses and under his skin if he didn't watch out. "Yes, ma'am, she's mighty something. I just haven't quite figured out what, yet."

"What am I going to do?" Every last bit of Dixie's cultivated poise crumbled as she collapsed into the overstuffed chair next to Miss Lettie's rocker.

"Do? I thought we were going to write some more on this story book you're making for my birthday." Lettie rocked slowly. She patted her spindly leg with one hand, in a beat at odds with her rhythmic swaying back and forth with her chair.

The sight of that action, combined with the constant, heavy throbbing in Dixie's temples, created a deep, whirling tide in her stomach that did not help her regain her focus. She shut her eyes to blot out anything but her thoughts. Those alone provided enough turmoil for her at present.

Her futile attempts to locate Greenhow had only added to the confusion and frustration set off in her by Riley Walker. And put her even further behind in her regular work schedule. She'd still be at the office now if she hadn't felt the pull of her responsibilities at home. Dinner had to be fixed, Grandpa and Aunt Sis checked up on, and Dixie had promised Miss Lettie they'd get back to writing her life's story starting tonight.

Dixie buried her face in her hands and stole a peek at the occasional table where the clothbound journal lay. Obligation demanded she keep her word to the dear old woman who had done so much for their family, but Dixie could not see the use of it. Not when most of Lettie's stories actually centered around Dixie's family and revealed so little of a personal nature about the retired woman's life, outlook, and experiences.

"Miss Lettie, do you mind if we put off working on the book for one more night?"

"Heaven's no!" She waved her hand as if to shoo the very notion of the thing away. "It's your creation, Dixie Belle, not mine."

"But it's supposed to be yours. Your story. So far most of what you've told me has been about my family, quaint anecdotes and observations on their lives, very little about your own." The antique mantel clock ticked off a few seconds before Dixie went on. "That's one of the reasons I haven't gotten back into the writing project since Daddy died. I haven't wanted to concentrate over much on the family history, but I would still like to hear about and record yours."

"Lands, I did tell you, now didn't I, how I come to live here in Fulton's Dominion, in the household of Mr. Samuel Prescott Fulton, all the way from my home in New Orleans when I was barely twenty-one years old?"

"You told me the circumstances that caused my great-grandparents to bring you here, yes. You went on quite a while about how they had lost their two boys before the age of five, so that when their daughter was born, they decided to bring someone in to care for her because Eugenia Fulton no longer had the strength or heart to do it."

"And that someone was me." Lettie touched her fingers to the top button of her favorite blue and white housecoat. "Hand chosen by Founder Fulton himself."

Very few people alive still referred to her great-grandfather as *Founder Fulton,* and the old nickname made Dixie smile just a bit.

"His putting his faith in me, trusting me with the raising of his child, bringing me into the house to live among the family and not off in a servant's quarters...well, a young person like you can't know what a meaningful gesture that was for the time. You come from good people, Dixie Belle, and you should know that."

"I do know. What I had hoped is that in helping me put together this account, I'd discover more about you and—" Dixie almost said, "and your family," but Lettie seldom discussed her own kin, and never unless she brought it up herself. "And your vantage point on things, like how it felt to leave New Orleans, and what kinds of things you enjoyed doing as a young woman in Fulton's Dominion. Or even what it was that Founder Fulton saw in you that made him—what'd you call it?—*hand choose* you?"

An enigmatic smile crept across those old, thin lips, a distant sense of wistfulness shone in those still-expressive eyes. Lettie stopped her rocking and sat up just a little straighter. "Perhaps in time, Dixie Belle, in time. When we're both of us ready."

"I'd ask you what you meant by that cryptic remark but I think I'd have better luck asking Peachie Too to perform an opera for me."

Lettie cackled. "Lah, can't you just see that disagreeable furball running hither and yon all over some stage a yappin' and a snappin' at the plump ol' behinds of them bellowing opera folks?"

"Laugh and change the subject all you want tonight, but I'm warning you, Miss Lettie, it's less than four months 'til your birthday. Sometime between now and then, I'd like to capture in this journal at least some of your thoughts and memories, you know, the lessons you've learned in a hundred years of living."

"Then let's just leave the book as it is, lamb—blank. That pretty much sums up what old Lettie has learned in her time on earth." Another raspy laugh crackled up from her narrow chest.

"That's not true, Lettie."

"The older I gets the more I know it *is* true. The longer I live, the more I learn how little I do know."

"You know about people, Miss Lettie." Dixie rose and went to the woman who had been a fixture in her family's life for over eighty years. She bent to give her a hug, ever mindful of how fragile the tiny powerhouse had grown. "You know about love and joy, and how to laugh and make other people laugh too, and you know how to sing and praise the Lord—"

"Now, those I do, child, those I do."

"That's not nothing."

"But it's not the kind of thing you can set down in a book, either. Seems most the lessons I've learned have to get passed along from one heart to another. And far as that goes, I think I've already done my job with you, pretty much."

"Don't you believe it; I still have plenty to learn from you." She gave the old dear a kiss on the cheek then strolled over to the window. She stared out at the small world of South Dominion Street through the intricate lace of imported sheers beneath the half-century-old portieres. "But days like this it does seem the only way life wants to teach me anything at all is for me to learn it the hard way."

Lettie snorted out her opinion of that assessment, then set to rocking again at a snail's pace. "Things can't hardly be that bad for a smart young thing like you."

"Bad? Maybe not." Dixie folded her hands together. "I mean, I have so much—I've always had so much—that it is a tad ridiculous for me to moan and groan about how *bad* things are."

"See, you *are* learning."

That picked Dixie's spirits up, a little.

"The thing is, everything is so crazy and now there's this... this...this...*man!*"

"Ahhhh."

"No! No ahhhh. This man...it's not like that, it will never be like that. This is a business problem kind of man. A man who has seized the opportunity of Daddy's death to move in on our companies like some vulture." Dixie gulped down some air, trying to rid herself of that shallow, breathless quality her hurried denial had taken on. "Oh, sure, he has a smile that makes your knees go weak as water and a way about him that makes you want to believe every dream you see shining in his eyes. But I won't be taken in by that. Riley Walker may be wonderful to look at, he may have shoulders like a bear, but I suspect he'd be just as dangerous to tangle with."

"He still sounds like a fine, handsome man."

"He is a handsome man, I'll admit that. But fine? Not in the ways that count." An image of Riley lifting Wendy up in his arms flashed in Dixie's mind. For a moment, she felt a pang of remorse over her harsh and hasty judgement. She recalled how glowingly the man had spoken of her father, of the plan they had supposedly laid to work together. "You know he had the nerve to try to tell me that Daddy had wanted him to go into business with him for *my* sake?"

"Oh, he did?"

"Don't say it like that."

"Like what?" Lettie blinked in big-eyed innocence.

"Like you believe his wild claim." She said it as much for herself as for the trusting old soul beside her.

"Why not?"

"It's just too easy, that's all. Daddy's gone and can't substantiate the story. I mean, I know now that they did meet, Mavis confirmed as much for me, but as to the nature of their talk? Well, I can't find anything to support this man's assertion that he and Daddy had any kind of agreement."

"Can you find anything to the contrary?"

"I can't find anything much at all, truth be told, and firing the attorneys has only made matters worse. At least in the short run."

Dixie moved to the sofa, a traditional top-of-the-line style that had been the mainstay of the Fulton line for thirty years. The upholstery, called *wheat on white,* looked almost opalescent bathed in the low afternoon sun. It was the kind of piece that reflected well on its owners, suggesting taste, elegance, unchanging style, and uncompromising standards. Dixie wanted to kick it as hard as she could.

Instead, she kicked off her heels. *As if some dirt and a few scuffmarks more or less would matter.* She swiped at a couple of downy tufts of apricot-colored hair. *I thought I banned that dog from the couch.* She plopped down and stretched out on the sofa. Banning the dog wouldn't do any good since Dixie wasn't entirely sure Peachie Too was the one shedding.

She let her body sink into the thick cushions and sighed. "Oh, Miss Lettie, I'm so tired and confused. I just feel like… like almost everything in my life is slipping through my grasp, careening wildly away, totally out of my control."

"Well, good."

"Good?" She jerked her head around to see if Lettie was even still listening. "I tell you my life is out of control and you say it's good?"

"You wanted to know about my experiences, lamb." She shrugged her shoulders. Or at least Dixie thought that's what she did. With Lettie's small frame inside that shapeless house-dress, it was hard to tell for sure. The old woman began rocking again. "My experience is that when we think our lives are out of control, that's when God does some of his best work."

"I don't follow you."

"Ain't much to follow. Fact is, God is always in control. Those times we step back and say to ourselves that things is out of our hands, that gets us out of the way and gives the Lord some elbow room to start working his wonders."

"You think one of those wonders he can start to work on right away is finding me a new lawyer to help me sort this all out?" She laid her head down.

"That sounds more like your work, Dixie Belle, not the Lord's."

"I'm not so sure. In order for me to do it I'm going to have to go out of town, and just hope to find the right one. Sure do wish the Almighty would point me in the right direction."

"Pshaw. What's it take to find a legal man? They's all over! Country is crawling with them, the way it looks on the TV. I even gots one in *my* family."

"You do?"

"You think a black man can't be a lawyer man, too? Or is it you thinks poor ol' Lettie can't have her a grandson over in Jackson with a fancy education? I had an education, you know, Founder Fulton seed to it that I had a lot of book learning."

"Yes, I know, ma'am. You told me." She rolled onto her side and propped herself up on one elbow. "It's just that you so rarely speak of your family. I know you and your daughter, Helen Betty, were estranged before…"

Lettie's brow crimped as if she had a flash of deep pain.

Dixie let the reference drop. "I always assumed your grandson lived far, far away. Now to hear out of the blue like that he is a lawyer and living in Jackson—"

"Shoo, that ain't important."

Dixie could see the woman's defenses go up. There'd be no more talk of grandsons or any of Lettie's relatives tonight.

"I'm just saying lawyers is everywhere."

Still, Dixie had a small piece of information she'd never had before. Lettie's grandson lived in Jackson. He was a lawyer. Dixie needed a lawyer. And even if it ended up he wasn't the man for the job, when Dixie walked in as a prospective client he'd have to listen to her pitch for a reconciliation with his grandmother. Wouldn't that make the best birthday present of all for her dear Miss Lettie?

"Besides, Dixie Belle, what you need first and foremost ain't the law, it's the Lord. What you need, my dear, is prayer."

"Oh, I have prayed, ma'am. I have prayed without ceasing, more than I think I have ever prayed before in my life." She laid back and covered her eyes with one hand. "I've asked the Lord to be my strength, to give me guidance, to send someone to help—"

"To send you help?"

Dixie's body went taut, her eyes squeezed shut so tight they burned. The word *no* formed on her lips but she did not speak her apprehension aloud.

"Did I ever tell you that story I love so much? 'Bout the man gots caught up in a great flood?"

"I think you have." She spoke so softly she knew Lettie could not hear. Even if she did, it would not stop her from telling the story again.

"See, this man, he saw the waters rising and had no way of escaping them 'cept to climb up top of his roof, but the water it just kept a'coming. So the man, he took to praying with all his heart that God have mercy and come and save him." As Lettie spoke, her rocking grew faster, then eased off and slowed down again. The low creaking of her chair gave off a natural sound effect for the building and ebbing tension of her tale. "Pretty soon, came a great peace over the man and he took it on faith the God had heard his plea and would be coming to his rescue directly."

Dixie crossed her ankles, then turned her head until the jacquard finish of the sofa cushion chafed lightly at her cheek. She could just barely see Lettie from this vantage. "Yes, I know, and then a rowboat came along—"

"Am I telling this or are you?" Lettie pursed her lips like she'd popped a sourball into her mouth and angled her sparse, wiry eyebrows down.

"You are, ma'am." Dixie tried not to show her amusement at seeing the old gal get her ire up. Miss Lettie still had a lot of life in her, and Dixie hoped to draw on her advice and guidance for a while yet to come.

"Well, like you said, 'round come somebody in a rowboat, tells the man to hop in and they'll go on to safety. No, says the man, God is coming directly for me, I'm going to wait on him." Lettie waved her hand in the air like she was sending the rowboat away herself.

Dixie smiled.

"The water keeps on rising. Soon enough another rowboat comes along and the man does the same thing." Lettie waved again. "Then one-a-them helicopters comes over, and even though the water is about to overtake him, lah, if that fool don't send that helicopter on its way too. Then you know what happens?"

"The man drowns and goes to heaven."

Lettie slapped her hands together. "The man drowns and goes to heaven! And when he gets there he asks the Lord why the Lord didn't come to the rescue and the Lord says—"

Dixie joined in. "I sent you two rowboats and a helicopter, what more did you want?"

A steely silence greeted her performance.

"I cotton, for somebody so smart—" Lettie shot Dixie a look that could have blistered paint—"I'd think you'd have sense enough to consider that this Walker man just might be—"

"Oh no." Dixie held her hand up, not wanting Miss Lettie to even finish that thought.

The old woman did not know Riley Walker. She did not understand the intricacies of business or Dixie's responsibility to make sure nothing endangered the livelihoods of her workers.

"If Mr. Walker is a rowboat, Miss Lettie, he's one who could very well leave me up a creek without a paddle." Her chest burned with anger and her head swam with all the potentially disastrous outcomes Walker could bring on her family. "Despite his efforts to convince me his intentions are to help, I only have to remember that somehow this man has aligned himself with Howard Greenhow. Howard desperately wanted to *help*, you know. To help himself to the family money. And with Riley Walker, he might very well have found a way to do just that."

If Lettie had any more to add, Dixie did not know. And she never would since Peachie Too came bursting into the room, barking like a record played too fast—either that or a dog breathing a tank full of helium. The animal snarled and bared its teeth at no one in particular. Then, catching sight of its tail poking out from beneath the tartan plaid fitted cape Aunt Sis had wriggled onto the dog this morning, it began to chase its hind end in a whirl of activity that made Dixie dizzy just to watch.

"Oh, my. Sis is home." Dixie sat up. "The Judge can't be far behind, and here I haven't even thought about what to fix for dinner."

She groaned, stuck out her stockinged feet, rotated her ankles a few times, then thrust both her hands into her hair. Zestfully massaging her head in total disregard for the mess wayward tresses would create, she shut her eyes and savored the feel of her nails dragging over her stress-sensitized scalp.

Aunt Sis's perfume wafted into the room before her footsteps even reached the threshold. "You'll just never guess who I ran into just outside my meeting of the Commemoration Day steering committee asking directions for a hotel and a nice place to eat tonight."

Dixie wriggled her toes and scrubbed more vigorously with her fingers, sending her hair bouncing over her face and shoulders. "As long as you didn't offer to put them up here and invite them home for supper, I don't really care Aunt Sis."

"Oh, but I did, dear."

"So we meet again, Miss Fulton-Leigh."

That mocking masculine voice went through her like a shard of glass. She stopped mid toe-wiggle and dared to lift just enough of the brunette veil from her eyes to confirm her greatest fear.

Riley Walker stood in the doorway of her home, big as life, grinning like he'd just won the Kentucky Derby without a horse!

"*You!*" Dixie seethed the word out through horror-clenched teeth.

"You mean you already know Mr. Walker, Dixie?" Aunt Sis tittered out a nervous laugh.

Dixie just sat there, her hands in her hair, her legs sticking straight out, and her shoeless feet extended at odd angles.

Riley stepped into the room.

"Well, don't just sit there with your jaw hanging open, Dixie Belle." Lettie's rocker fell into a quiet rhythm with the ever ticking clock. "Get yourself up and do something. I do believe your rowboat has arrived."

Eight

◆

Perseverance must finish its work so that you may be
mature and complete, not lacking anything.

JAMES 1:4

"THE ONLY REASON I AGREED TO ALLOW YOU TO COME ALONG
and help me get supper ready is so there wouldn't be any witnesses." Dixie let the swinging kitchen door fall shut with a
whoosh that just barely missed her unexpected guest's backside.

He didn't even flinch. "I'm not too worried about witnesses,
Miss Fulton-Leigh."

He very slowly laced one arm over the other across his
chest, which looked somehow even broader than she remembered. Probably the starkness of his white shirt and the absence
of his elegant tie, which had lent a civilizing effect to all that
brawn....

"Anything happens to me I reckon you know you'd be the

prime suspect, witnesses or not." He dipped his chin and a lock of his curly black hair fell forward onto his tanned forehead. "Seeing as you're the only person I know who isn't utterly dazzled by my exceptional wit and charm—and my uncommon humility, of course."

Brawn tempered by a gentle good nature that she could see twinkling in his dark eyes, and which brought a genuine warmth to that rakish grin. Dixie wished she could just—

"Spare me the nonsense, Mr. Walker. The truth is I brought you in here because I don't want anyone to overhear what I have to say to you."

"Hmmm. Strange that you didn't have that fear when you tried to discuss our new business partnership in the drugstore earlier today."

"We don't *have* a business partnership, and that is something I will discuss openly and often with anyone who cares to lend an ear." She swept her gaze upward over the pale yellow walls of the small kitchen, a modern marvel for the late eighteen hundreds when it was built. Oh, the many discussions this place had heard. The arguments, the plans, the tears, and laughter and so much more that had drifted up from this spot toward the high ceilings and beyond.

Yet never once, she suspected, had any of those conversations been so pointed, so concise, so outright rude as she was about to be. But then, she doubted any of her predecessors would ever have found him or herself in this predicament! Oh no. Only her. "I cannot *believe* Aunt Sis invited you home with her, and you accepted! This is so typical."

"Your aunt is prone to bringing in strays?"

"My aunt is prone to many things." She pinched the bridge of her nose. "What's typical, though, is that some member of my family has acted without thinking things through, leaving me to come along behind and clean up the mess."

He laughed, just enough to let her know he was having fun with her but not so much as to imply he was delighting in her dilemma. "Wendy and I can clean up after ourselves, if that's any help."

At the mention of Wendy, Dixie softened. Just a smidge.

Riley must have sensed that as he stepped toward her and lowered his voice. "You know, acting on an impulse is not always a bad thing. In fact, my personal belief is that if the impulse is well grounded—"

"Puh-*lease*, Mr. Walker." She held her hand up to stop him. "You've met my Aunt Sis—"

"And her little dog, too."

"Does *anything* about that woman scream *well grounded* to you?"

"Just her taste in relatives."

"You are making what I have to do very difficult." She shut her eyes but could still feel him near her like a deeply banked fire that radiated through a chilled winter room. That scared her, scared her more than she knew how to handle. This man could spell the end of everything she held dear, and letting herself fall under his spell could only make matters worse. She had to fight it, keep her mind fixed on the danger he represented and not be lulled into complacency by the thrum of his rich, deep voice.

"What do you have to do, Miss Fulton-Leigh? Besides prepare dinner?"

"Mr. Walker, I have to—and let me first say this is offered without any personal animosity and with all due regard befitting this particular situation—I *have* to tell you to get out of my house!"

Riley leaned one shoulder up against the wall, crossed his arms, then settled one ankle over the other, content to let his body language tell her he'd settled in for the long haul. "Seems like your version of Southern hospitality is missing a few letters, Miss Fulton-Leigh. It reads more like Southern hostility."

"Well, isn't that very clever of you to come up with that?"

"I thought so…" He restrained the grin that wanted so badly to break out.

"And that would be an interesting thing to note if you were working the jumble puzzle in the newspaper." She moved toward the door again as she spoke, extending her arm in a sweeping motion as if showing him the way out. "Or perhaps if you are ever a contestant on Wheel of Fortune—"

"Not interested." He did not budge from where he stood.

"Beg your pardon?" Her smile tightened.

"In going on a game show." He shook his head. "Not interested."

She opened her mouth, then shut it, scowled, and cocked her head, sending her still irresistibly tousled hair tumbling against her flawless neck. "I'm sorry, but I don't understand that—"

"Think about it." He pushed himself away from the wall and strolled in her direction, his arms still clamped over his chest. When they stood side by side, he leaned close enough to speak quietly, but without the implied intimacy of a whisper, in her ear. "Why would I need a glamorous game show? With all that tension?"

He hit the last word hard and Dixie jumped, just enough so that only someone standing as close as he would notice it, but she did jump.

He went on. "That frenzied sense of anticipation?"

She set her lips in a grim line and glared at him from the corners of her eyes.

"The prospect of walking away with everything or being left with nothing but embarrassment and disappointment? Not to mention an enchanting hostess dripping charm and with the uncanny ability to get worked up over absolutely nothing at all?" He could tell by the set of her jaw just how badly she wanted to respond to that implication-packed bombshell, so he hurried on to make sure she didn't get the chance. "Why would I want to go on a game show, Miss Fulton-Leigh, when I can stay put and get all that right here in your home?"

If looks could kill…well, Riley thought, she might not have done him in but when he looked in those beautiful eyes, it did occur to him that he had seen warmer glints off the teeth of jagged-edged buzz saws.

"You are reprehensible, do you know that?" she whispered.

"My mother calls me a troublement." He tried not to seem too proud of the title.

"If only she would call you *home*." Dixie held her ground.

"She can't. She isn't at our home. She's in the hospital."

Dixie started at that. "Oh, I'm sorry, I didn't realize…" She touched her fingertips to her lips as if she wished that could somehow take back her flip remark. "I hope she's all right."

"Broken hip. She's a fighter, though, she'll be fine with therapy and time to recuperate." He actually felt bad because Dixie so obviously felt bad. "That's why I have Wendy with me this trip and why I have to take care of as much of the business of getting set up in our new home now as possible. When Momma is ready to join us, I'd like it to be one smooth transition into our new place so she doesn't get all in a fit over packing, moving, and what have you."

"I'm sure your mother will appreciate your thoughtfulness.

It's always nice when someone takes another person's situation into account while making plans that involve that other person."

"Subtle," he muttered, then lifted his hands in mock surrender. "Listen, Miss Fulton-Leigh, when your aunt invited me to come to your house, I never imagined it would come as a personal imposition on you. I just assumed…well, let's just say it never crossed my mind that you'd be stuck with the extra cooking duties."

"I won't be…that is, I *wouldn't* be, if you were actually staying." She crossed the floor in front of him to a painted door with a glass knob. "I'm not cooking anything from scratch tonight."

The warped old door banged against its frame when she shimmied it open to reveal a long, narrow staircase descending into complete darkness.

"Taking me to the cellar are you? Not only do you not want any witnesses, you don't want anyone to find what you've done with the body."

"Don't be silly. Give me credit for knowing better than to hide the evidence of my misdeeds in my own basement, Mr. Walker."

He chuckled.

"After all, I haven't lived my entire life in a family of lunatics without picking up a few pointers along the way."

His laughter died in his throat, making something of a choking sound as he swallowed hard. There was that reference again. In all the excitement of his decision today, he had forgotten about the vague rumors of eccentricities and his mother's warnings. Beyond the frivolity of Aunt Sis and the shoplifting grandfather he'd heard Dixie refer to, what more could there be?

Riley had met John Frederick face to face and had found the man to be of sound mind and exemplary spirit. And so far, he saw absolutely nothing lacking in Dixie's character, except for that obvious shortsightedness on her part in not taking a shine to him immediately. Then there was the Judge, the man from whom Riley had taken the reins of control just today when he became the chief executive officer and senior stockholder in Fulton's Cartage. Riley knew little of that man except what he'd seen on paper—a bold signature across the papers authorizing Howard Greenhow to negotiate the deal on his behalf.

Still, the man *was* a judge. Riley took comfort in that reminder. They didn't let just anyone become a judge…unless, of course, your family ran an entire town! An uneasiness began to twist low in Riley's gut. He raked his fingers back through his hair.

"Mr. Walker? Hello?" Dixie snapped her fingers and he realized she'd been trying to get his attention.

"Um, yes. What is it Miss Fulton-Leigh?"

"I said I have to go downstairs now, to get something from the freezer for dinner tonight."

"Oh, sure." He swept out his open hand in a stereotypical *ladies first* gesture. "Let's go."

"*I'll* go, thank you. It won't take long, I just have to bring a casserole or something up from the freezer so I can warm it up."

"Well, anything for the cause of warming things up, ma'am." He stepped to the door, just inches away from her so that she would either have to move away or shove him down the stairs to be rid of him. "Why don't we start with that cold shoulder you're intent on giving me?"

"I do believe now you're the one who's got his words out of whack, Mr. Walker." She pulled herself up to her full height, her hands behind her back, chin level, and her gaze fixed on his. "The thing you seem most interested in doing is *worming*, not *warming*. As in worming your way into my business, my family, my home—"

"Say, you're pretty good with letters yourself. Maybe later on this evening we can tackle that jumble puzzle together."

"Why don't I just give you my edition of the paper and you can take it with you when you leave?"

Without her heels, the top of her head barely reached his chin, which only fueled the already primitive protective instincts he harbored toward her. She had no idea, he imagined, how precarious her situation was, how he alone had stood between her and Greenhow and who-knew-what havoc the lawyer would have liked to have unleashed on her and her companies.

"That would be the *morning* paper, then, correct? I believe your aunt's invitation was to put Wendy and me up for the night."

At the mention of Wendy, Dixie tore her gaze away from his. She placed her hand on the interior wall of the stairwell and spoke as she crept down the first few steps. "Leave the door open. The fixture over the stairs is broken, so I need the light to see the way to the switch by the freezer."

Riley caught her by the arm. He stood half in, half out of the doorway, not yet fully committed to coming after her but unwilling to let her get away. Somehow he had to get through to her, had to make her understand that he was not her enemy.

"Why have you made your mind up that my presence here spells disaster for your company, Dixie?" He took extreme caution to make sure his grasp on her was gentle, hoping instead, to keep her from running away by the power of his voice and his message. "Why won't you even listen to my side of this? Why are you so resistant to my efforts to help?"

"Help? There's that word again." Dixie gripped the handrail.

"Is it so frightening a word to you?" He stepped over the threshold. The door banged shut behind him, plunging them into a darkness broken only by the dim evening light from a curtained basement window below. "Are you so scared of letting anyone come in to try to help you that you'd sooner lose everything than take a chance that it might work out?"

"I am *not* going to lose everything."

He could sense her chest rising and falling with the passion of her conviction.

"No, of course not." He relaxed his hand on her arm.

"My great-grandfather founded this town."

"I know." He came down a step so that now he could see the fire in her eyes as well as hear it in her voice.

"My family has been self-sufficient in business since this town's founding, and in Fulton's Fine Furniture and its companion businesses since before I was born."

"Yes, but now—"

"*Now* nothing has changed. This town has come to rely on our companies and, by extension, our family for jobs, patronage, and the tax revenues we pay the city and county. Not to mention the charity and community support we have been happy to provide, whether it meant new robes for a church choir, uniforms for our high school baseball team, or decorations for the downtown square on Commemoration Day."

He moved down to the step above her. "So, you're saying this is a control issue?"

"I'm saying it's a *responsibility* issue. My family has accepted this responsibility for over a hundred years. All that time folks around here knew they could trust and rely on the Fulton family to act with honor, fairness, and common decency. Now I have the reins of power less than ten days and a stranger steps in and tries to take that away? A stranger who isn't even from here, who has no idea who we are or what we stand for?"

"Is that why you're so resistant? Because you see me as an…as an outsider?"

"I see you, Mr. Walker, as a man who has come, not to me directly but through a man who clearly would put personal gain over charity and goodness and perhaps even ethical behavior. Resistant? To that? You bet I am."

Dixie charged on down the stairs, fueled by a mass of emotions that ranged from unvarnished fear to outright uncertainty over what she really needed to do concerning Riley Walker. No footsteps followed. Perhaps her speech had given him reason to pause, if not retreat.

She grimaced. No, Riley Walker did not have the makings of a man who would easily retreat. *That* she did know.

Not until her feet hit the concrete of the basement floor did she realize she'd forgotten to put her shoes back on. She hugged her arms close to her body and shuddered at the sudden shock of cold biting at her stockinged toes. She managed the few shuffling steps it took to reach the light switch, then flicked it on, unsure if she would find Riley still standing on the staircase or not.

"Wow. It's like a wonderland down here." The wooden stairs groaned under Riley's weight as he came down them one halting step at a time.

She blinked to help her eyes grow accustomed to the brightness of the pair of bare bulbs glaring down from the crossbeams.

One heavy footfall and the moan of wood against wood repeated in maddening slow motion, making Dixie stop and turn, not to see what was taking the man so long, but to find what had taken him so aback. Something had gotten this man's attention and left him in silent awe.

Her gaze fell on the wild array of furniture parts, old advertising signs, trunks and suitcases, bottles and baby things strewn here, propped up there, and even hanging from the low, unfinished ceiling. She'd long ago begun taking the collection of trash and treasure for granted, but as she surveyed it again, she could well imagine how one might react to the first glimpse of what represented a century of her family's daily life.

"What can I say? My family has a hard time letting go of anything."

"You're telling *me* that?" He laughed.

Such a good laugh. Like it came from a place of real joy that existed deep in his being. Could he really be just what he said he was? Could he really just hope to help her? Why would anyone do that? Why would he invest his money just to help her? Could he possibly be that rowboat Lettie suggested, or was he the first swell in a wave that would overtake her and those who depended on her?

That kind of thing couldn't be decided in the basement while everyone waited for supper. Later tonight she'd think more about it. For now, she could only give a brief prayer that the answer would come soon.

Straightening her shoulders, she waved her hand and kept the conversation focused on the collection of junk and away from the conflict between the two of them. "You think this is something? You should see the attic."

"I'd love to. Want to take me up there after dinner?"

"You do not give up, do you?" She turned her back on him.

"I don't make decisions lightly. But when I do commit to something, no, I don't give up on it unless I absolutely have to." The steps creaked, then his boots scuffed over the gritty concrete surface of the floor.

The freezer door's seal let out a quiet pop and then a gasp as she tugged it open to stare inside. She was not going to pursue this line of discussion and that was that. "We gave away most of the food folks brought after Daddy's death to people who needed it more than we. Two hams and a smoked turkey went to families who are struggling, and the rest went to the church to supplement a fellowship dinner. But we did have the foresight to save some casseroles for these evenings when work and…unexpected circumstances…kept me late."

Riley said nothing but she heard him moving about, sifting through things, picking something up then setting it back down.

She thought of reiterating that they only had a few casseroles left and they were small ones at that. But as much as she wished she could convince Riley not to stay, she could not poormouth her way out of serving him and his daughter a meal. It seemed ungrateful for all she and her family had been given to even pretend to deny or downplay their abundance. And it seemed just plain mean to exaggerate their circumstances and chase off Riley and with him sweet little Wendy, then sit down to a table filled with food she had neither bought nor prepared herself.

She sighed. "If you should decide to stay for supper, are there any foods you can't or won't eat?"

"Horses!"

"*What?*" She pulled back to look right at him and discovered him gazing at a dusty showcase of ribbons and trophies.

"Do you still ride?"

"I never did." Dixie curled her fingers more tightly around the cool metal handle of the freezer door. "Those were my mother's. That other stuff, there, that's all mine. I'm afraid you won't find an award or a medal in the lot, though."

She hadn't meant for the casual comment to sound so apologetic. Then again, she wasn't exactly sure why she'd said it at all. She didn't really want this man who had already intruded too far into her professional and now private life looking through her childhood keepsakes...did she?

The man bent at the knees, squatting low until he brought himself level with the clutter of old toys and mementos. He examined a box filled with an odd assortment of cups and dishes. He tapped his blunt fingertip along the spines of some old, worn books. Then he came to the small, white table with pink ribbons and blue lamb decals on it. Dixie had held hours worth of tea parties on that thing, and when he ran his hand over the top of it with a kind of gentle reverence, a most disconcerting shiver tripped up her spine.

"I've got to shut this freezer door." There. If he'd noticed her shiver that would give a perfect excuse for it.

She reached into the frosty shelves and selected the largest of all the casseroles that remained. One step back and a well-timed bump of her hip set the door swinging closed. It fell shut with a *wham,* so hard it rattled the copper Jell-O molds stacked on top of the unit, which did nothing to quiet her jangled nerves.

She hugged the casserole to her and found the chilled air that rose from the rectangular pan had a cooling effect on her fortitude as well. She breathed in the scent of the freezer's cold and the dankness of the musty basement. Head high, she pivoted on her bare heel, full ready to deal with Riley again.

"My baby..." She couldn't help it. The murmur had escaped her the second she saw what he now held in his hands.

"It says *Belle* on it." He held up the large, muslin doll with the black yarn braids and her name embroidered on her red-and-white gingham apron.

"Baby Belle, that's what I called her." Dixie approached with subtle caution, avoiding the halos of brightest light directly beneath the exposed bulbs. She did not want Riley to see how much she cherished the old belonging. She simply was not ready to show him any weakness, especially one so private. "Miss Lettie made her for me shortly before my mother died."

"She looks like she's been well loved." He stretched his arm out to offer the doll to her. "And well cared for."

"Actually, I hardly played with her at all." She pulled the freezer dish closer to her but found it harsh comfort.

"Is that why she's in such sterling condition?"

He was trying to engage her, to get to her on the most personal of levels…but when Dixie saw the delicate handwork of the doll's achingly familiar face, and the way Riley's work-toughened hands held her with undeniable tenderness, she didn't care what his motive was. She set the dish in an empty spot on a nearby shelf and reached out to take the oversized doll.

"I never played with her much. Thought I was too old for dollies by the time Miss Lettie gave her to me the Christmas before I turned ten. Though I had dearly loved and worn to pieces every baby doll she'd ever given me before." Dixie fingered the doll's twisted yarn bangs. "This one, I sat on top of my dresser and never gave another thought to, until…"

He leaned forward, his gaze intent, his jaw set, his large hands now resting between his knees, fingers entwined.

"The day of my mother's funeral." Dixie could not look at him as she spoke. Yet she could not force from her mind the picture of his face when he'd handed her the doll…those strong features awash with almost palpable kindness and empathy. So many emotions crowded up in her that she had no idea what she was saying or why. She just went on, letting the words pour quietly out. "As we got ready for my mother's funeral, I picked up Baby Belle to take with me and I did not let her go for the next two years."

"Really?"

"Well, I didn't take her to school with me, but pretty much everywhere else I went, Baby Belle went, too. My family didn't make too big a deal out of it or even seem to notice. Miss Lettie did, though." She swallowed and blinked away any dampness in her eyes. "I think she understood more than any of my blood kin ever did how very much I missed my mother."

"You have a very special bond with her."

Dixie wasn't sure if Riley meant she had a special bond with her mother or Baby Belle or Miss Lettie, but since the statement held true of all three she simply nodded. "During those two years, Miss Lettie, she took some of my mother's clothes and used them to make a whole wardrobe for my doll. They're in that trunk there, the blue one, by your knee."

"Pretty big trunk for a little doll's clothes."

"Guess you think I'm awfully spoiled, huh?"

"Miss Fulton-Leigh, you are talking to the father of an only child, a man trying his best to raise a motherless daughter himself."

Dixie started to run the edge of her thumb over her mother's pearls, caught herself, then folded her hands together instead.

"Because you've refused to listen to my side of things, you don't realize that main reason I ever even entertained your father's initial business offer was because of Wendy. Because of Wendy, I *need* the opportunity that being your partner provides."

This was no sales pitch, no slick story spun out to endear him to her, to make her lower her defenses to him. The raw edge to his every halting word told Dixie as much.

"Miss Fulton-Leigh, I am fully prepared to uproot my entire existence, to relocate my home, and take on new business responsibilities all for the sake of my little girl. I would do anything within my powers to see to her safety, well-being, and future. I am certainly not going to call you spoiled because you have a big trunk filled with doll clothes made from your late mother's things."

Poor little Wendy! It was all Dixie could think. No, not *all* she could think. She marveled at this man, as well, and what he implied by his fervent confession. "Would it be presumptuous of me to ask what happened to Wendy's mother?"

"After the way you've refused to talk to me about anything civil much less personal, yes, it'd be extremely presumptuous of you."

"Oh."

"However, given that I still hope that the relationship between you and me can improve and grow, I'd be glad to share it with you." He glanced over to the casserole dish on the shelf nearby. "But you'll have to settle for the short version for now, I think."

"Agreed."

"Wendy isn't really…that is technically…" His brow creased and he fumbled with his hands. "My sister, Marcia, abandoned Wendy two days after she was born. Just walked out of the hospital without so much as a good-bye to my mother or a second thought about what would become of her newborn."

"Oh, Riley…"

"I can't say it came as a big surprise. Marcia has had a lot of problems but we had hoped that she'd overcome them, especially for Wendy's sake." Riley lifted his head like a man scanning the horizon for something he knew would never come. "That's why my mother and I brought Wendy home and began taking care of her, hoping Marcia would get herself together and come back. By the time we accepted that wasn't going to happen, well, I already thought of Wendy as my little girl, so we just went on that way. Her calling me daddy and me loving her like my own."

"And Wendy's biological father?"

"Her biological…" He swallowed so hard she could see the movement of his Adam's apple. "Thank you, very much, Miss Fulton-Leigh for making that distinction. You don't know what it means to me."

Anyone with eyes could see what it meant to him, but she didn't say so.

"Wendy's biological father wasn't interested in raising a child. He gladly signed over his rights to her, gave us as much medical information about his family as he could, then hit the road. But my sister never did sign away her parental rights." Riley ground his fist into his palm, his jaw clamped down so tightly that she could see the muscle tick in coiled tension. "In a little less than eight weeks, I am going to walk into a courtroom and ask the state to do that for us, to sever Marcia's rights so I can adopt Wendy properly."

A foreboding gripped Dixie. She cuddled Baby Belle close and waited for Riley to decide if he would go on.

"This is one of the most important things I've ever done, Dixie."

She could only nod.

"And I haven't entered into this decision without a lot of deliberation and endless hours of heartfelt prayer."

"Prayer…" That Riley Walker was a man of faith suddenly

seemed so apparent that she flushed with embarrassment at all the horrible things she had thought of him before. Her concerns had not all vanished, but they had paled next to this newfound side of the man.

"I've had to draw some hard conclusions over this and take what to some might seem drastic actions."

"Buying into my company?"

He nodded. "When I walk into that courtroom, I've got to prove beyond the shadow of a doubt that I have provided for Wendy the best home life and the most stable environment possible. Moving here and becoming a part of your organization is how I hope to do that for her."

He did not look her in the eye, but she could not take her gaze from him.

For one terrifying and brilliant moment, Dixie looked at this kind man, this caring father's anguished face, and she saw things from a broader perspective. In that heartbeat of time, she began to wonder if Lettie had it wrong. Perhaps Riley had not been sent to help her so much as they had been meant to help each other.

She stood and looked around at nothing in particular. "I, uh...I think we're going to have some pretty hungry people waiting for us upstairs if we don't get this casserole in the oven soon."

She laid her carefully preserved doll down on top of the trunk, then took up the still-frosty dish in both hands and started for the steps. As her foot reached the first tread, she paused, then turned to look over her shoulder. "Why don't you grab Baby Belle and her clothes trunk and maybe that box of play dishes and bring them up? I have the feeling Wendy will be plenty bored with all us big folks quick enough and might like something to play with, especially if ya'll are going to spend the night. Unless you think she wouldn't…"

"I think she'd like that, Dixie." He stood, her precious play-things in his arms. "I think she'd like that very much. Thank you."

"You're welcome." She smiled.

He grinned.

Her heart did that annoying flippity-flop thing that only this man's smile seemed to inspire. She cleared her throat. "But don't go reading too much into my relenting about tossing you out of my house, you hear?"

"Yes, ma'am."

Even as she turned to go up the stairs she could hear the amusement in his tone. She clutched the casserole dish more tightly and went on. "I am only doing this for Wendy's sake."

"And I appreciate it."

"And I am warning you, Riley Walker, if I find out that there is one shred of falsehood in anything you told me tonight, or if I even suspect you have tried to inflame my sympathies to strengthen your position in order to get control of my company—"

"Not a chance. You can rest assured of that."

"I *will* be assured, Mr. Walker, but I won't rest until I am."

Nine

◆

*If any of you lacks wisdom, he should ask God, who
gives generously to all without finding fault,
and it will be given to him.*

JAMES 1:5

EVERYTHING WAS GOING TO WORK OUT JUST FINE. RILEY KNEW IT.
He knew it down into his very bones.

Dinner preparations had gone smoothly with Dixie handling the hot foods, heating the entree and browning the rolls, on account of the temperamental oven, she'd explained. Riley took on the cold things, the cutting up of a salad and stirring the sugar into the iced tea. Meanwhile Wendy had occupied herself with three new fascinations, Dixie's doll Baby Belle, the feisty little Miss Lettie, and that awful dog named Peachie Too.

Wendy had taken to all of them with an instant enthusiasm and affection that both Miss Lettie and Peachie Too returned in kind. Wendy assured him that Baby Belle was her first new best friend in her brand-new hometown, but Riley had to take the child's word for that since he did not speak, nor even hear, the language of rag dolls.

With Baby Belle beneath one arm and Peachie Too prancing at her heels, Wendy had helped set the table under the often befuddled direction of Dixie's grandfather, "Smilin' Bob" as he was introduced to Riley by Sis, whose real name, it turned out, was June.

When Riley had joked about needing a program to keep up with everyone, Miss Lettie had croaked out a laugh and given his hand a pinching shake. "You don't know the half of it, young man, not the half of it."

He'd have liked to quiz the delightful old imp about that. In fact, one look in those ancient eyes and he figured he'd found the one person who could pretty much tell him anything he wanted to know regarding anyone he wanted to know about. If anyone had answers for him about this family and its peculiarities, this woman who had raised three generations of them was it.

Unfortunately, she had not felt up to staying on and visiting. Riley feared that Wendy's energetic attentions had worn the old woman out, but Lettie batted that notion away with both hands. "Go on, I love little children. I'm just tuckered out and want to go to my room now to rest awhile and watch my stories that Sis's going to run on the machine for me."

Sis had explained the she recorded TV shows and replayed them later. Miss Lettie liked to stick to her own schedule, Dixie's aunt had told him, which kept her perpetually out of sync with almost everything, including family mealtime and regular television programming.

"But you come calling on me after supper, young lady."

Lettie wagged one crooked finger in Wendy's direction. "And I'll tell you a story. You promise?"

Wendy had promised.

Sis had whisked Lettie away.

Riley and Dixie had called everyone to wash up for supper while the two of them set the serving dishes onto the crisp, white tablecloth. When everyone joined hands around the table and Dixie asked him if he would give the blessing, he couldn't help but show his confidence in his words of thanksgiving.

"Father, bless each one of us through this food, which keeps us healthy, and in our faith, which makes us whole. For all your goodness in bringing us together and all your grace in our shortcomings, we thank you. Be with us now and in the days ahead as we create new bonds and strengthen old ones. Guide us and protect us and hear our thanks and praise. In the name of Jesus..."

"Amen." They all said in unison.

"Play ball!" Dixie's grandfather clapped his hands together.

Wendy squealed with delight.

Dixie rolled her eyes and tucked her linen napkin into her lap while Aunt Sis swooped down on the casserole dish, serving spoon at the ready. "Let me get a portion for Peachie Too first, so I can set it aside to cool."

Dixie scooted her chair close enough to Wendy to help the child tuck her napkin in, then served the little girl some salad. Heads together, they shared a giggle, then began to eat.

Food was passed and plates were filled. Things got quiet for a few minutes except for the scritching of silver forks over china and the occasional pop of ice in the tea glasses.

Then Sis's poodle sprang up on its hind legs and began spinning around, making a sound that Riley could only compare to plaintive yodeling. Sis shushed it. "You'll get your dinner, my sweet thing, soon as it cools down. Peachie Too wouldn't want to burn her widdle tongue, now would she?"

While Sis spoke, the dog's caterwauling wound down to a soft *woo-ooo-ooo*. Two seconds after Sis went back to her meal, the wrenching cry went up again.

Dixie's chagrin at the commotion showed not in her delicate features, but in the white-knuckled grip on her knife as she spread jam on a roll for Wendy. Riley caught her eye and tried to reassure her that it did not bother him, giving her a smile and a sly wink to tell her he understood.

She looked down, then up again, as if testing to see if he had taken his gaze from her. He had not. If he had his way, he *would* not, not all evening long.

Around them, the subtle charm of the old mansion created a welcome backdrop. Candles flickered at the center of the table, casting the surroundings in a cozy, inviting glow. The aroma of hot rolls and creamy buttermilk salad dressing filled his senses.

Riley let out a long, contented sigh. Except for the psychotic yodeling poodle, the scene had a Norman Rockwellesque, American family dream quality about it. If Riley let himself, he could just picture—

He sat bolt straight in his chair. He had done quite nicely so far without the fantasy of this beguiling brand of home and hearth intruding on the uncomplicated reality of his life. He certainly did not need to start entertaining those kinds of thoughts now. Not when his mind should stay sharp and focused on his new business and on Wendy's adoption.

He reached for his tall, crystal glass of sweet iced tea. He'd driven a small wedge into Dixie's defenses tonight and it had made him cocky, allowed him to relax a bit too much. Yes, she was a lovely woman with a gracious home and a fearlessness that came from some compelling inner flame. Yes, she was fierce about facing life and its demands.

Yet there was so much about her, her business, and her family that Riley still did not know. Like where was George R. Cunningham, this mysterious Judge? Obviously he did not share the family home, something Riley could not hold against the man. When would Riley meet him and how would they work together to bring Fulton's Cartage up to its full potential?

"So, Mr. Walker, come over here from Deepwoods, Mississippi?" Dixie's grandfather rapped on the table with his spoon. "Our Miss Lettie tells me that you made your fortune selling rowboats to rescue operations."

"What? I..." Riley looked to Dixie for help making head or tails of that pronouncement.

"No, no, Grandpa, that's not right." Dixie put her hand to her cheek. "You've got Mr. Walker confused with a joke Lettie was telling—"

"Well, tell me the joke, son, and I'll see if I can't *unconfuse* you."

"I don't know the joke, sir."

"There's your problem!" The round-faced man tapped his spoon to the table again, his red, round cheeks puffing out as he laughed quite congenially over apparently nothing at all. "How can I help people when people refuse to help themselves?"

"If they could help themselves why under the sun would they *need* your help?" Sis plucked up the elegant bowl into which she'd scooped the first helping of noodles and chicken, then lifted it in the air as if she were going to make a toast with it. "Rowboats? My goodness, imagine getting everything all twisted around like that. That doesn't even make sense. And here you have three-fourths of this town calling you…"

Everyone looked to her.

Riley could almost feel them all simultaneously holding their breaths, waiting for Sis to announce what three-fourths of the town was calling Dixie's grandfather.

Sis eyeballed the food, sniffed it, tipped the bowl left to right in the palm of her hand—in general, quite unaware that she'd left everyone dangling.

Riley started to say something, anything that might prod her into finishing her sentence or at least get the conversation going again. "I was just going to ask—"

Suddenly, Sis disappeared beneath the table.

After that, whatever Riley would have said just did not seem to matter anymore.

Dixie seemed to jump at the chance to throw out a diversionary tactic, dabbing her napkin to the corner of her mouth and cooing, "Grandpa, you know that this man is—"

Kissing sounds carried up from somewhere beneath their meal, stopping Dixie cold. She cleared her throat and finished, "Mr. Riley Walker, right?"

"I know the man's name. I know his name," Smilin' Bob insisted in a quickfire scolding tone. Then just as quickly, the look on his face shifted. He stroked his thumb and forefinger along his jowly jawline. "Where do I know his name from, though?"

Peachie Too's growl arose from a place not too far away from Riley's feet.

"Aunt Sis introduced you to him. She'd invited him, and little Wendy here, to—"

"Wook at the precious puppy's pwetty teeth." Sis's odd combination of pouty baby talk and a cultured Southern accent rose above her pet's continued snarling.

"Spend the night in our home," Dixie concluded.

Smilin' Bob nodded. "I know all that, darling. I'm trying to recall where else I might know the man's name from, besides meeting him an hour or so ago. Did you really think I didn't remember shaking the man's hand when Sis carted him home?" He chuckled and leaned toward Riley. "You'd think I'd get more respect in this house. Worryation, gal! I may be a forgetful old fool, but—"

"You can say that again!" Sis muttered with enough vigor to make herself heard above the sundry thumping and bumping below that rattled the silver on the table and made the stemware tremble.

"Yes, well." Smilin' Bob shifted in his seat.

Suddenly Sis let out a quiet but expressive *oomph*.

"Sister?" The white-haired gent looked quite surprised even as his twinkling gaze flitted from Dixie to Riley and even over to include Wendy. "Sister? Are those your hindquarters down under there? I was just crossing my legs and my foot must have slipped."

Sis sighed like a gust of ill wind.

Riley glanced at Dixie, inclined to laugh at the antics but wanting to take his cue from her.

She had her head in her hands.

He swallowed.

"Grandpa, Sis has fed her dogs under this table for as long as I can remember and yet you still pull that 'is that you under there, Sis?' routine every third day of the week. If you aren't crossing your legs and kicking her, you are dropping olives or croutons into her hair."

"Just trying to improve on a good thing," he explained to Riley, his face as innocent as a newborn babe's.

"When are you going to realize it's not funny anymore?" Dixie demanded.

Supportive as Riley would have liked to have been of Dixie's point, the image of Sis rising up from the floor of the elegant dining room with olives perched in her bouffant hairdo, like tiny eggs in a nest, got to him. He laughed out loud.

Dixie glared.

Smilin' Bob smiled.

Wendy went right on gobbling down her food.

"Anyway, the thing is, of course I remember greeting our guests, Mr. Walker and his little daughter." Smilin' Bob reached out and patted the child on the head. Then he turned to the limp doll sitting in the vacant chair between himself and Wendy. "My, but this is a well-behaved child. Very quiet and hardly eats a thing."

"She's a doll!" Wendy clamped her hands over her mouth while her little shoes slapped into each other as she wiggled her legs and giggled. "I'm the little girl. *I'm* Wendy Walker."

The man made a big show of looking over Baby Belle then Wendy. "Well, so you are. Pleased to meet you again Miss Wendy Walker. Have I given you one of my cards?"

He started to reach into one of his jacket pockets, then the other. Then he patted his hands down his sides, his face a mask of confusion and concern. Just when Riley was about to tell him not to bother with it, hoping to ease any discomfort the obviously muddled man might feel, Smilin' Bob raised one hand in the air.

"Ahh, there it is." He produced a perfect, white business card, seemingly out of thin air.

Wendy clapped her hands.

Riley chuckled.

Dixie rolled her eyes at the act, but a big grin shone on her face.

Smilin' Bob acknowledged it all with a bow, then handed

Wendy the card with a flourish of his hand.

Despite the warning about the state of Dixie's family, Riley found it almost impossible to think ill of this jovial character who'd been so sweet with Wendy. Smilin' Bob seemed far more daft than dangerous, making Riley think the whole shoplifting thing might just be another kind of mix-up.

"So, now, Mr. Walker, tell me more about these rowboats."

Or if it wasn't a mix-up, it came more from a mental condition than a moral failing.

"I have no idea what you—"

"Grandpa, there are no rowboats! Honestly!"

"Daddy, I'm done eating, can I go see Miss Lettie now?"

"Miss Lettie! Excellent suggestion!" Smilin' Bob threw his napkin onto the table. "She is the one who knows about these rowboats. Let's go see Miss Lettie."

"Can I, Daddy?" Wendy already had Baby Belle in a neck-hold, ready to jump off her seat and go with Dixie's grandfather.

"It's just down to the end of that hallway." Smilin' Bob pointed.

Riley looked to Dixie. In light of his own agenda, he liked the idea of getting Wendy away from the table. That way he might finally be able to talk to Dixie. He'd gotten past a few of the woman's formidable barriers today. Maybe this was his chance to really get some concrete information at last. If nothing else he could try to arrange a time to meet the rest of the family.

"Miss Lettie did ask her to come in after supper," Riley reminded Dixie. "Do you think it's all right?"

"If Miss Lettie's resting, you have to promise to come straight back here." Dixie wagged her finger at her grandfather even as he slipped from his seat then moved to pull out Wendy's chair so she could come along. "I don't want you going in there and getting her all riled up over nonexistent rowboats, especially if she's resting. Do you hear me?"

Smilin' Bob muttered what Riley could only assume was an agreement.

Meanwhile, everything under the table must have gone well because the growling had given way to sound worthy of a lion sinking its teeth into the day's fresh kill.

Sis popped her head up so quick it made her hairdo wobble. "Hold it right there! I just got our Lettie settled in good and I won't leave it up to Mr. Slippery Foot's judgment as to whether or not he is disturbing her. I'll go with."

Wendy ran to Riley and threw her arms around him. "You come, too, Daddy."

"In a few minutes, sweetheart. I'd like to stay and help Miss Dixie clear away the dinner things, maybe help with the washing up first." He kissed her cheek and then the cheek of the doll she thrust out toward him. "Baby Belle, you and Miss Wendy behave yourselves like proper young ladies in Miss Lettie's company."

Wendy laughed, spun around and grabbed Smilin' Bob's offered hand. With him tottering at her side, she skipped off through the arched doorway.

"You love her very much, I can tell." Dixie stood.

"It's been a long time since I've seen that light of joy in her eyes." Riley stood, too. "It's not that she's an unhappy child, you understand, quite the opposite. I just haven't been around her in long enough stretches lately to see just how happy, how wonderful she truly is."

Dixie began stacking up the plates around her.

"I'll take up the silverware," he said, starting to do just that.

"Don't feel you have to hang back with me, then, Mr. Walker. Go on, be with your daughter, enjoy this special time together." She picked up Wendy's plate, and Riley's attention went to the stark white business card left on the table there.

"Don't worry, she and I will have plenty of time together from now on." He followed in her wake, gathering the knives, forks, and spoons onto the tray that had held the rolls. "I just have to find a place for us to live here in town, get her and her grandmother settled in and assume my new duties at—"

The dish in her hand clattered against another place setting as she roughly piled one on top of the other. "*Please* don't start up with that again. We were getting along so well."

"Yes, well enough that I thought we could finally approach this discussion." He lightly pitched a serving spoon onto the heap of silver. "Why can't we just talk about this like two mature adults?"

"Because we are not two mature adults. We are two people at cross purposes in a potentially messy situation with a lot at stake." She clunked the plates down and stood behind the empty chair at the head of the table. "I cannot talk about this and risk giving you information that might come back to hurt my case. Especially not until I have seen with my own two eyes what Howard Greenhow has done."

The candle's flames jumped and danced as if reacting to the rising tensions between them.

"Look, it was all legal, if that's what you're implying." He picked up the napkin lying at the place where Wendy had sat and wiped his hands on it. "I had done my research before I ever showed up here. Now granted, the deal changed a little after—"

She lifted her head high, but her chin trembled as if she were holding back great emotion.

Riley ran his fingers back through his hair, sighed, then dropped his hands to his hips. "Dixie, I went over those papers with a fine-tooth comb today. The deal is signed, sealed, and airtight."

"Sounds more like a crypt than the formation of a lasting partnership."

"Fine. It's clear you aren't going to listen to me now. But eventually, you will have to get past all this because our companies are going to have to work in unison."

"My family's companies already work in unison very nicely, thank you. And...*no!* The deal Howard Greenhow brokered for you wasn't to become an equal partner in each enterprise!" She put her hand to her forehead. "Why did I just assume that?"

"Maybe because your father had first talked to me about buying 20 to 25 percent of each concern, but—"

"What have you and that awful Greenhow done? What did you mean when you told me we were going to be partners?"

"Just that. That our success would depend on us working together, as partners, your business and *mine.*"

"Is that why you came in with Sis? You bought into the outlet store?" She shook her head. "Oh, Mr. Walker, I'm afraid Mr. Greenhow has bamboozled you. You see, the outlet store, while it does bring in a nice profit, is not the hub or heart of our operation. And even if you owned it in its entirety, you certainly would not be anything like a real partner in—"

"I came in with your aunt because I met her on the street and my realtor introduced us. Actually the person I have bought controlling interest from is another relative of yours."

"Oh my." Even in the golden hue of the candlelight he could tell she had gone pale. "You've got control of our delivery and transportation branch!"

"Uh-huh. You can make all the fine furniture you want, but with my company to haul, ship, and deliver it." He held his hands open. "That's not a threat, Dixie, that's just the way it is.

And that's why I keep saying that you and I have to figure out how to work together as true partners, with the judge, too, of course."

"The Judge. Why didn't I see that coming?" She shut her eyes.

"I'm hoping you can arrange for the two of us to meet tomorrow."

"Meet? *Tomorrow?* What do you mean?"

"Mr. Greenhow worked as the go-between in this, we never met face to face. My decision was based on my arrangements with your father and my own pressing need to move ahead with the negotiations. Since I have controlling interest and will act as CEO for the time being, a personal meeting was just courtesy, after all, and there wasn't time for it. It's all very legitimate, I assure you."

"Oh, I have no doubt." She just stood there for a moment staring, but not seeming to be really looking at anything. Then, slowly, she started to shake.

"What are you laughing at?"

"You."

"Me?"

"You *and* me, really. Here I've been so worried that you were in cahoots with Greenhow, it never occurred to me that he could be taking advantage of you every bit as much as he was of me."

"Taking advantage? How? What do you mean?"

"Mr. Walker? The name on the papers you signed, my other relative that you hope to meet, the one who is now your partner? Can you tell me what that name was?"

"Of course I can. George R. Cunningham. Why?"

"No reason, except…" She gathered up the plates she'd abandoned before, pivoted on her heel, and headed toward the kitchen. "Except before you go feeling all superior over having gotten into such a shrewd business arrangement with the founding family of Fulton's Dominion, you'd better take a peek at my grandfather's business card."

Riley did not want to do it. Did not *have* to do it, if he were honest with himself. The minute she'd suggested it, he knew what he would find. Still, discouragement lay like lead in the pit of his stomach, and a dull, foreboding throbbed behind his eyes as he picked up the card and read aloud, "George Robert 'Smilin' Bob' Cunningham. Principal Judge, Miss Fulton's Finest Future Furniture Fanatic (baby and toddler division), Chief Justice Dominion Days Bail and Jail Fundraising court, Little League umpire, Mediating matters of all magnitude since 1978!"

Ten

Humble yourselves before the Lord, and he will lift you up.

JAMES 4:10

THIS WAS JUST TOO GOOD.

"As my grandfather might say, Mr. Walker, you fall asleep in Delilah's barber chair—" Dixie pressed her back to the kitchen door, dinner plates in one hand, Peachie Too's crystal supper dish in the other—"you got no call to go bellyaching when you wake up with a new haircut."

"Isn't that a piece of shrewd advice!" Riley flicked his wrist and sent the business card sailing across the table. The small rectangle landed atop the bowl of fresh fruit, teetered on a tangerine, then tipped and slid between an apple and a bunch of bananas. "Pardon me if I don't rush out to have that embroidered on a pillow as a keepsake, Miss Fulton-Leigh."

"Well, maybe you should check into doing just that." She

165

had not set out to sound so haughty, but the way he'd discarded the fitting counsel as easily as he cast aside her grandfather's card struck a chord in her. "Or maybe you'd really do better with something more permanent. A nice engraved plaque, perhaps, or I've heard tattoos are all the rage now—"

His face clouded. "I cannot believe you can stand there and make light of this."

"*Me?*" She started to gesture to herself but realized her hands were full. She ducked inside the kitchen and in two quick steps she had set the dishes on the counter, pivoted and caught the door before it had stopped swinging. Poking her head back into the dining room, she said, "You've got some nerve scolding me for not taking this seriously! As I recall, as long as you thought you had come charging into my life like some knight on a white steed, acting in the name of all you saw as right and reasonable, well, you seemed all too happy to treat everything like some big jokefest."

He puffed his chest up. "Yeah, well, that was before—"

"That was before you realized that Greenhow had made just as big a monkey out of you as he had me. Now suddenly it doesn't seem like a laughing matter, does it?" She let the door fall shut between them, the heavy swish and thump of the thing as appropriate a close to the conversation as anything she could have come up with on her own.

The deluge of hot water rushing in to fill the deep, white sink drowned out her tongue-tied sounds of utter frustration. On one hand she had wanted nothing more than to see this very thing happen—for Riley Walker to be thwarted in his attempt to move in on her family business. On the other hand, some small part of her did not want it to come like this. The only reason Riley would back down now was because he thought her grandfather was a nut.

She grabbed the liquid detergent and squirted a long stream of green soap into the churning water.

If this was a victory, it was a shallow one at best. And in the end, one without any real winners. She would still be in every bit as big a mess as she had been before, trying to run three businesses on her own. Everyone in town would still be dependent on her decisions, and she still did not have a lawyer that she could trust to help her comb through the plans left in chaos by Daddy's dying. And then there was Riley.

She slid the plates into the sink and turned the faucet off with one hard crank of the handle. Standing with her hands immersed in the steaming water, she stared into the fragile, quivering bubbles. *Riley*. He said he'd changed his entire life for Wendy's sake, and now to have this happen. What was the man going to do?

She dragged the moist air into her lungs, ignoring the artificial lemon scent that stung her nostrils. She thought of Riley's compelling eyes, ready wit, and clear devotion to his family that rivaled…that rivaled pretty much all common sense. She exhaled slowly but the tightness in her chest did not ease. What on earth was that man going to do now?

The faintest tapping from the door behind her jarred Dixie's thoughts back to the reality of the moment. She raised her hands from the water, started to wipe them on her apron, only to remember she'd been so worked up she had not put one on. She turned toward the drawer with the kitchen towels in it, but the continued tapping drew her attention away.

"What?" She shook her hands over the sink to fling away the bubbles but they were too thick. Feeling a fool for having acted so impulsively out of her mixed feelings, she thrust her hands behind her back. "What is it? Did somebody want something?"

Slowly the door cracked open, not much, but just enough to allow a small white object to inch through the opening.

Dixie squinted. She cocked her head to try to make out what the peculiar white—and now a bit of yellow—contrivance could be. Her grandfather's card, she concluded after a few seconds study, stuck like a flag on the end of…"A banana?"

Riley pushed his way on through the doorway, a grin as wide as the ol' Mississippi itself on his face. "It's a call for a truce." He held the fruit toward her. "From one monkey to another."

"If you think this is funny, Mr. Walker, then…" She glanced at the banana in his hand, held up like a staunch little flagpole made just for this circumstance, to carry forth his makeshift sign of surrender. Dixie couldn't help but chuckle. "Okay, it's funny."

"Truce, then?" He held out his hand, his gaze hopeful but hard.

"Truce." Dixie returned that gaze with one she hoped he would read as strong but sympathetic. She swung her hand out to grasp his.

Their palms met.

The soap bubbles squished and popped and oozed between their fingers.

Riley glanced down.

Dixie winced.

He shook his head. "Well, at least this is going to be a clean break."

Dixie straightened her shoulders and let her hand slip from his. With all the suds on their warm skin he could not have held it if he had wanted to, but he did not seem to want to. Why that only rankled her already frayed nerves, she would not stop to mull over now.

"Actually, Mr. Walker, it could become quite messy, if you think about it."

"Messy? I don't see how. Unless you're planning on contesting my backing out of the partnership."

This time she did cross the floor to the towel drawer. She tugged on the old ceramic knob. It jerked to one side, then she wrangled it to the other until, after several lurching starts and coaxing jiggles, she got the thing open.

Dixie stared down into the neat rows of fine, Egyptian cotton towels. "I'm afraid I don't have anything to say about it, Mr. Walker. You've struck a deal with my grandfather, it seems, not with me. And as you've gone to great lengths to assure me, it's airtight."

Riley set his improvised flag of surrender aside. "No deal is airtight if one of the participants can be proven to have, um, shall we say, sprung a leak?"

She grabbed a towel from the drawer and shook it so fiercely the soft cotton snapped in the air as it unfurled from its sharp folds. "Just what are you implying, Mr. Walker?"

"Oh, c'mon, don't get all coy with me. You know what I mean. Your grandfather there." He gave a sharp gesture with his thumb in the general direction in which the old man had last been seen. "'Smilin' Bob,' 'the Judge.' He's a wing and a leg short of a full fried chicken dinner."

"He's eccentric." She wadded the soft fabric in both her hands. "But he is competent, *mentally* competent, and I don't think you could prove otherwise."

"Then why wasn't he helping you run the business?"

"It's not his forte." She gave her reply through gritted teeth.

"Oh, yeah, right, not like judging baby contests and mediating matters of all magnitude since 1978!"

"Maybe you should have read that card before you came

butting into our business. Maybe you should have asked some questions." She swiped away the last of the moisture and bubbles from her hands as she rushed on. "My goodness, Mr. Walker, you could stop pretty much any school child or distracted passerby on the streets of Fulton's Dominion and ask them about my family and you'd get an earful—most of which will be quite amusing and yet startlingly accurate."

"I was desperate, okay? You know I'm in a fix with Wendy's adoption. I'd sold my mill, so I had no job, no position in the community. We were living in too small a house that I'd never moved us out of because the mill took all my time in a town that was a fine place, especially for a man, but wasn't my ideal for Wendy. My mom was injured, my social network stunted. I had to do something to make our lives look normal and as positive as humanly possible, and I had to do it yesterday."

"I beg your pardon?"

He had to have heard her polite call for a clarification, but he rushed on all the same. "I thought I knew what I was walking into after speaking to your father. I believe a man is responsible to act *on* his faith and act *in* good faith. I believed I was doing both. I thought I was helping both our families by doing what I did."

There it was again, that justification, that oh-so-heroic means of implying that she shared some part in his travails. Dixie clenched her hands at her side. She set her jaw.

"If my actions were rash, Dixie, they were at least well intentioned."

"Your actions, Mr. Walker, were *greedy*."

"What?"

"You heard me. Greedy. Nothing but plain, old grab-at-something-you-ain't-worked-for greedy. You hadn't made your life, what did you call it? Normal and positive? In six years of being Wendy's father you had not created the kind of life you thought reflected well enough on your role. Me, I take one look at the child, see how she treats others and the way she lights up around you, and I'd say you worried for nothing."

"Thanks," he muttered. "I think."

"But you had it in your head you had to present the court with some kind of picturebook life. So when push came to shove, you decided you could waltz into my life and buy those things you had neglected to build for yourself, to siphon them off of my family and all its trappings of stability and—"

"Stability?" It came out sounding like he'd just scalded himself. "This group?"

"That was your mistaken assumption, not my assertion, but yes, in many ways my family does seem to have the stability yours lacks. Otherwise, why us?"

"It was business." His eyes narrowed.

"Well, it turned out to be bad business, didn't it?" She tossed her hair back in a move that was far more pride then primping, then leveled her gaze at him. "And it certainly has put you between a rock and a hard place."

"How so?"

"Well, you're making noises like you want to back out on Grandpa. All because he doesn't suit the image you wanted to buy into, as it were." Her pulse picked up in sheer exhilaration in the confrontation. All day she had dreamt of bringing Riley Walker down a notch.

Well, not *all* day, she admitted to herself. There had been moments, flashes of gentler feelings, of understanding, even attraction. But those had no place here. She had a point to make and she would not back down from it. If Riley had made a mess of things, he had no one but himself to blame and she was not going to let him pass the onus of responsibility off onto her or her dear grandfather.

"The way I see it, a man who invests his fortune and future to get controlling interest of a place one day then tries to get out of it the next because of something he never bothered to check out beforehand—that doesn't scream *stability,* either, does it?"

She was right. He knew it. She knew it. But no power on earth was going to make him admit it. Not today, not in the heat of this exchange, not with so many thoughts crashing together in his mind that he could not concentrate on anything but his own anger and embarrassment.

"There's no sense in us going over and over my motivations, Dixie. It doesn't change anything and it doesn't set us on the path to correcting this problem. You wanted me out all along. Well, congratulations, you win. I want to get out every bit as much as you want to be rid of me. In fact, given this unexpected turn of events, I think maybe it would be best if Wendy and I stayed elsewhere tonight." He gave the kitchen door a mighty shove and in two long strides he was back in the dining room.

The door whooshed and clunked, swinging back and forth, back and forth in smaller and smaller increments over the threshold until a sudden noisy *wham* broke the thumping rhythm. "Oh, no you don't."

It took every ounce of irritation Riley possessed just then to keep him from smiling at her response. He honestly had not intended to evoke it, but he had suspected all along that she would deliver something like this. He pinned her with a glare. "You're just not *content* unless you're contradicting me, are you?"

"I'm not content unless I am doing the right thing, Mr. Walker. If that happens to make you look like the north end of a southbound mule in the process, well, that's just a happy coincidence." She raised her chin.

The neat little row of pearls he'd noticed before accentuated her slender neck and complemented the flawless color of her skin. That he could take note of such things when other men might have been contemplating circling that pretty neck with both hands, told Riley something that scared him far more than any business deal gone sour ever could. Dixie Fulton-Leigh had gotten under his time-toughened hide like no other woman had before. Now, more than ever, he knew he had to get out of there.

"I simply will not allow you to take Wendy and leave. You are the invited guests of this household, and I will not be any part of you running off with that precious child of yours into the night when we have perfectly fine—"

"Spare me the melodrama, please. Into the night? Where do you get that stuff?" His laugh came out unnecessarily cruel. "You won't allow me to take my child and go? Well, Miss High-and-Mighty Princess Snooty-Patootie, I'd like to see you try and stop me."

Dixie stayed on Riley's heels as she followed him down the dark and narrow hallway that lead to Lettie's room. She tried to reason with him but she didn't manage to get more than a few syllables out before the sound of Wendy's darling voice reached them, and Riley pulled up.

His arm out to block her passage, he held them both back. He peered inside the room, then glanced back at her with a look that said he wanted to stay and listen a second to his six-year-old discussing matters of great import with Dixie's one-hundred-year-old retired maid.

"I liked that story, Miss Lettie, can you tell me another, please?" Wendy seemed quite careful indeed not to jostle or disturb the old lady lying next to where she sat cross-legged on the wide bed.

Still, Miss Lettie braced herself with one hand on the pillow that Sis had propped behind her back, as if she expected the child to start bouncing and somersaulting like a gymnast on a trampoline. Even so, there was a faraway light shining in those dark old eyes that Dixie had not seen in a very long time, the light of joy in the company of a young child.

Seeing that, Dixie gladly obliged Riley's wish to linger on the fringe of the serene scene.

"*Another* story?" Lettie laughed. "No, lambkin, I don't think ol' Lettie gots it in her tonight. Old 'uns like me and the Judge, we tends to wear right thin when it gets to the very last nub of day."

A nudge from Riley sent Dixie's gaze over to the overstuffed chair where Grandpa sat, head back, mouth open, snoring to beat the band. Despite the tangle of emotions this evening had stirred up in her, she found herself sharing a laugh with Riley over the sight. "Chief Justice of log sawing, huh?"

"Does that mean I have to go now?" Wendy asked, her head bowed slightly over the limp figure of Baby Belle draped in her lap.

"No such of a thing. Not at all. I'm all run out of stories to tell you right now, but that don't mean you can't tell *me* one."

"I don't know any."

"Then tell me about this baby doll of yours you've come toting in here."

"It's not mine, it belongs to Miss Dixie." She held the doll up. "She said you made it for her when she was a little girl."

"Yes, yes. That's right, now I remember. I made so many

dolls for that little gal, I almost forgot which one was which. But this one, she's special. That's the doll I made for her just before the accident."

"Why did you make so many dolls for her? Did her daddy not know how much little girls liked dolls and never buy her any?"

Riley shuffled his feet. He looked down.

"Her daddy could have bought her any doll they sold at the finest stores, lambkin, but she preferred the ones I sewed up for her because they was made with love."

"Are you Miss Dixie's mother?"

Lettie cackled up a laugh. "Only a pure heart could ask such a question child. No, I'm not my Dixie Belle's mother. I helped to raise her, though, just like I raised her grandmother. Raised her mother, too, right alongside my own little girl, Helen Betty."

"Is that the lady with the funny dog?"

Again Lettie laughed. "No, darling, Helen Betty has gone on to live with Jesus in heaven like so, so many people I have loved and cared for in my lifetime."

Dixie thought of the grandson that Lettie had not seen in so long. Now more than ever she knew she had to do something to bring about a reunion. And soon.

"I'm not blood relation to any of the folks in this house. They're my family by fate, by the will and grace of God, and by some measure of mutual consent, I reckon."

"I don't understand."

"Well, the way I sees it, the Lord has brung us together here for a whole lot of reasons and we've all of us made our home together, now. All of us that's here, we've all had a heap of love but we've all known our share of loss."

"I like listening to you talk, Miss Lettie. Tell me some more."

"Oh, a sweet little thing like you don't want to hear about nothing I have to say. You're too young to understand about grieving for thems what's gone away or gone on."

"My mother's gone away," she said quiet but distinctly. "She left me for my daddy and my grandma to take care of. Sometimes thinking 'bout her leaving makes me feel real bad, Miss Lettie. I know how that feels—all sad, and lonely, and wishing you knew how to make it all better."

Dixie reached out to pat Riley on the back, but her hand came to rest on his arm instead. She just left it there.

"Faith in the Lord and trust in the healing powers of time makes it better for most of us, lambkin. You probably can't understand that now, but remember it, 'cause one day it might just help you see your way out of the darkness we all of us pass through in this life."

Wendy nodded quite seriously, her soft, dark hair swaying with the emphatic movement.

"Faith and time helped me when I lost my Helen Betty, my only child, first when she moved away with that no-account husband of hers, Walter Summers, and then after...the accident."

"There it is again," Riley muttered. "The accident. It seems to be a defining moment in your family's personal history."

Dixie said nothing. What could she say—to deny it would be to deny all the pain and anguish this family had endured because of that one eventful night. To acknowledge it meant an explanation that Dixie was not ready to issue to a man she wasn't sure she could trust—or would ever see again after they dissolved his partnership with Grandpa.

"After the accident, I lost touch with my grandson. I ain't seen him since his mother's funeral. Yes, this household sure has known its share of good-byes." Lettie began to stroke Baby

Belle's hair as she spoke, her head lifted high and her gaze fixed somewhere in the unseen distance. "Miss Dixie, she's done just lost her daddy and years before that her mother went on to glory land along with Young Bobby, that was Miss Sis's husband, and—"

"Where's the glory land and why don't they ever come back to visit?"

"It's heaven. They can't come back because they've gone on to a better place."

"Oh. I thought maybe they didn't come back for the same reason my mom don't come back."

"Doesn't," Dixie whispered under her breath, unaware of what she was doing until the correction reached her own ears.

"What reason is that, child?"

"I don't know for sure, but if you knew why Young Bobby and Dixie's mother didn't come back, it might have been the same reason as why my mom stays away."

Riley pushed his hand back through his hair. He shifted his feet. The wooden floorboards creaked and his whole body went taut. He waited a second, then another, then slowly dared to look into the room. Lettie and Wendy sat, undisturbed by the noise, fussing to smooth down Baby Belle's ruffled petticoat.

"Will you tell me about the accident?" Wendy asked softly as her small, nimble fingers worked in unison with Lettie's gnarled ones to straighten out a row of yellowed lace.

Riley looked at Dixie. Even in the dim light of the hallway she could see the compassion burning in the depths of his eyes.

Still, Dixie's stomach knotted. She did not want to hear this story again. She started toward the door, determined to go in and break this all up with some cheerful excuse about Miss

Lettie needing her rest or Wendy needing to go to bed or that the house was on fire…anything to divert the conversation away from this painful memory.

Riley caught her by the arm. "Let Miss Lettie talk, Dixie. Look at her, she really seems to be going someplace with this, and it seems like it's making a connection with Wendy. I've never known her to open up about her mother like that to anyone. Please, let her talk."

"It's not an easy story to hear, Riley." She looked away. "Or tell."

"I trust Miss Lettie to handle it well, to tread lightly where she should and to be frank when frankness is called for. Am I wrong in doing that?"

"No, you're not wrong." She fought back the urge to either dash off down the hall or to stand there, frozen, with hands over her ears while she sang loudly and most likely off-key.

"It was a long time ago, long before you was born even, when Miss Dixie was just a tad bigger than you are now, as I recollect."

Wendy settled in, nestling close to Miss Lettie while the old woman croaked out the tale in her ancient voice. "There was to be a party, you see, an anniversary celebration for the Judge, there, and his wife, Miz Samantha Eugenie."

Lettie jabbed a finger in Smilin' Bob's direction.

As if he knew they were talking about him, he let out a long, laborious snore, then blustered and blubbered before quieting down again and falling back into the more familiar, rhythmic buzzing.

"Now, so many folks was invited to this here party that they had to find a place big enough to hold everybody so they decided to have it out to the new place they'd just built, where they kept all the trucks and such, out to the Cartage company."

"Cartage, that's a funny word."

"Just a fancified way of saying *hauling*, I reckon. You know how folks like to put on airs and make it sound like what they does and what they has is better than what everyone else has or does."

"My daddy is going to run that cartage place. Should I tell him to just call it plain hauling?"

"Your daddy's going to run that place?"

"Yes ma'am, he's the main chairholder now. I thought he was going to make the sofas with Miss Dixie but he told me today he is going to run the trucks for the Judge."

"Oh, my, that is good news. Good news indeed. Praise the Lord." Lettie lifted up her hands.

Wendy watched with wide eyes then she, too, lifted her hands and echoed, "Praise the Lord."

"He is merciful and just." Lettie's eyes were now shut, her face practically beaming with inner peace and joy, her hands still uplifted.

"He is merciful and just." Wendy kept one eye open.

"And he knows our needs before we know them ourselves. He hears our prayers and answers our pleas for mercy and relief. Amen."

"He knows our…prayers and…mercy…for…relief. Amen." Wendy stammered out the few words she seemed to have picked up. "Miss Lettie, why are we praising the Lord?"

"Because the wise man praises God in all good things. Your daddy coming to take over the Cartage is a good thing. It's like, well, it's like God sending a rowboat just when you think the flood of tribulations is just about to overtake you."

"Rowboat?" Riley raised an eyebrow. "What is it with this family and rowboats?"

Dixie pressed her lips together.

In the room, with the hazy halo of light from Lettie's stained glass lamp, Wendy and Lettie shared a smile.

Then Wendy wriggled a little so that she could stay close to Lettie but still look her in the face when she asked, "Why is my daddy like a rowboat? Miss Dixie said it was a joke, but I don't get it."

"Oh, it ain't no joke, lambkin. Your daddy taking over is a godsend, and when I tells you the rest of the story about the accident, you'll know why."

"When you stopped, you had said they was having a big party."

"That's right. Everybody was to get there early, then Geneva, Dixie's mama, was to make up a reason for her mama and daddy to come out to the truck depot. Then she and her brother— who everybody called Young Bobby, even though he was a man fully growed and married to Miss Sis for many years—they was to come on in a car ahead of their folks. That way they could let us all know when their parents would get there."

"It was a surprise party!"

"Yes, it were meant to be one, that's right. But the weather weren't good. The road out to the new building hadn't been paved over yet and it were all rutted and muddy. Something went amiss." Miss Lettie stroked her thumb over Baby Belle's face.

Dixie put her hand to her own cheek, wishing she could rush in and take comfort from Miss Lettie. And give it back to her as well.

"One of the trucks clearing out to make room for party goers..." Miss Lettie curled her hand around the doll's braid. She took a deep breath before going on. "Lost control on the road between the depot and town."

"Oh no, Dixie." Riley looked to her as if asking for confirmation of the awful truth. "They were killed in a wreck with one of the family's own delivery trucks?"

She could only nod.

"Only the driver of the truck was spared." Lettie's jaw trembled with an emotion only those who knew the whole story could fully comprehend. Then she blinked, and dragged the back of her hand over her leathery brown cheek and sighed. "But that night, Geneva, Young Bobby and…the other passenger in that truck…went to an even bigger and better party in heaven instead of the one they'd expected to throw for their parents."

Riley started to put his arms around Dixie's shoulders.

She went rigid. She did not want this man's sympathy. A few moments ago he'd been ready to run roughshod over her and everyone associated with her in order to get his way. She would not accept his contrived benevolence now.

Riley must have felt her resistance, for he withdrew without saying anything.

"After that night…" Miss Lettie began again to toy with the doll's yarn hair as she spoke in a lighter tone, but still with hushed anguish. "Miz Samantha Eugenie took to her bed and never recovered. We lost her not long after, her poor little heart just not strong enough to sustain her through the great loss of both her babies at one time. From that day forward, the Judge, well, he never was the same."

"I like the Judge the way he is now." Wendy tipped her head to one side and blinked as she made what appeared to be a quite serious regard of Dixie's grandfather. "I think he's funny and I like it when people call him Smilin' Bob and when he fights with Aunt Sis and when he growls at Peachie Too and does magic tricks—"

"He is a character, I'll give you that. And sweet as bees knees to me."

"Bees knees." Wendy giggled.

"But sweet don't run the business, lambkin, nor does magic tricks or the brand of general tomfoolery that old man is so fond of. I've known that man for nigh onto sixty years and I will tell you, child, he's as smart as a whip to this very day. Much smarter than folks 'round here give him credit for."

Dixie shot Riley an I-told-you-so look that in any other situation would have made her blush at her own smugness.

"But it's not in the Judge anymore to take over and run the business that brought about the loss of both his children."

Riley tensed. His dark brows angled down over his eyes as if he were doing long, difficult calculation. He began to fidget, starting to—but not quite—folding his arms, then stuffing one hand in his pocket, then running his thumb down his jawline.

"For a long time that didn't matter, though." Lettie's voice was soft and craggy but it carried just fine into the stillness of the narrow hallway. "Because Dixie's father took care of everything. John Frederick Fulton-Leigh has gone on to the other side and now…" She let the word trail off, as if implying the uncertainty of what would become of things.

Dixie understood that uncertainty tenfold. Lettie's reminder of it all only served to humble her. How arrogant she'd been when Riley had come with his offer of help, how self-righteous and demanding in thinking only of how it would look for her to be the one who lost the family business. How ridiculous she had been to let fear rule her decisions instead of faith. She had known better…and now—

"And now—" Wendy perked up, her eyes shining—"now me and my daddy have come here to help everyone."

"Yes! Now you and your daddy have come!" Lettie patted the girl's hair and grinned that gapped-tooth grin. "Isn't God good in the way he provides for his children if they will just humble themselves before him?"

Dixie held her breath. She could feel the musty air in the hallway on her tingling skin as the clear and reverent truth in Lettie's claim resonated in her being. The knot in her stomach relaxed. She understood and, closing her eyes, turned to Riley.

"Dixie, I'm so sorry—"

She opened her eyes, hoping he saw the sincerity there. "Oh, me too, Riley, that's just what I was going to say. I'm so sorry I acted like such a...a Princess Snooty-Patootie."

He laughed. "I'd say what I acted like, but I'm not going to use that kind of language."

She smiled at that. "So, now what?"

"Well, first we need to talk—really talk—this over."

"We need to assess the situation and look at it from all angles."

"We need to understand the ramifications of any actions we take before we commit to anything."

"We need to make plans."

"We need a lawyer."

"I just fired mine," they both said at exactly the same moment.

"You, too?" She clutched at his shirtsleeve. "But aren't you in the middle of an adoption proceeding?"

"Long story." He shook his head.

"Is that code for don't ask?"

"It's..." he put his hands on his hips and turned his face toward the ceiling. "It's code for ask me again later. Okay?"

"Yes, you're right. We have enough on our plates at the moment. We need..."

"We need a rowboat." He chuckled.

"Maybe we should ask Lettie about where to get one since she seems to be our resident expert."

Dixie glanced in to see that Wendy had slid from the bed and was holding the TV remote in her hand, poised and at the ready. Lettie snuggled under the covers, obviously preparing to go back to watching her stories until she fell asleep, as was her usual routine. Dixie pondered the frailness of the woman she so adored as Lettie moved with great effort to get comfortable. Dixie would gladly rush in and offer aid, but Lettie would only shoo her away. The old woman was far too proud to accept any help, so proud she would sever all ties with her own flesh and blood rather than—

"Wait a minute!" Dixie snapped her fingers. "That's it! Or it *may* be it. It's a place to start anyway!"

"Suddenly I wish I had my white flag again, because I give up on trying to make hide nor hair out of what you just said, Dixie."

"Lettie told me today that her grandson is a lawyer in Jackson. I was going to go over and see if I can't arrange a reunion."

"You think he'd act as our advisor?"

A flutter of anxiety rippled through her. She swallowed as if that might wash it all away, or at least push it back down so that she might answer Riley with some measure of confidence. "I…it's hard to say. I don't know the man."

And you don't know everything that stands between his family and mine. Dixie chose not to say it out loud. Why bring up old ugliness? Unless it became an issue, the secret of the tragic connections between Lettie's family and her own would not come from Dixie's lips.

Riley stole a peek in the room again. "But even if he doesn't want to work with us, at least it's a good place to start for recommendations, don't you guess?"

"Yes." Dixie stood tall. "Yes, I can't imagine that Lettie's grandson would be anything but forthcoming and helpful even if it turns out he has no desire to get personally involved."

In the next room the television clicked on.

Grandpa sputtered awake.

Wendy told him they had to get going and leave Miss Lettie to enjoy her stories.

Riley took Dixie by the hand. "C'mon, let's slip off before they come out here and know we've been eavesdropping. I have a notion Miss Lettie could still tear into us but good for being so rude."

Dixie smiled as she let him lead her back down the hallway toward the front parlor. "You're not scared of her. You're just using that as an excuse to hold my hand and I know it."

"Well, I don't notice you turning lose of me." He curled his hand more firmly around hers.

"Maybe that's because I finally know we're in this together." She tightened her own fingers. It felt good…just to have someone to finally share in her burdens. Nothing more. Her heart raced. *Nothing more.*

Eleven

Be patient, then, brothers, until the Lord's coming.
See how the farmer waits for the land to yield its
valuable crop and how patient he is
for the autumn and spring rains.

JAMES 5:7

"HERE YOU ARE! SIS TOLD ME I'D FIND YOU IN THE KITCHEN. ARE you ready to—" Riley froze at the threshold, his arm out straight to brace open the swinging door. "What are you doing still in your robe? We've got a big trip ahead of us if we hope to get over to Jackson, find and speak with Lettie's grandson, then get home again before nightfall."

Outside, the low rumble of thunder seemed to underscore his impatience.

Dixie slid her spatula under the lacy edges of one of the eggs frying in the cast-iron skillet. "I'll be ready in no time, just let me finish up with the breakfast and then I'll grab a quick shower and dress and be ready to hit the road."

"Breakfast? What are you doing cooking breakfast?"

"It's the first meal of the day, and it is now just a few minutes past seven in the morning. It's not such a difficult leap of logic to put those together." She held her tongue just so, rotated her wrist, and then flipped the egg in the pan without disturbing the deep yellow yolk.

"No, I mean why are *you* preparing breakfast?" He folded his arms and anchored his feet, using his broad back to hold the door wide open.

The morning light, muted by overcast skies, added a depth to his features that the brightest sunshine had erased—or at least, de-emphasized. She could see the lines of care etching outward from the corners of his deep eyes and the small creases that framed his smile, faint but always evident in his tanned cheeks. His damp hair looked even thicker, the waves and curls more unruly at the ends where he had tried to comb them back and down. The sight of him here, in her kitchen, dressed and ready to face the day sparked a subdued and startling excitement in her.

"Surely you don't put in a full day's work and still fix all the family meals." He looked around the room as though he almost expected to see someone else helping her. "If that's the case then we're going to have to make some changes starting immediately." ·

"You offering to take over the duties?" She held up the spatula. One fleeting, brilliant burst of lightning illuminated the kitchen windows. "Because if you are, you'd better get yourself over here pronto—the grits need stirring, the bacon needs crumbling, and the rest of these eggs should be over easy, thank you."

"Grits? Bacon? Eggs? Don't tell me you've got cheddar cheese and butter, too."

"I have."

He stepped forward, practically licking his lips. "Just tell me what I can do to help."

She pointed to the pot of pale, creamy grits bubbling on the stovetop. "Stir. And if you have some ill-informed opinion about how this all should be handled or how we do things in this household, kindly keep it to yourself."

"You're not a morning person, are you?" He moved close enough that she could feel both the heat of the stove and the warmth of his skin through the thick layers of her chenille robe and the long flannel nightgown underneath it.

The thin layer of bacon grease in the skillet popped and sizzled.

"What I'm not, Mr. Walker—"

"Riley. We agreed last night that since we're going to go ahead with our partnership, we'd operate on a first-name basis."

Thunder rolled in the distance.

"Riley." The name did not come easily to her. She liked the formality of last names, especially when standing in such close proximity to the man that towered over her and made her feel...well, just made her *feel*. Everything from panicky to protected, from angry to assured. She licked her lips and focused on the delicate task of turning the eggs so that they stayed intact. "The thing I am not, Riley, is calm or confident. I'll admit, that may have affected my mood."

"Calm or confident about what?" He earnestly did not seem to know what she was talking about.

"About...everything. What if this is all a big mistake? What if all the plans we made last night bring nothing but disaster for us and everyone we hope to benefit by them?"

"And what if they don't? What if they are the best things we've ever done, the best decisions we've ever made?" He swirled the wooden spoon through the grits in long, even strokes. "We've looked at this from every angle and gone over it as much as we could with your grandfather and Sis. I've approached my mother and she's..."

"She's..." Dixie raised her brows.

"Well, she's got a broken hip. How much trouble can she give us? She can't run away and she won't be doing much kicking and screaming for a while."

His jokes and wide grin did not assuage Dixie's concerns. She grabbed up a plate and began lifting the perfectly fried eggs from the black skillet bottom onto a pristine white plate with tiny pink roses twining around the rim. "Your mother is not crazy about the idea of coming to live with my family until we can get everything squared away, is she?"

"Well..." He lifted the spoon and let a glop of the thick corn mixture plop quietly back into the pot. "The word *crazy* did come up."

The plate clattered as Dixie set it aside on the counter beside the butter dish, egg shells, and the crockery jar of saved bacon grease. "Is she scared to come and stay here?"

"No, no. Not at all, she's just, well, she's heard some things about your family, that's all. But I know once she's spent a little time with them, seen how they are with Wendy...once she's met *you*..."

Dixie looked up from the clutter of the kitchen and right into Riley's eyes. Her breath caught in her chest at what she saw reflected there. She pursed her lips to say something, but at that precise moment, Riley's gaze dipped to brush over her mouth. She could not have spoken then if her life depended on it.

He wanted to kiss her.

Dixie was no fool. Neither was she a simpering child. She recognized all the signals, all the subtle nuances of flirtation and attraction. She also knew the pain of mistaking such things for real affection.

Riley stepped toward her, reaching out with one hand to push her hair.

Lightning and thunder crashed together just outside the windows. The clouds huddled dark and dangerous now, heavy with a held-back downpour.

Dixie held her breath. Riley wanted to kiss her, and for all the alarms going off in her brain, the haze of emotion blurring the very way she viewed it all, she was going to let him. She tipped back her head, went up on very tippy toes and—

"Land-a-goshen! What are you two doing in here?" Sis rushed in, flapping a placemat from the dining room ahead of her all the way. "Can't you hear that alarm going off? Can't you see the smoke?"

Aunt Sis grabbed up the broom leaning against the nearby wall and took one well-aimed bat at the blaring smoke alarm. It gave out a sickly whine then plummeted to the floor, barely missing the dog's water dish.

"I have a feeling she's done that before," Riley muttered. In one sure move, Riley reached over and flicked off both burners on the stove.

"I...I must have forgotten to turn the burner off when I finished with the eggs." Dixie's cheeks were hot as fire themselves, both from what she had done and from what she had *almost* done. She stepped away from Riley as though he were the source of all the smoke and commotion. In a way, he was.

Sis went right on fanning the placemat, coughing and choking as she cried, "How could you let this happen, Dixie? You, of all people, know how it's possible in one careless moment to make a mistake you will regret the rest of your life!"

"Yes, ma'am. I do. Thank you for, um, intervening before I did just that." She spoke to Aunt Sis but her eyes remained on Riley.

Sis whipped the mat in the air one last time. "Oh, I am going to do a lot more than intervene. I am going to take over for you."

"That could prove interesting." Riley's smile inched up higher on one side.

Dixie shivered at the hint of a secret that neither one of them had acknowledged—the kiss that never was.

"Interesting?" Sis pulled open the usually stubborn towel drawer with one hard, purposeful yank. She snatched up a towel and slung it over her shoulder, then nabbed an apron hanging on a hook by the refrigerator. As she cinched the cheery red and yellow ties around her waist and made a big bow, she scowled at the mess on the stovetop. "If you're worried that I'm not up to the job, Mr. Walker, you needn't trouble yourself. Dixie's job has kept her travelling for a long time now. In her stead, I assure you I do just fine keeping the family clean and fed and as healthy as can reasonably be expected. Dixie only does the cooking when she's home because she enjoys it so much."

"Really?"

"Oh yes." Without looking, Aunt Sis answered as if Riley had spoken directly to her, though his teasing gaze had been fixed quite firmly on Dixie. "Our little Dixie is quite the homebody. More so than I ever was or am inclined to be, but one does what one must to contribute to the overall well-being of one's household. Something I am sure you appreciate."

"Yes." He kept his gaze fixed on Dixie, his voice hushed.

"I'm just chocked full of appreciation, ma'am."

"Good to hear, sir." She attacked the stove with vigor, moving the skillet to the back, shifting the plate of eggs closer to keep them warm, then testing the grits by churning the spoon through a few times. "I hope that means you harbor no reservations about my helping care for your mother during her convalescence with us."

"Me? No, I don't have any reservations at all Miss Sis."

"Call me Aunt Sis—*Aunt*. You may as well."

Riley raised his eyebrows.

Dixie put her fingers to her lips, and tugged her robe closed high at the neck. "Aunt Sis, I think you're making an assumption based on one unintentional moment…"

"Everyone does," Sis explained without looking at them.

"Everyone does what?" Dixie dreaded the answer but she had to ask.

"Calls me Aunt Sis, relative or not. And since Riley and his mother and his daughter will be living with us, he ought to, too."

Dixie exhaled. She felt a perfect fool on so many levels already this morning—and she wasn't even out of her pajamas yet! This did not bode well for her day.

"Now, you two skeedaddle. I have some last-minute things to attend to, then I'll bring breakfast on out to the table."

"I'll stay and help." Dixie had no intention of walking out that door side-by-side with Riley, not after she'd almost kissed the man, not after she'd literally set off the smoke alarm with the recklessness of her behavior. "You go on out, Riley. Tell everyone we'll be there straightaway."

"Tell them yourself. I don't need anyone in here distracting me while I…*create.*" Aunt Sis placed her hand in the middle of Dixie's back and gave a light shove.

It was a feat of tremendous grace as well as grit-your-teeth-and-save-your-pride-at-all-costs pig-headedness that kept her from stumbling face first into Riley's chest. Instead, she staggered, bumping her hip against the corner of the cupboards. It smarted but she did not let her pain show.

"Are you all right?" Riley leaned down to be eye-level with her.

"I'm fine. Fine." She flung her hand out, meaning to give an elegant flourish toward the kitchen door in silent suggestion that he lead the way out. The gesture threw her off balance. She took a step back to regain her equilibrium, careful not to tromp on the poor, lifeless smoke alarm, only to land the heel of her fuzzy pink house shoe in Peachie Too's water bowl.

No, she thought as she lurched along after Riley into the dining room with one soggy slipper and an ego to match, this did not bode well for her day at all.

"Be doers of the word, not hearers only…" Riley guided his truck through the pounding rain down the main road leading out of Fulton's Dominion.

"I beg your pardon?"

"Nothing. I'm just reminding myself why I am doing what I am doing."

"You're quoting the Bible."

He smiled. "Yes, I am, because when it gets right down to it, the reason I'm in this brand-new truck headed to Jackson to meet with a man I've never heard of until last night—a man, I might add, who does not even know we are coming to call on him—is faith, Dixie."

"Faith? You mean you have faith it will all work out?"

"No, well, yes. Yes *and* no." If he had worked a *maybe* in there he'd have had all the bases covered. Why hadn't he voiced his convictions properly from the first? "I do believe it will work out, one way or another, and it might not be to our immediate liking. However, when I say faith is responsible for my being here now, I mean because I made it a practice to act on my beliefs. I acted on what I felt God would have me do. And, in short, that set me on the road to Jackson today."

"Well, let's see, there *is* a verse about helping widows and orphans…"

"That could fit, I suppose, but it's not what I'm talking about, either. You see, I decided a long time ago that if I didn't act on my faith then it was, like it says in the book of James, dead. I've heard folks use a lot of terms for that quality in me from being a man of action to being a workaholic."

A sly smile tipped up the corners of her mouth. She nodded like a woman who had just figured out some great mystery and was reveling in her achievement. "Ah-ha, so Lettie was right."

"Right about what?"

"You *are* a rowboat."

"That could be a good thing, because if this rain doesn't let up we may need a rowboat." He chuckled. "I know one thing for sure, I'm a lot more likely to be the guy in the rowboat in that story than I am to be the man on the roof."

"It's not a sin to be the man on the roof, Riley. It's no great shame to need help sometimes. Isn't that the very lesson you wanted me to embrace?"

"I'm not afraid to ask for help when I need it—*if* I need it."

"Uh-huh."

One hasty glance her way told him she had his number. In truth, she'd had it the day she'd stood in front of his truck in that empty parking space. She'd called his bluff and stood right up to him, something very few people ever did. Most likely they were afraid of getting mowed down as he plowed ahead toward his goal.

He'd thought he had her pegged that day. But now, sitting here, he realized he had only just scratched the surface. This woman could switch in the blink of an eye from high Southern belle in a full-blown hissy fit to an unyielding businesswoman to someone capable of nurturing anyone in need from Wendy to Lettie to...

Riley fixed his grip on the steering wheel and pressed his shoulders back against the seat. He had no place thinking any such thing about Dixie Fulton-Leigh. She was his *business* partner. She had graciously opened her home to him and his family so they could get their lives in order before Wendy's adoption hearing. He would not do anything to jeopardize either of those situations. The pull of attraction he felt for Dixie spelled danger on so many levels it made his senses go on all-points-alert just to imagine the outcome.

For the first time in a long while Riley could honestly say that he had not just hope, but real confidence. He could stand up at the adoption hearing now and show that he had provided his daughter with the best home in town, complete with an eccentric but doting collection of caregivers and a dad who would be home every night in time for supper. He also had secured Wendy's future by becoming part of a thriving, time-tested business concern. And he'd provided the child with a fine role model of womanhood in Dixie. As Carol had so succinctly put it, if he made a mess out of this he would most truly be in a "world of hurt."

They drove without talking for a good long while. The rain came in sheets, then let up. The thunder rattled the windows and lightning scored white-hot across the sky. Then the clouds let loose again. And so it went.

In the midst of the deluge, it seemed almost unbearably intimate in the close quarters of the truck's cab. The silence hanging between him and Dixie only made it more so. He could hear her steady breathing, feel every move she made as she fidgeted with her hair, her dress, her mother's pearls. It fascinated him how she sometimes simply skimmed the strand with her fingers, as if that simple act focused her, put her in touch with who she was and where she had come from.

Dixie was unlike most women Riley had known. She wasn't driven and willing to run over anyone in her way like Carol, nor was she hard and manipulative like his sister, Marcia. Dixie was on her way to being someone extraordinary, he could see it in her flashes of fearlessness, in the strength of her faith, even in her moments of weakness. Dixie was a lovely flower, a seed planted deep in winter, who was just now pushing her tender green leaves up past her latest adversity.

Dixie was—he paused to steal a look at her as he slowed for a four-way stop—was asleep. He smiled. The poor thing had every right to be exhausted. She'd been through so much these last few weeks…and most of it all alone.

"Get your rest, Sweet Dixie Belle." He knew the gentle thrumming of the rain on the roof of the truck would keep his voice from disturbing her. "I'm here now. Our partnership is firm, and so is my resolve not to let emotions get in the way of either of us reaching our goals."

"Well, we're here and it's going to be smooth sailing from here on out." Dixie scanned the unevenly spaced white-lettered names on the black felt directory in the building's lobby. Her head throbbed and her stomach rumbled from hunger, but she had insisted they come directly here as soon as she'd found Lettie's grandson's office in the phone book. She wasn't taking any chances on more things going wrong with this well-intentioned mission.

"Glad someone is still optimistic about this misadventure," Riley grumbled.

"Look, how many times must I apologize for not knowing that the Eudora Welty Library and the downtown library were the same place? I thought the first one had something to do with that celebrated author, so when I told the person we asked for directions that we needed to look up information on lawyers at the library and they directed us there…it was an honest mistake. Besides we got it straightened out."

He ran his hand back through his hair, sending droplets of rain splattering onto the floor. "Eventually."

Dixie ran her finger down the glass covering the office roster until she saw the name she'd been searching for. "Here he is."

"Are you sure that's Lettie's grandson? Maybe you should have asked him over the phone if you had the right man."

"And give him the chance to refuse to even see us and let us make our case? No, sir. I did not come all this way to let that happen."

"Maybe he wouldn't have refused to see you. Or just maybe he'd have told you up front that you have the wrong guy."

"It's *not* the wrong guy. Look at that name." She stabbed her finger at the neat row of letters.

"Fulton Summers," Riley read aloud. "My, but your family's influence does have a far reach."

"There were only three Summers listed under lawyers in the book, and only one of them with the first name Fulton. It has to be Lettie's grandson." Dixie raised her head, letting the gesture tack on her nonverbal *so there*. "And for the record, I'm not at all surprised to see something of my family reflected in the man's name. His mother and mine were close as sisters once upon a time, before—"

Dixie cut herself off. She'd told him all he needed to know about the matter. Speaking about the rest of it would only put her in a poor state of mind for meeting Fulton. She tapped the glass with her fingernail. "That's not important now. Look here, office number 308. That's where we're headed. When I called Mr. Summers, he said he could see us as soon as we could get here, and we weren't exactly zippy making our way over here."

"Not unless you count all the time we wasted zipping down one-way streets downtown trying to figure out how to get where we needed to go."

"But that's all behind us now, Riley. We're here!" Despite her physical discomfort and the nagging reminder of what still stood between Fulton Summer's family and her own, her spirit had begun to lift. She tugged at Riley's rain-dappled sleeve and took a step backward toward the elevator doors behind them. "We've done it! We've actually found Lettie's grandson and in a few minutes we'll be planting the seeds for a long overdue reunion. Maybe we'll even kindle a new relationship that's going to benefit all of us personally and professionally. Don't tell me you're not just a little excited about that."

He held his hands up, his footfalls leaden but compliant as she dragged him along. "Anything that gets me back on track with the adoption is pretty exciting to me. It may sound mercenary, but I can't help but think that having the grandson of one of the people who will be influencing Wendy represent us in court will be a positive thing."

Dixie pressed the up button on the elevator, then looked around the simple but clean lobby. "It's not a very fancy place, is it?"

"I've seen worse."

"Yes, but I mean for a *lawyer*. When you compare this building with the one of Greenhow, Greenhow, Byson, and Pryor…"

"Considering we're looking for pretty much the opposite experience as we had with them, I'd say we're off to a good start."

Dixie smiled. Riley's approval in this situation meant a lot to her, and not just because if things went smoothly here they'd agreed to hire Lettie's grandson to do their legal work. "So, you have a good feeling about this?"

The elevator groaned to a stop, announcing its arrival with a harsh electric buzzer. The doors rolled open.

Instead of answering, Riley motioned for her to get on the elevator.

"Riley?" She stepped into the dark, paneled space, foreboding closing in on her. "You *do* have a good feeling about this, don't you? You wouldn't even consider using this lawyer for Wendy's case if you didn't have a good feeling, would you?"

"I don't make my decisions on emotion, Dixie." He stepped inside and turned to face the doors as they swished shut. He pushed the button marked 3 and the elevator whirred and groaned then hurtled upward. "I act on the information at hand and out of a sense of faith."

"Yes, but…"

"The fact is that, the way I want it handled, my case is a very routine matter that any competent family lawyer could oversee. And it's my business with whom I chose to deal. It's not for you to worry about."

"Oh?" It was neither the answer nor the attitude she expected to hear. "And what do you think I *should* worry about, Riley?"

The elevator slowed. The number 3 flashed in green over

the doors, then blinked out. The old contraption jerked to a stop, made a noise that Dixie imagined was somewhat akin to a beached whale, then dropped into place at the selected floor, leaving her heart in her mouth and her stomach roiling.

"Riley?" The door slid open.

He looked down, put his finger under her chin, and whispered, "I don't think you should worry about a thing, Princess, not a thing."

Her thrill to that reply rivaled any reaction she'd had to the wild ride in the cantankerous elevator. Dixie took his words to heart. She let her worries slip away as they marched through the door marked 308 and gave Riley's name, as they had over the phone, to Fulton Summers's secretary.

Moments later, they were in his office.

"Oh my!" Dixie's astonishment escaped her lips before her brain had a chance to reign it in.

"I take it you've been caught off-guard, Ms. Walker?" Fulton stood, seeming neither agitated nor surprised.

"Actually, I'm Riley Walker." Riley thrust out his hand.

Dixie wondered whether Riley were trying to diffuse the tension created by her idiotic outburst or hoping to make a quick ally in the other man and distance himself from Dixie entirely.

"Glad to know you, Mr. Walker." The lawyer gripped Riley's hand.

"Nice to meet you too, sir." Riley gave a nod and released the handshake. "And this is—"

"I am so sorry." Dixie rushed forward the moment Fulton's hand was free. She seized it and began pumping vigorously. "That must have sounded the height of rudeness, just coming in here, throwing up my hands and…" She re-enacted it with a comical flare. "Oh my!"

Riley cleared his throat.

She was overcompensating, she knew, but unable to stop herself. This encounter simply had to go well, had to produce a positive outcome. Just had to.

"It's just that I wasn't prepared for—"

"A black lawyer?" He pushed back his open suit jacket to put his hands on his hips.

Dixie stopped cold. The excitement with which she had approached this meeting fell to the wayside in one instant. She was not angry, but she would not brook any implication that she was prejudiced, either. There might be other reasons why she and Fulton Summers would clash, but race was not one of them. "No, Mr. Summers, it's not the color of your skin that took me aback. What I was unprepared for was just how familiar I find your features. How much you must look like my Miss Lettie. Letticia Gautier, that is, she's—"

"My grandmother?"

Riley moved in close behind Dixie. "She's the reason we sought you out, Mr. Summers."

She welcomed the comfort of his nearness.

"Is she dead?" Fulton said it so coldly that Dixie shivered.

"No! No, she's *not* dead," she came back with almost a huff.

"Oh. I see." He dropped into his seat and rubbed his eyes with one hand, causing his gold, wire-rimmed glasses to bob up and down on top of his thumb and forefinger.

Dixie's hopeful enthusiasm plummeted. She studied the man behind the old but immaculate wooden desk. He wore his black hair cut very short and it had begun to recede on either side of his smooth forehead.

He had Lettie's facial structure, and though his skin was just a hue darker it was equally rich and flawless. And yet, upon closer inspection, she saw little else of Lettie in him despite the strong pull of familiarity about him. There was a hardness around his mouth and a beaten-downness to his posture that had come over him when he slumped into the chair upon learning his grandmother was still alive.

Where Lettie radiated inner joy, her grandson cast around him something else…not anything sinister or even unsettling so much as—sad. There was a deep, deep sadness about this man.

"Mr. Summers." Dixie eased down into the chair directly across the desk from the man she hoped to warm to on Lettie's behalf. "I've come here because your grandmother is a very old woman. Very old. Near as we can calculate she will be one hundred years old in three months and a few days and—"

"Stop right there." He held his hand up, not even looking her way. "If you've come here on my grandmother's behalf, to try to plead with me to reconcile with her before it's too late, you're wasting your breath, Ms. Walker. Let me tell you right now, that is *never* going to happen."

Twelve

What causes fights and quarrels among you?
Don't they come from your desires that battle within you?
You want something but don't get it.
You kill and covet, but you cannot have what you want.
You quarrel and fight.
You do not have, because you do not ask God.
When you ask, you do not receive, because
you ask with wrong motives...

JAMES 4:1–3

"NEVER?" DIXIE TIPPED HER HEAD, FOLDING HER ARMS AND straightening her shoulders until her backbone was positively rigid. She'd have arched one eyebrow the way characters were always doing in books, if she had the slightest idea how to do it. "Excuse me, Mr. Summers, but did you just tell me *never?*"

"Oh, boy," Riley muttered under his breath behind her.

"Mr. Summers, I think you should know straight off that I don't believe in never, not the way you're using it. I believe in never-ending loyalty and compassion, never let them see you sweat, and have been known to utter the phrase *never mind* and even *never again* in certain exasperating cases."

Riley laughed.

"But where somebody I love is concerned, the idea of never trying to bridge the gap between us, never putting my personal grievances aside long enough to make amends for whatever wrongs stand between us, never seeing the eyes that hold only hope and love for me? It's not in my vocabulary, which means I'm willing to do whatever I can to erase it from yours, as well."

Fulton's face lighted like the slashes of lightning beyond the window. "Dixie Fulton-Leigh! Why didn't I recognize you the moment you walked through that door?"

"Your reputation precedes you." Riley moved around to the seat next to hers, but did not sit in it.

The lawyer shook his head. "Not reputation, Mr. Walker, memory. You see, I've met Miss Fulton-Leigh before."

"You have? Where? When?" She tried to place the man's face, his name, his mannerisms, anything that might give her a clue as to what he was talking about. "I have to apologize again, Mr. Summers, but I don't recall—"

"Oh, you wouldn't."

Dixie tensed at what seemed an indictment of her character. "I'm sure if we had met, that is, I don't see how I would have forgotten meeting Miss Lettie's grandson. Even if our paths had crossed under unfamiliar circumstances, such as for business or something entirely unrelated to our families, the name Fulton Summers would have struck a chord in me."

"I'm sure it would have." He met her gaze and the sadness she had sensed in him before seemed harder now, though tinged with a soul-deep weariness...something with which Dixie readily identified. "Ironic, isn't it, that I was named to honor the family that tore my own family apart?"

"That...?" Dixie looked to Riley, then back to Fulton. She struggled to swallow, to keep her emotions in check. "If anything, Mr. Summers, I'd say just the opposite. The irony is that you were named for the family later devastated by the action of your own father."

"I didn't...I wasn't..." He blinked and for that instant his eyes felt to her like eyes she'd looked into a thousand times before. Then he looked away. "I wasn't thinking about the accident at all when I said that, please believe me. I'd never have brought it up like that knowing how painful it could be for you."

She could see in every aspect of the gentleman's reaction that he was speaking the truth. Having just dismissed a lawyer who had sought revenge as his parting shot, Dixie appreciated the kind of man that made Lettie's grandson.

"I believe you, Mr. Summers."

"Since *you've* brought it up, though, you know that's just what it was, don't you? An *accident?*"

"Yes." She barely managed to make herself heard. The little girl within her—the motherless daughter who had lost her beloved mother in that one blinding moment—sprang up then and Dixie battled to keep her beneath the surface.

This wasn't about that night. This was about everything *but* that night. And no matter what she felt or thought about the awful incident, it had left its scars on the man before her as well. She could not forget that.

"Yes, Mr. Summers, I personally hold no one to blame for what happened, and if it's all the same to you, I'd rather not dredge it all back up again."

Fulton nodded.

Riley shuffled his boots, his hands clasped in front of him, standing as though he were waiting on the fringes of the conversation. Did he expect an invitation to sit? Or was he feeling some need to stay out of the way? She felt his gaze on her profile, but she refused to turn to acknowledge his curiosity. Not about this.

Instead, she adjusted her strand of pearls, sliding the clasp back so that it rested against the back of her neck, and made a quick survey of the room. Matted and framed degrees and certificates hung neatly on the wall behind the desk. Intermixed were newspaper articles that featured Fulton in some way, plaques of recognition from two civic organizations and one marked "Coach of The Year." There were photographs of Fulton shaking hands with important looking people and one of a group of girls in uniforms grinning from behind a huge soccer trophy. In all they formed a lovely mosaic of the richness of this man's life. Lettie would be proud…if she only knew.

Fixed again on the task at hand, Dixie sat up straight and took control of the conversation once more. "You said that you and I had met before, Mr. Summers?"

"Yes." He looked down at his desk, thumped his knuckles on the calendar a few times, and then sighed. When he looked up again, he wore the most sincere smile, but it did not chase away the somberness in his compelling eyes. "You were in kindergarten. I remember that because you tried to show me what you were learning in class and, being a seventh grader, the information annoyed rather than impressed me."

"Why do I suspect she persisted anyway?"

At Riley's comment, Fulton's smile broadened. "Of course. The whole time I was at her house she tagged along behind me singing the alphabet song—over and over and—" Fulton laughed, just a little, then his face grew serious again. "The thing I remember most was how you kept asking me to point to things so you could tell me their color."

Dixie did not know if it was the word *color* or the way Mr. Summers said it that put her on edge.

"So I tried to find things that were the strangest shades possible, which wasn't hard to do considering the decorating scheme in your front parlor."

"Some things never change." Riley folded his arms, practically daring her to contradict him.

"I pointed to an old-fashioned beaded lampshade, some peculiar Chinese figurines, and a piece of modern art that I am at a loss to describe to this day except to say that it sure did have plenty of exotic colors to it."

Now Dixie did turn to Riley. "Aunt Sis had taken up painting."

"Ah." He must have taken this as his cue to fully join them. He pulled back the chair next to hers then settled himself down in it.

"You rattled off your answers, pink and puce and royal blue—you knew a name for every thing I pointed to." Fulton pushed his glasses up. "Then I pointed to myself."

The air of tension in the room, which had begun to ease only slightly, instantly went so brittle that Dixie thought she heard it crackle like static electricity on a dry, winter day.

"And I will never forget what you said and did then." He leaned forward, his elbows on the desktop. He laced his long fingers together and put his chin on his hands. "You said *brown*. And just as quickly I said black right back at you. *Brown* you insisted, and I was every bit as insistent, if not more so. That went on for quite a while until I pointed to you and told you you were white. And you said 'No I'm not, I'm tan.'"

"It sounds like me. I can remember thinking that exact thing, but I still don't recall our meeting."

"I don't expect you did."

Dixie gripped the arm of her chair. If that had been Riley speaking, she suspected he might have tacked on his favorite nickname: Princess Snooty-Patootie.

"I wasn't at your house more than fifteen or twenty minutes," Fulton said.

"Oh, so it was just a brief meeting?"

"Well, I was there long enough for you to be able to go and get your great big crayon box, whip out the black and white crayon and prove your point to me that we were neither one, but more different tones of the same color that you called *brown*. I tried to explain that the world did not see things that way, but you had your mind set. You sure were a stubborn thing back then, one who wasn't much inclined to give up your viewpoint."

"Like I said, some things never change." Riley folded his arms.

Fulton's laugh surprised her. If she'd had to guess, she'd have ventured that Fulton Summers would laugh in halting starts, his mouth closed, his face almost unaffected by his humor. The depth and warmth of his spontaneous chuckle put Dixie so in mind of his grandmother's infectious joy that she laughed, too, pleased to bear the brunt of any joke that broke down these walls, even if just a little bit.

She raised her finger and struck a pose she knew would do their adolescent concept of her proud. "I am taking that as a compliment, from both of you."

"We expected nothing less." Riley dipped his head to her.

"So, this one brief visit was the only time you were invited to my house, Mr. Summers?"

"I was never *invited* to your house, Miss Fulton-Leigh."

Her good humor came up short. "But you said you were there, and, after all, Helen Betty grew up in that place. I know our mothers were close as kin at one time. I can't imagine that—"

"My grandmother issued that edict. She had no use for my father from the very start. She knew about his drinking, that he held in contempt much of what she counted dear, including her religious beliefs. My mother married him anyway, and my grandmother set down the ruling. My father was never to set foot in her home."

"*Her* home?" Riley sat forward.

"My home *is* her home, Riley, just as it is for Aunt Sis and Grandpa." Dixie's quiet conviction hurried her words out through her tight lips. "Just as it will be for you and Wendy for as long as you need it."

"Whatever the reason, it's clear my grandmother does think of your house as *her* home and your family as…well, obviously she holds them in high esteem."

She didn't get the impression that Fulton condemned her family for his grandmother's actions or opinions, but she also sensed that he did not particularly share Miss Lettie's regard.

"My issues are not with you, Miss Fulton-Leigh—it is still Miss Fulton-Leigh? Or is it Mrs. Walker?" He looked to Riley, then Dixie.

"Oh, no, we're not married." Riley threw both hands up as if ready to physically repel the idea. "We're—"

"Mr. Walker here is the new primary shareholder and CEO of the trucking division. He bought the controlling interest from my grandfather after my father died a few weeks ago."

"I hadn't heard. I don't get much word from Fulton's Dominion anymore. I, uh, I am, of course, very sorry for your loss. Very sorry."

She believed he meant it. Whatever he felt toward her family, Fulton Summers seemed a kind and decent man. She saw on the wall and in the awards sitting in his bookshelves evidence of education, hard work, dedication, and charity. This was, without a doubt, just the sort of man she needed to help her and Riley untangle themselves from Greenhow. Just the kind of man Riley could use on his side in Wendy's adoption case.

Dixie had to make the connection now for her and Riley's sake, as much as for Lettie's. "Mr. Summers, we really need—"

"Pardon me for interrupting, but it seems pointless to let you go on." He held one hand up. "As I've said, my issues are not with you, but I'm afraid you've wasted your time by coming here. I only wish you had made your intentions clear when you called me. I could have saved us both the trouble."

"If I had told you who I was, would you have seen us?"

"Would I have devoted time I might have spent counseling a genuine client about a real legal matter talking to you about lost causes?" He shook his head. "What do you think?"

"I think you haven't heard us out." Riley leaned back in his chair, as though hunkering in for the long haul.

"I've heard all I need to." Fulton stood.

"Then at least do us the courtesy of recommending another lawyer." She knew that would command his attention.

"What for?" His eyes narrowed behind the thin, oval frames. "You want to hire one to play the part of me for my grandmother?"

"No. Truth is, we need legal counsel."

"When you say we…?"

"My whole family and all our business concerns."

He sat down again.

"As well as a personal matter." Riley's face went positively grim. "Do you have experience with adoption?"

"Wait. Stop right there." Fulton put his head in his hands, his voice strained when he finally spoke again. "I don't get this. What are you saying to me?"

"We're saying we came here today on a dual mission, to find Lettie's grandson *and* a new lawyer. I know it's terribly simplistic of me, but I was hoping that we might find them in the same person."

"Me?"

"If you can handle the workload. If it's the kind of law that interests you."

He blew out a long blast of air, rubbed his knuckle over his chin, then adjusted his glasses. "Adoption? No problem, I've done my share, even foreign adoption and some fairly tricky ones."

"Great." Riley clapped his hands together. Under other circumstances, Dixie thought he might have actually shouted *hallelujah!* to the heavens.

"Family legal matters, the same. No problem, if the family has no problem with me doing the work."

"If they do, they'd have me to answer to, Mr. Summers, and that includes ornery old Miss Lettie."

"This I would sell tickets to." Riley gestured broadly, his good mood uncontained.

Fulton laughed that wonderful laugh of his. "But I do have some concerns about the business. I'm not a corporate lawyer."

"Neither was anyone at Greenhow, Greenhow, Byson, and Pryor. It's routine stuff, Mr. Summers, contracts and negotiations on a business that's run almost unchanged for thirty years. And nothing is pressing right now except tidying up as we extricate ourselves from our previous lawyer. So you'd have time to familiarize yourself with our needs and find out for yourself if you think you want to take it on or want to simply stay with the family side of things."

"You'd let me do that?"

She'd walk through fire for this man's grandmother. Now, having met him, she would do whatever she could to mend the rift between the two of them. "Yes. I would. Is that awfully frivolous? Choosing a lawyer based on a tenuous family tie like this?"

"A lot of my clients chose me because they picked me out of the phone book, others because my office is close by, some because I go to their church, coach their kid's soccer team, or because someone they know recommended me." He shrugged. "How did you choose your last lawyer?"

"My dad went with old Mr. Greenhow because they were Boy Scouts together."

"Ahh. The boyhood connection, I'd forgotten that one." For the first time in this meeting mirth lit his dark eyes.

"Beats the way I got *my* last lawyer." Riley crossed his stretched-out legs at the ankle. "Met her when someone set us up on a blind date."

"There's a story there, no doubt." Fulton's chair gave a tight little squeak as he moved in it.

"No doubt." Dixie stared at Riley.

"I'd love to tell you all about it, Mr. Summers. And I will if you'd let me do it over a nice, hot meal." He hooked one thumb under the waistband of his jeans. "What do you say? Lot of business is done over lunch. It'd give us more time to talk, answer each other's questions."

Riley looked over at Dixie and gave her a wink.

She pretended not to notice. She was suddenly very much aware of how little she knew about Riley Walker.

Last night they had talked until all hours and spoken of so many things, revealed themselves to each other in so many ways. She understood his strong sense of duty, his unbending rules of honor, loyalty, and trust, and his devotion to Wendy, his mother, and even his wayward sister. She had shared with him that her father's philosophy of good stewardship included generosity, and her own conviction that with the blessings she had inherited came much responsibility. Through the long night they had laughed a lot and come near tears a time or two, but they had never once mentioned things like past loves—or present ones, for that matter.

"I suppose a lunch would give me more time to consider." Fulton's voice pulled Dixie back to the topic at hand. "If you're sure it wouldn't be awkward for you, Miss Fulton-Leigh."

"Awkward?" She shook her head. "Not at all. In fact, I'd welcome the chance to spend more time with you."

"What she's saying is that she's not done with you yet, Mr. Summers." Riley put his feet flat, as if ready to stand.

"Not done with me?"

"She's had a few years since your last run-in with her to perfect that stubborn, determined side of her sweet, genteel nature. So far you haven't given in and said you'd go pay a call on our beguiling Miss Lettie, or officially said you'd come on board as our legal counsel." This time Riley did stand. He looked down at Dixie, then over to Fulton, then at her again. He held his hand out to help her from her chair. "It ain't likely that Miss Dixie Belle Fulton-Leigh is going to let you out of her sight until she has an answer."

She gave him a glower that her smile probably completely undermined, rose from her chair on her own, then turned to Fulton. "Much as I hate to admit it, Mr. Summers, he is right. I'll keep after you for that answer, even if I have to resort to following you around town singing "The Alphabet Song" until you cave in."

"On the one hand, I guess I could be offended that you are, in essence, throwing me a bone because of some genetic link rather than on my own merits." Fulton lifted the basket of bread the waitress had just left and flipped back the napkin on top to offer Dixie first choice. "On the other hand, and you could not possibly know this, you are throwing me a lifeline that I don't see how I can refuse."

"Then don't." Dixie plucked a golden corn muffin from the basket and held it up like Eve proffering the apple, only without the sinful undertones.

Riley chuckled under his breath and shook his head. That was his Dixie—

His eyes widened. *His* Dixie? Where had that come from?

He fit his palm around his cold, smooth glass of water and mulled the question over in his mind. He'd promised himself on the drive over not to think of her that way and yet here they were, a few hours later, and she was *his* Dixie. At least for one unguarded moment in his mind she was.

Slowly, he lifted the glass. The story about meeting Carol had done it. The way that absolutely innocent tale had seemed to prick at Dixie's disposition had encouraged him to indulge in plain old masculine pride that she might, just maybe, care about who he had dated and the details of his love life. He chugged the water down, the chunks of ice gouging his throat as he swallowed hard, then harder.

His gaze fixed on Dixie. The delicate way she put the muffin to her lips made him think of the kiss they'd almost shared, made him wish…

"Care to help yourself, Mr. Walker?"

He gurgled, sputtered, coughed, then coughed again. *Cool, Walker, very cool? Why not just start drooling and walking into walls around her, really cap off the suave act?* He turned to Fulton, his hand up. "No, thank you. I seem to have enough trouble with plain water. Adding bread might do me in."

"Okay, then." Summers helped himself to a roll and set the basket aside.

Turning down the offer of the bread did leave Riley at a disadvantage for what to do with his hands. He put the glass down, then picked it up again, chose not to risk another near-choking incident and set the thing down with a definite *clunk*. "A lifeline, huh?"

"I beg your pardon?" The man's hand froze halfway to his mouth, the bread in his fingers dripping melted butter back onto the plate.

"You said we had no way of knowing it, but we were throwing you a lifeline that you didn't see how you could refuse." Riley edged his chair close to the linen-covered table.

"Yes." Summers put the bread down. "I guess I did." He looked away.

Riley saw a flash of anxiety shoot through Dixie's eyes, then cool into concern as she watched Fulton take a deep breath and appear to compose himself to explain his comment.

"If you'd rather not get into this over the lunch table—" Riley offered an out for everyone's sake.

"No. No, it's not that, I just want to say it right, do it justice." Hands folded on the table, he sat straight-backed. "The barefaced truth of the matter is that I need the income the work you're proposing would bring in. I need the immediate money your adoption case will provide, Mr. Walker, and the steady income of ongoing work for your business and family, Miss Fulton-Leigh. And I *need* the work. I need to immerse myself in my life's vocation again, be productive, know that I'm making a difference for others, to start to live again...if you will."

"I don't understand." There was hesitance in Dixie's voice.

Riley felt the same thing, he just didn't say so. He didn't know what to say. Twenty minutes ago in this man's office, he believed he had found the person who could help him make Wendy legally what she had always been in Riley's heart—his little girl. Riley's heart now thudded hard and heavy with apprehension.

Fulton's mouth twitched. He bowed his head.

The waitress started to approach with a water pitcher but Riley waved her away.

"I'm sorry." Fulton's earlier cultured and commanding tone was now so quiet Riley could barely hear the man. "It's just that it's been so recent, for me. Everyone else tells me it's been long enough. Time to get on with my life."

Mercenary as it might seem, Riley found himself practicing ways to wiggle out of using Summers on Wendy's case. How could he risk his child's future with someone in an emotionally fragile state?

"But people don't know how fresh my wife's passing still feels to me." Fulton picked up his glass of iced tea, then set it down again. He touched the overturned coffee cup, the flatware, then wiped his hand on his napkin even though he hadn't had any food at all yet. Finally, he looked at Dixie. "Even after a year I still miss her every day. Maybe more now so because the first year I kept thinking, 'This is how it feels to miss Regina on Christmas.' 'This is how it feels to miss Regina on her birthday.' Now, I find myself saying, 'This is how it feels to miss Regina...forever.'"

"I am so, so sorry." Dixie put her hand on Fulton's dark blue jacket sleeve.

"Thank you. You certainly are no stranger to loss yourself, Miss Fulton-Leigh." He patted her hand lightly and as quick as the beat of a bird's wing.

"I don't want to preach at you, but I hope your faith is such that you have confidence that you'll see Regina again someday."

"That is some comfort, yes. But that alone doesn't raise a little girl to be a good, strong, able wonderful woman like her mother." He cleared his throat and then trained his attention on Riley. "So after we lost Regina to a rare complication of Lupus, I took a year off from my practice just to make sure my daughter was well grounded, that she knew she had a daddy she could count on."

All Riley's doubts vanished. This man wasn't emotionally unstable, he was a grieving daddy to a little girl for whom he could never be both mother and father. From that moment on, Riley wanted nobody but Summers on his side.

"As you can imagine, it's been hard building my practice back up after an extended leave of absence. Of course, I, too, have some of those boyhood/friend clients who've stuck by me, and the referrals have begun to trickle in now and again." He exhaled and his shoulders pulled up straight as though a weight had lifted off them. He even managed a reserved smile. "Not quite ready to try that blind date method of rounding up potential clients, Mr. Walker, but if the two of you do decide to hire me, then I guess I won't have to resort to that. Not just yet anyway."

Fulton reached into his pocket and pulled out a smooth, black wallet. Tenderly, he flicked through the photo sleeves, stopped, and fixed his gaze on a picture for a few seconds before showing it to them. "Regina. She was actually very, very sick by the time she had that made. Went to one of those places where they do the lady's hair and make her up like a movie star."

"She's very pretty." Dixie brushed her fingertips over the plastic-sheathed photo.

"Regina *was* very pretty." Fulton rotated the picture so Riley could see. "Inside and out. She sang in the church choir, pitched in down at my law office, and worked as a substitute teacher when she could manage it just because she loved kids and learning so much. On top of that, she took such good care of our little girl. Here's Sarah's picture."

"She doesn't look much older than Wendy." Dixie tipped the picture toward Riley.

"Wendy is my daughter." Riley had his own wallet open and on display faster than a gunslinger could clear his holster in a shoot-out. "She's six, going on thirty-six."

"Sarah is eight." Fulton put his wallet back into his pocket.

"When you come to visit Lettie, the girls can play together." Dixie flashed a bright smile that did not mask her steely determination. "Do you know how much it will thrill your grandmother to wrap that great-grandchild up in a big ol' hug?"

"And you thought she'd let the topic pleasantly fade away, didn't you?" Riley gave Dixie a grin, but his joke did not seem to shame her one bit.

She kept her gaze on Fulton, clearly waiting for a reply.

His gaze did not waver an eyelash from hers.

They looked like a pair of bulls staring one another down over a patch of prime pasture. At first, the two of them made a study in contrasts of skin color and gender, but the longer they sat eye-to-eye in silence, the more Riley began to see a similarity that he couldn't quite pinpoint. The way they held their mouths? Or was it something more vague, like the way they carried themselves?

"You know, the more I look at you two, the more I have to say—"

They clapped their cool but openly agitated gazes on him.

"The more I have to say where's our waitress?" Riley glanced around the hushed restaurant, saw the woman he had hurried on her way before, and signaled her with a subtle *all's clear* nod so she would begin to serve the meal.

The waitress brought their salads and refilled their glasses.

Dixie pushed her cherry tomato across the shallow bowl of shredded lettuce with her fork. "Normally, at a business lunch, I'd never even mention asking the blessing. I'd just say it silently for all of us and tell myself that had it covered."

"You want us to say grace together?" Summers looked skeptical.

"Dixie, we're in a restaurant." Riley shifted in his seat.

"So acting on your faith, that just applies to charging in and rescuing people? To making rash business deals?"

He took her hand and said nothing more.

She held her other hand out to Fulton. "I'll be quick and quiet. No singing, I promise."

He laid his hand into her outstretched fingers.

She did not press for the two men to join hands and that was wise of her. Riley felt united enough in spirit with this man he'd just met.

"Dear Father," Dixie whispered. "After Daddy died I asked you for guidance. I asked you to send help. I believe that you have done that and we are here together because of your hand on all our lives. I thank you now for your goodness in *all* things, for our food, our fellowship, for the relationships we cherish, those we hope to heal, and those that we have forged today. Amen."

"Amen," both men murmured. Fulton dropped his hand to his lap but Riley could not let go of Dixie just yet.

"You honestly think we could do this." Summers did not

make a question of it. "That we could put our past behind us and move forward. You sincerely believe that, don't you, Miss Fulton-Leigh?"

"Mr. Summers, your grandmother is like my own grandmother. Your mother was like a sister to my mom when they were young. I think they would want us to try to move beyond the…history that was not of our own making and work together, don't you?"

His gaze dipped downward. He did not reply.

"This is the right thing to do, Mr. Summers, I can feel it." Riley loved the way her eyes shone with that conviction. "It's been recently brought to my attention that if I know the right thing to do I am obliged to do it or it's as though my faith is not alive."

Riley gave her hand a squeeze.

"My faith *is* alive, Mr. Summers, and I believe God has brought us all together because we need one another."

"All right." He raised his head high. "All right, let's do it— but on one condition."

Dixie's chin inched up.

Rather than let them launch into another lockhorn session, Riley turned to Summers. "What's your condition?"

"Miss Fulton-Leigh, you cannot keep pressuring me to meet with my grandmother. I will do that in my own time, if at all. Do you understand?"

Dixie cocked her head. "When you say *pressure,* do you mean—"

"She understands." Riley cut her off. "Does this mean we have a new legal representative?"

"Yes." Fulton held out his hand.

Riley took it.

Dixie shot Riley a daggered glare, but turned her hundred-watt charm on as she shook their new lawyer's hand and smiled. "You are not going to regret this, you know. Not for one single, solitary minute. You'll see. Everything is going to work out just beautifully."

Riley wanted to believe her. More than that, he *needed* to believe her. There was only one…no, *two* things he needed more: the strength to keeping working toward the resolutions they all hoped for, and the faith to accept the outcome, whatever it might be.

Thirteen

---◆---

Who is wise and understanding among you?
Let him show it by his good life,
by deeds done in the humility that comes from wisdom.
JAMES 3:13

"DID YOU MAKE THIS SOFA, MISS DIXIE?" WENDY BOUNCED ON the edge of the sofa in the front sitting room.

"Honey, I told you I don't actually make the sofas, I just..." Dixie followed the child's movements, her own head bobbing. The hairbrush in her hand waved up and down, never so much as grazing the dark brown hair she was attempting to smooth into some semblance of neatness. "Honestly, sweetheart, trying to brush your hair today is like trying to put one of Peachie Too's hats on Aunt Sis at the supper table."

"You couldn't do that!" Wendy pointed an accusing finger.

As Dixie had hoped, the flaw in her thinking got the six-year-old to stay in one place long enough for Dixie to get the brush through her hair and a barrette at the ready to hold it in place. "You can't put anything on Aunt Sis during supper, not a hat nor nothing, 'cause Aunt Sis don't sit still for a minute then."

"Doesn't sit still." Dixie swept the child's hair back from her face and snapped the gold clasp in place.

"Doesn't sit still. Not for one minute."

"There! Now you're all set for when your grandmother comes to move in with us today." Dixie sighed, but that did not alleviate an ounce of her anxiety over Verdi Walker's imminent arrival.

For the past two weeks, Riley's mother had stayed in Deepwoods with a family friend, using that time to recover from her surgery and establish her physical therapy routine. It had taken some bold reassurances on Riley's part, but he had finally convinced his mother that the Fulton family descendents lived a peaceful existence and were, in the bigger scheme of things, not so peculiar as some people had said.

Every other day Riley had made the three-hour round-trip drive to visit his mother, check her progress, and get things in order. He brought over only what they would need and packed the rest up to go into temporary storage. He'd always made a day trip of it, planning his leave of absence to coincide with the time Wendy was in her first-grade class at her new school, which she loved. Last night was the first time he had been gone overnight, leaving Dixie in charge of his precious daughter.

They'd had a wonderful time, playing with Baby Belle and Peachie Too. Wendy had made quite an adventure of going through Dixie's closet, dressing up in the fanciest clothes, shoes, and costume jewelry and even smearing on a little lipstick when Dixie had turned her back for one moment.

Dixie made a quick inspection of the child's face to make sure she hadn't missed a spot of that during last night's bath. After all, Wendy had gotten the stuff everywhere—on her hands, in her hair, and even a little on her lips. When Riley and Verdi walked in that door in a few minutes, Dixie wanted everything to be perfect. She wanted to show Mrs. Walker and Riley that Wendy was in good hands. Dixie looked at the little girl and her heart swelled. She touched the child's cheek, then leaned over to plant a kiss on the top of her head.

"Aunt Sis would look funny in one of Peachie Too's hats."

"You think so? Funnier than usual?" Miss Lettie's furrowed face expressed teasing thoughtfulness.

Wendy giggled, both hands over her mouth.

"Sure is good to hear the sound of children's laughter in this house again!" The old rocker went to creaking out a slow, methodical tempo.

Dixie nudged Wendy off the sofa, then wet her lips and seized the opportunity to work in the subject of Lettie's great-grandchild. "You know, Miss Lettie, Wendy doesn't have to be the only child laughing in this house—"

"Oh, I know it, lamb. I pray for that all the time, and now Mr. Walker has come to stay with us." She patted her gnarled hands together just above her lap. "I hope you two has a whole house full of children and that I'll be alive to see every last one of them borned."

Dixie stared at her, her well-planned comments vanishing in the face of this startling comment. "Miss Lettie! Riley and I aren't… We never…" She put her hand to her suddenly aching head. How did you tell a frail, elderly woman who'd just wished to live long enough to see you have children that she should forget it without sounding like she might as well just give up and die now because it was never going to happen?

"Miss Lettie, Riley and I aren't even married."

"I know, not yet you're not, but—"

"Dixie and my daddy are getting married?" Wendy leapt in the air. "Hooray! Hooray!"

"No, honey, we're not. Miss Lettie is just a little confused about—"

"Can I be in the wedding? I know just what I'll wear." Wendy whirled around and darted up the stairs.

"Don't change your clothes, Wendy, I've got you dressed just right for greeting your grandmother!"

"C'mon, Aunt Sis, help me get ready," was her only reply.

"No lipstick!" Dixie demanded.

"I have to wear lipstick," came Aunt Sis's protest.

Dixie turned to find Miss Lettie humming happily and rocking.

"Now just look at all the mischief you've started!" Dixie shook her head.

Miss Lettie tapped her foot and hummed a little louder.

Dixie shut her eyes. She wasn't angry or panicked, not yet, but she certainly didn't possess Miss Lettie's abiding calm about the situation. Any minute now Verdi Walker would come into this house and get her first impression of them.

"Here comes the bride..." Sis was belting out the words to the tune Dixie now recognized Lettie had been humming. Dixie's aunt descended the staircase in grand fashion, Peachie Too snarling in her arms. Looking a bit like a slightly deranged Southern belle reliving the triumph of her debutante ball, the woman drifted downward slowly, singing *la-la-la* in place of the lyrics.

Sis caused such a racket, the Judge popped out of his office—the sitting room just to the right of the staircase—and hollered. "Can't anyone get any work done around this place?"

Wendy appeared at the top of the stairs in one of Dixie's old formals, a half slip on her head like a bridal veil, and carrying the bowl of potpourri from the bathroom as a flower girl might carry delicate rose petals.

The sight set Lettie laughing like a hen cackling on the nest.

"Quiet, ya'll, please!" Grandpa flung his arms out and stomped his foot as if making a call to an invisible little leaguer. "I am trying to practice my umpiring technique for heaven's sake!"

Above the chaos of Lettie cackling, Sis la-la-ing, Peachie Too barking, and Grandpa stomping, waving his arms and calling out "Safe!", Wendy tossed back her satiny white headcovering and announced to the world, "*I* am practicing for Dixie and Daddy's wedding."

"If this is your idea of a peaceful, ordinary family, son, then I don't think I raised you right!" Dixie spun around to see the look of stunned horror on the face of an older woman standing next to Riley in the open doorway.

"Welcome, Mrs. Walker!" She brushed past Riley, who looked befuddled but not particularly surprised by the goings-on, and took his mother by the arm. "Do come in. We're so happy to have you here with us. Please, make yourself at home. I'm just sure that it won't be very long at all before you feel like you're one of the family!"

"Every time this phone rings, I almost jump out of my skin." Riley clicked off the cellular phone in his hand and pitched the thing gently onto a crumpled-up canvas tarp in the middle of the floor.

"Who was it this time?" Dixie glanced up from where she was rolling a length of pale blue wallpaper out on their makeshift worktable. Riley took in her overalls, gray work shirt such as the company truck drivers wore, and her hair pulled back into a ponytail underneath a red baseball cap, and held back a grin.

"Just Mavis going over some rough spots in last week's paperwork." He pushed up the sleeves of his faded maroon sweatshirt. "Almost a month of seeing my writing on the forms and she still can't tell my fours from my sixes."

"Guess you're thankful that's all it was." She measured the long strip of thick paper once, stood back and scrunched up that adorable face of hers, then measured again.

"Yeah, ever since Fulton ran those ads, I've lived in dread that Marcia would call. Or worse, just show up."

In a show of good faith, and to meet certain legal require-ments, Fulton had placed a notice in the newspaper of any town where they knew Marcia had lived or worked. In theory, this would give her one last chance to come forward and either defend or resign her rights to Wendy. In reality, Riley felt it was asking for trouble. "Funny, that's one of the things I used to pray would happen, that Marcia would call or one day just come home. That she'd pull herself together and want to make amends for all the grief she'd caused Momma. I thought she might realize what a terrific kid she'd left behind and grow up enough to be a part of Wendy's life again, not to take her from me, but to lend another layer of love and support."

"I don't doubt for a minute that you always truly longed for that to happen." Dixie flopped the paper down, practically sprawling her upper body over it to get it to lie smooth, then shot him as serious a look as her position allowed. "If there's one thing I've learned sitting across from you over a couple of meals a day, at your side every Sunday in church, and in ses-sion with you at a few never-ending meetings at work, you put the people you care about first. Even before your own wants and desires."

He'd kept his vow to stay away from her, even though every day he spent in her company—especially days like today when she looked at him that way—made him long for something more with her. Still, their present conversation only reinforced to him how much was at stake. So many people were counting on them for so many things that he didn't dare risk being distracted...not even by Dixie. He would be content with the friendship that had grown strong between them.

She was watching him carefully. "I know you want Wendy to get to know her mother, Riley, in the right way, at the right time."

"Momma still prays for that every day. But me..." He crossed the plush pastel carpet of the small but airy sunlit room, took the wallpaper bedeviling Dixie, unfurled it onto the workspace, and held it down for her to cut. "Dixie, am I a selfish jerk that I hope with all my heart we *don't* hear from Marcia before we go to court?"

"If you are, then you're not the only selfish jerk in this household. You aren't even the only selfish jerk in this room!" She laid the straightedge down and scored it with the cutting tool. "We've all come to care so much for Wendy. I can't tell you how much having her here has meant to all of us. She's like the daughter I some days think I may never have."

"Don't say that. You'll have a family, Dixie." It made his heart ache to imagine otherwise. That Dixie might end up only caring for her older family members until they'd gone on and she was all alone in this big house, in this whole world...no, he couldn't stand the idea. And he did not believe God would ever let that happen. "It would be such a waste if you didn't have a husband and children of your own."

She looked up at him, her eyes shaded by the brim of her

hat, her voice husky as she spoke. "I hope you're right, Riley. I've always wanted those things. You know, Daddy pushed me into being so career- and business-oriented. He felt he had to. And while I can pretend that's why I haven't met the right man yet, I know it's not true. I'm just not the kind of woman men today are looking to marry."

"Oh, yeah, men really tend to shy away from women who are smart, beautiful, funny—"

"Bossy." She tipped her head back.

"Confident."

"Old-fashioned."

"Virtuous."

"Always have to have the last word."

He sighed, nodded, and let her have that very thing. If this went on much longer his vow of self-denial would mean nothing. He'd find himself down on one knee for sure, promising her that she would never end up alone as long as he drew breath. And that was one promise he could not make, not now—not yet.

She went on. "As far as Wendy and Marcia are concerned, let's just say there are plenty of prayers going up that this all works out for the best." The razor edge of the cutting tool growled against heavy paper as she made her final pass over it. "We all want what's best in this situation, of course, and everybody thinks that means getting this adoption over with once and for all."

"I think even my mother would agree with that one. And it's not like I don't want Marcia to ever see Wendy, you know." He caught the roll of paper as it fell away from the sheet on the table. "Like you said, 'right time, right place.'"

He put his hands to his hips and scanned Wendy's new bedroom. From the fairy-tale canopy bed with Baby Belle perched on a hand-crocheted coverlet to the brand-new wallpaper with white fluffy clouds they were hanging in the room's windowed alcove today, he could not have imagined a nicer place for Wendy to say her bedtime prayers and dream the sweetest dreams.

Dixie poked her tongue out, seemingly unaware of the action, as she fed the prepasted wallpaper slowly into a trough of water.

That she would spend a sunny April Saturday afternoon working to help make Wendy feel so special and welcome in what was, at best, a temporary home, touched him more than all the womanly wiles ever worked on him since he first noticed girls. She'd done it. Without even meaning to, she'd gotten to him. Big time. If he knew what was good for them all, he wouldn't do a thing about it.

"Here, let me do that." He stepped forward.

"Fat chance!" She angled her shoulder to block his access to the paper, which reminded him of a giant slimy noodle as she pulled it from the water and began folding it in accordion pleats. "You're the ladder climbing, heavy lifting, keeping-your-decorating-tips-to-yourself part of this operation, remember?"

"How could I forget? After last time?" They had finally gotten those curtains up, he recalled, but not before they almost tore the house down.

"Then just stand back, pal, and let me do my work." She flapped her elbows a few times.

"And your job would be…? Demonstrating the chicken dance?" He mimed birds' beaks opening and closing with both his hands.

"Watch it, mister." She glanced at her watch, ignoring him a bit too flagrantly. "I've got five minutes to kill while the paste sets up. Don't make me have to get in my rowboat and come over there and dunk you."

"I'd like to see you try it. Just make sure you know how to dogpaddle before you do, though." Riley laughed and turned away, craning his neck as he surveyed the alcove to make sure the walls were clean and ready to take the paper.

Behind him, Dixie huffed.

He went right on inspecting the wall.

Her tennis shoes crunched over the plastic dropcloth beneath the worktable.

He could just imagine her pacing, pouting, glowering at him to try to make him pay attention to her again. He feigned intense interest in a speck of dust in the corner of the alcove.

The plastic rustled some more, then all went quiet.

She'd given up awfully easy… He stood stock still, listening.

Quiet. *Too* quiet. Maybe he should just—

"Hey!" He slapped his hand to the side of his neck just seconds after the splat of warm, watery goo landed there. He pivoted to find Dixie standing a few feet away, her hands dripping with water from the paper trough.

"Oops, sorry!" Her eyes were big and her smile grew wide. "Guess I splashed you a little while I was dogpaddling by."

Laughter bubbled up from within him. "Okay, okay. You got me. You proved you could do it and you got me."

"I got you!" She sang out in triumph, then, fingers still dribbling pasty water, launched into a victory version of the very chicken dance he'd teased her about earlier. "You think all you have to do is order me around and I will do your bidding."

"Since when?" He laughed right out at that. How could you not laugh along with anyone usually so dignified acting like a nut and enjoying herself so much while doing it?

"Since when?" She flapped and wriggled. "You have always tried to set yourself up as my boss, Riley Walker, ever since you ran that stop sign and we—"

"*I* ran the stop sign? Oh, that tears it." In two steps he'd overtaken her. Latching one arm around her waist, he pulled her to his side so abruptly that she would have lost her footing if he had not had everything firmly under control.

Dixie gasped for air. "Oh, my!"

"Any more gloating and you'll be doing a *Southern fried* chicken dance, m'dear." He tugged her cap off, then lowered his face to within a few inches of hers and gave her a grin he was sure rivaled that of even the most roguish of Southern scoundrels. "You do know how to make Southern fried chicken, don't you?"

She blinked, her lips slightly parted. "I—"

"You have to dip the whole thing in batter first." One arm supporting the small of her back, he dipped her backward.

She clutched at his shoulders with both hands.

He laughed, then looked up from her flashing eyes to the waiting trough of water.

Her eyes widened even more. "You wouldn't dare!"

Even with every card stacked against her, she held her ground. What a stubborn...irritating...amazing...wonderful woman this was. He let his gaze fall on her mouth...felt his grip on her tighten...and drew a ragged breath as he looked into her eyes again.

She licked her lips. "You wouldn't dare." It was a whisper this time.

He felt himself smile. "Oh, yes I would. I *shouldn't*, but I can't help myself, Dixie."

The kiss startled and enlivened Dixie, made her happy and terrified all at once. Just like Riley, himself.

When he began to pull away, she curled her fingers into the

soft cloth of his sweatshirt and drew him back for one more sweet, fleeting kiss. Then her hands relaxed and she let the shirt slide beneath her damp palms as he stepped back, his head still bowed.

"Dixie, I—"

"No, let's not talk it to death, Riley. We both felt that building up for days now, weeks even, and I think we both realize that while we might have enjoyed it, it just can't…" She strangled on the words.

"It can't happen again."

Though that's exactly what Dixie had intended to say, to hear it in his low, resonate voice, cut at her emotions like a dull blade hacking away at a tender flower. She shut her eyes and moved back a step and then another until the side of the worktable pressed against her hip.

"We're living under the same roof. Our businesses are interdependent. Our families have come to care about and count on one another." She held her hands out, palms up and close to her body, making a stilted attempt at a shrug. Her throat got tight and her eyes stung, but she pulled a soft smile up from somewhere deep inside herself. "We can't lay all that on the line for some misplaced romantic notions. What if it didn't work out? I don't exactly have a terrific track record with things working out."

"Me, neither, though I've always remained friends with the women I've dated."

"Then maybe we should just cut out the middle part and do just that—remain friends." She took a deep breath, nudged her smile wider, then wider still until it worked as much on her as it was meant to work on Riley. Her spirits buoyed a bit. She stuck out her hand. "It's a deal then. We'll just stay friends."

"Deal." Though he shook her hand once it was hard enough

to send a tingle all the way through her. Or should she blame his touch alone for that? Or the fact that she saw a hint of sadness in his eyes as he let his hand fall from hers. "Friends it is, then."

"Good." She nodded.

"Good." He put his hand to his neck, then pulled it away and frowned. He moved toward her. "One thing we need to do first, I think."

He was going to gather her up in his arms and kiss her senseless...and she was going to let him do it despite her brave bargain to be just friends.

Which only went to prove she'd already lost most of her common sense.

Riley took another step.

Her heart raced. She raised her chin.

He reached his arm out.

Dixie braced both hands behind her on the worktable.

Riley stepped close, he shifted left then right.

How sweet that he felt so unsure. She went up on tiptoes just enough to show she would not reject his advance.

"Ah, that's it," he murmured, then lunged forward. One second later, he was wiping his damp neck with one of the rags Dixie had tossed onto the table. He narrowed his eyes at her. "Okay, then, friend, we'd better get this paper on the wall. And while we're doing that, maybe we should go over some ground rules."

"Ground rules?" Embarrassment and confusion, not emotions Dixie welcomed, clashed in her mind. She snatched up the red cap Riley had taken off her head just before he'd kissed her and jammed it down low, until it grazed her eyebrows. Maybe the brim would hide the blush on her cheeks with its shadow. "Ground rules for what? For hanging paper?"

"For our friendship." He lifted the wet folds of paper in his arms and strode to the alcove. "You'd better hold this while I get up this ladder."

"Yes, of course." She hurried over and when he got to the rung that enabled him to reach the top of the wall he held his hands out. She helped him apply the sky-blue paper dotted with white, fluffy clouds, her thoughts and feelings stormy. "Give me a for instance on these ground rules you're proposing."

"Okay." He kept his eyes on his work. "For instance, no kissing."

"Of course! *No* kissing." She grabbed a wide brush with stiff, yellow bristles and began to work the bubbles out from the center of the wallpaper sheet. "And no jealousy allowed, either. You know, in case one of us would want to go on a date with someone else."

He laughed. "You got your eye on someone?"

"What do you mean *me?* You could just as easily—"

"Nope." He moved his own brush over the carefree clouds in long, even strokes. "I'm in no position to start *any* new relationship right now, even if I wanted to. But I am flattered that you'd be jealous if I did."

"Me? Ha! I could care less who you see or date or even talk to." She flicked her wrist and ended up splattering tiny droplets of watered-down paste everywhere. She ignored it and went on working, saying aloud what she truly, sincerely, almost nearly had convinced herself she believed in her heart. "So I guess that makes the jealousy issue a moot point, old buddy of mine, because I'm sure not going out manhunting anytime soon. Like I said before, I don't exactly have a terrific track record with things working out."

"Fine, then." He seemed totally absorbed in working out a

long, rippling crease over a particularly fat, cottony cloud.

"Fine." Well, what more had she hoped for, she asked herself as she worked her sticky fingers over the textured paper, checking for imperfections. That he'd deny the validity of her statement? That he'd rush to reassure her that many, many of the things she attempted worked out very well indeed, things that mattered far more than rotten romances? How could he, in good conscience, do that? What, in the little more than a month that he'd known her, had worked out right for her?

She still had not convinced Fulton to meet with Miss Lettie or to even let Dixie tell the dear old woman that she'd found her grandson. Guilt over that had slowed the work on Lettie's birthday book to a halt—not that Dixie had gotten anything much done on it beforehand, either. In fact, with time running out, it was likely she'd have to abandon the whole idea of writing Lettie's life story entirely. Chock up yet another monumental flop for Dixie.

She gritted her teeth and swiped her hand across her faded blue overalls to get rid of some wayward paste.

The downstairs phone rang. Peachie Too barked. General commotion ensued. *Nothing out of the ordinary there. Aunt Sis will handle it.*

Above her on the ladder, Riley was putting the finishing touches on a near-perfect job. It did not surprise her that his first effort at hanging wallpaper had turned out flawless. Riley did everything well.

She put her fingers to her lips...*Everything.*

"Ready for the next panel." His feet landed on the carpet with a cushioned thud. "Mind if I cut and measure this one?"

"Please do. I'm sure you'll do a better job than I ever could."

"I didn't mean it that way, I just wanted to try to do it for myself. You've done a great job, Dixie. I hope you didn't think I wanted to bully my way in and take over."

"I know." She waved him off. Riley did not need to bully his way into taking over anything, he simply threw himself into the work so thoroughly that there wasn't any need for anyone else. At least that's how it was fast becoming at work.

In their first week at it, Fulton and Riley had straightened out the mess her daddy had left. It only made sense the two of them could do that since most of it, she had quickly learned, either related to the deal Daddy wanted set up with Riley or was falsely created by Greenhow to convince Dixie to let him take over the management of the business. Dixie still ran the furniture manufacturing plant and oversaw the outlet store, but the deeper they got into things, the more she saw why her father had always kept running the businesses as a one-man operation. After thirty years, Fulton's Enterprises was pretty much a well-oiled machine, the kind of thing Riley could run on his own and still be home for dinner every night by six, just like her father always had been. Dixie's contribution amounted to very little at work, and since Sis had everything under control on the home front—

"Riley! Riley? Hon, do you still have your little phone up there with you?" Aunt Sis called up the stairs with all the timbre and sophistication of an operatic cow bellow.

"Yes, ma'am." Riley had the decorum to walk to the doorway so that he didn't have to holler through the hallways.

"Well, pick it up, won't you dear, you have a phone call."

"A…?" He looked to Dixie, pointing. "It's right by your knee in that tarp. Do you mind?"

She scrambled to locate the small black phone in the layers of canvas tarp.

"Aunt Sis, how do *you* know that I have a call on my phone?" He turned his attention back downstairs.

"Because I answered the phone down here and the person asked to talk to you."

"So you gave them my cell phone number?"

"Cell? I know the guest room you're in is small, sugar, but do you really think of it as a *cell?*"

"No, no. My room is lovely, really. My cell phone is my cellular phone, the one you told me I had a call on."

On her feet in no time at all, Dixie started to take the phone to him, then remembered they were just a couple of pals now and decided not to cater to him but do what a regular guy-type friend might do. She gave it a gentle underhanded pitch. "Heads up!"

"Thanks." He held his hands open and caught it with great ease. He also dropped it with great ease. But it did appear to Dixie that he had some amount of trouble holding in what he really wanted to say about that as the phone bounced on his toe, then onto the floor, then went skidding out onto the hardwood floor of the hall.

Dixie couldn't see what happened from there but she heard the *thunk-a-thunk-a* of something tumbling down step after step, then the clatter of plastic reverberating in the high-ceilinged entry way at the foot of the stairs.

"Is this the cell phone you were talking about, dear?"

Riley sighed. "Yes, Aunt Sis."

"Then I'll just answer it myself."

Dixie looked away so Riley wouldn't catch her laughing.

"Hello? Hello? No wait, that's not right. There now. Hello?" Sis's struggle carried up the stairwell, loud and clear. "Riley, honey, is it supposed to be in three pieces?"

"I heard a crash. Is everything all right?" The Judge's voice carried upward.

"Everything is just fine, Smilin' Bob-Busybody, I have everything under control. I'm taking care of things just fine." The tremor in Sis's voice belied her confident claim. "Now why don't you go on back to your naptime."

"I'll have you know I was in my office doing important business," Dixie's grandpa blustered.

"Do you think what I do around this house isn't important? You think I wouldn't much rather be heading my committees and chairing my boards and generally seeing to the cultural well-being of my beloved Fulton's Dominion than trying to juggle the schedule of a house full of—"

"Would you two pipe down in there? Wendy and I are trying to get Miss Lettie caught up on her stories in here," Riley's mother, Verdi, called from one of the downstairs bedrooms.

Peachie Too barked.

Sis wailed something about not being appreciated. "Even my own precious princess puppy-toes has turned against me!"

"I had to drive to Jackson to get that phone, you know." Riley said it too softly for anyone but Dixie to hear, not that they would have heard or cared as they squabbled quite blissfully on.

"I'm sorry. I never should have thrown it."

"Hey, your throw was impeccable. It was my catch that stunk." His gaze met hers. "I guess I was distracted."

By me?

"You know, worried about who'd be calling me here." He answered as though he'd known what she was thinking, then raised his head, drew a deep breath, and stepped into the hallway. "Aunt—oh, you're here."

"Here's your phone, dear. I can't work these new-fangled technological things. I'm an artist, you know, not some mechanical wizard." Her poppy-red lower lip trembled. "You'd better hurry and answer your phone, dear, that lady is waiting."

"Aunt Sis, my phone hasn't rung and...what lady? Waiting where?"

"I don't know where she was calling from. Long distance, she said."

Dixie fit the pieces together, which was more than Riley would be doing with his phone anytime soon from the looks of it. "Okay, I think I know what's going on here. Aunt Sis, Riley's cell phone is not some cordless extension of our phone here at home. He can't just pick it up and talk to someone who calls our number. So what we need to know from you is, did you hang up on the lady who called?"

"Gracious, no. That would have been rude."

"Great." Riley handed his cell phone to Dixie. "I'll just go downstairs and get—"

"I told her good-bye first."

"You what?" Riley froze.

"I didn't just hang up on her, I told her good-bye first."

Dixie physically put herself between Sis and Riley. Not in her wildest imaginings could she believe that Riley would do anything to harm her often-off-kilter aunt, but after so many weeks of living in this household with two families—had it really been almost three weeks since Riley's mother arrived?—Dixie had learned one thing: she was a born buffer. Grit and grace, her only redeeming attributes it seemed at times, served her well these days.

Riley moved in behind Dixie and she could feel how tense he was...as she felt the heat of his body and heard the quiet rasping of his hard breathing.

Dixie stood up as straight as she could. "Told *whom* good-bye, Aunt Sis? Did you get the woman's name?"

"Oh, yes. I didn't write it down, if that's what you're asking but she identified herself to me immediately upon my answering. What nice manners, you know, folks don't do that much anymore. Just is so-and-so there or let me talk to thus-and-such."

Dixie sensed Riley's building tension over the mystery woman. She knew his anxiety had penetrated her own calm composure when she took Aunt Sis by the shoulders and gave her a shake. "What was the woman's name, Aunt Sis. It's important that you get this right. Was it Marcia?"

"Mar—oh, my no."

Riley exhaled.

For some reason Dixie did not share in his relief as equally as she had his stress. She tried to tell herself that had nothing to do with her own conflicting feelings about a woman calling Riley. *No jealousy, remember? We're just friends, nothing more.* Women could call him all day and it should not matter to Dixie in the least.

"The name was Carol, dear."

Blind date, ex-lawyer, dated for almost three years, Dixie thought then squeaked out, "Carol?"

"Thanks, Aunt Sis." Was it Dixie's imagination or did Riley sound just a bit too happy when he said that? "Did she give you any other message?"

Dixie set her analysis of Riley's reaction aside and honed in on Sis's response.

"No, I thought you could just pick up your phone up here so I didn't ask if she wanted to leave one."

"If she has anything really important to say to you, she'll call back, Riley. I know I would." Oh, dear. That came off snippy and quite superior even to her own ears.

Riley, however, did not notice. Dixie knew this because he'd already dashed into the room, plucked his wristwatch and car keys up from the worktable, and was on his way somewhere.

"I'm not going to wait for her to call back. It's too, um… busy here to take the call anyway. I think I'll scoot down to the main office and call her."

"Oh, you're going downtown?" Dixie tugged her ball cap off in a flash. "Mind if I tag along?"

"Uh…um…" Riley blinked at her as he wrestled the silver watchband over his hand and in place on his wrist. "I thought you had work to do here?"

Her? Stay here and wallpaper his daughter's room for him like some sorry Southern version of Cinderella while he went off and made contact with his old girlfriend on the phone in her daddy's old office? Not very likely.

No jealousy. Just Friends. Her own rules came back to haunt her. She hushed them up as she whipped the rubberband right out of her hair, shook her hair onto her squared shoulders, and smiled. "I'm at a good place to take a break. Besides, I needed to go downtown today."

"You did?" Aunt Sis's hair listed to one side as she cocked her head. "What for?"

"I can't tell you what for Aunt Sis," she said through a locked smile. "It's…a surprise."

"A surprise? What for?"

"I can't tell you because it's an irthday-bay urprise-say for Miss Ettie-lay."

As she suspected it would, that shut Sis up while she tried to decipher the code.

Riley laughed and stuck out his crooked elbow. "Well, all right, hurry up then if you're coming. But before we go any-where together I have to add another stipulation to our ground rules."

Dixie slid her hands around his arm and fell in step beside him. "What's that?"

"No more pig Latin out of you, young lady."

"Why? Because pork rinds are a Southern aphrodisiac and Latin is one of the romance languages?"

"Did anyone ever tell you, Dixie Fulton-Leigh, that you are a troublement? Pure and deliciously simple, a troublement?"

"I do my best." She smiled at him and kept on walking. Riley would never know the irony she felt at having finally found something she was impossibly good at—caring about him with all her heart—and knowing it was the one thing she'd promised she would never pursue.

Fourteen

Anyone who listens to the word but
does not do what it says
is like a man who looks at his face in a mirror and,
after looking at himself, goes away and immediately forgets what he
looks like.

JAMES 1:23–24

"SO JUST WHAT KIND OF BIRTHDAY SURPRISE DO YOU HOPE TO FIND for Miss Lettie in the office?" Riley's keys rattled as he opened the door to the upstairs office that had once been John Frederick Fulton-Leigh's domain.

His first two weeks on the job, Riley and Dixie—and even Fulton, a time or two—had worked here alone or together, refiling, learning the ropes, separating the old ways from the new and the plans from the realities. Then Riley had noticed Dixie was spending more time downstairs on the sales floor of the outlet store or running errands for the family, always at the ready for anyone and everyone whether at work or home. She kept informed on all the day-to-day goings-on of the business but really had very little to do beyond signing papers, going over financial information, and attending a couple of meetings a week. That was all her part of the businesses required. Riley's end of things required more hands-on and paperwork to keep up with state and federal regulations, union requirements, upkeep on the vehicles, and much more. Still and all, it was the kind of work that kept to a tight schedule and, barring emergency, left him weekends and evenings free to spend with Wendy, Momma and…well, anyone else he might care to spend his time with.

Fulton no longer needed to come over, but he remained a mere phone call away. So John Frederick's office, simply because Riley came in to work there every day, seemed to have become *his* domain.

He pushed open the door and stood aside, allowing Dixie to step in ahead of him. He really did not care why she wanted to come up to the office with him instead of sticking to her first, adorably weak story of simply needing to come downtown over something regarding Lettie's birthday plans. Deep down, he liked having her here with him when he returned Carol's call. Having someone else in the office with him would provide a built-in excuse for not talking too long if his ex-lawyer, ex-not-quite-girlfriend had only called to chat. If Carol called for some other reason..∴

But what other reason could there be? He tossed his keys onto the large desk and moved around to the leather chair behind it. If it were anything else, Carol knew to contact Fulton. She hadn't spoken directly to Riley since his move more than a month ago.

Still, he didn't mind ribbing Dixie a little about her almost transparent excuse to eavesdrop on the conversation between him and the woman he had once dated. "I don't believe I caught your answer, Dix."

"What?" She jumped like a cat catching a glimpse of itself in a mirror.

"What did you hope to find here for Miss Lettie's birthday? If you'll give me some idea, maybe I can help you locate it."

"Well, actually, it's…um…" She moved her hands as if indicating the four sides of something small and square.

"A box?" He held in the urge to chuckle as he began opening desk drawers, then slamming them shut as if searching in earnest for the object. "You've hidden a gift box in here?"

"No, it's really more of a…" She waved her hands like a person describing a cloud or something large and fluffy. The whole time her gaze darted around the room.

"More of a—" he mimicked her motion to a *T*—"A wig? A pillow? An enormous mound of freshly sheered sheep's wool?"

"No! More of a…a…" Her gesture got bigger.

"I've got it." He stopped his swirling hand motion all together and snapped his fingers. "A thinly veiled excuse for getting up into my office and listening in on my phone call to Carol!"

"A concept!" Somehow, she managed to sound both insulted and caught red-handed. "I wanted to come up here to see if anything struck a chord and helped me come up with a new concept for Lettie's birthday. All right?"

"A concept and a clandestine conversation. Lucky you." He dropped down into the chair, grabbed up the phone receiver, jabbed in Carol's home number, then kicked back and placed his new tennis shoes on the corner of the desk. "You've come to just the right place to find both."

She gave him a look that could have blistered a stone.

Riley laughed out loud. No petty priss-and-pout routine for this gal, no sir. She did not play those games to try to persuade or manipulate him. She did not pretend to be something she was not to get what she wanted from him. Did she know, he wondered, that in refusing to do just that she had gotten to him in ways no other woman ever had?

The phone rang for the fourth time in his ear.

"For your information, I really do need to come up with a new concept for Miss Lettie's birthday present."

"I believe you." The fifth ring…the sixth.

"And as for your conversation with…what's her name, I…I have to admit, I'm dying to know what she wants."

"Well, looks like you may have to linger on your deathbed a while longer." He hung up with one finger, then methodically pressed in the number of Carol's workplace. "Because she's not answering at home. She doesn't usually go into her office on Saturdays, but I'll give her a try there, just in case."

"If you want me to, I'll leave." She didn't so much as shift her eyes toward the door.

"Naw, no reason to. You go right on looking for your birth-day concept. I don't mind the company."

Dixie began to work her way around the room. She seemed totally unaware of him, or of the way the sunlight lit her face to warm the color of her lips and reveal the finest of lines beside her beautiful eyes, the evidence of how readily she shared her smile. She walked the length of the bookshelves, a study in contrasts, with her ever-present pearl necklace peeking out from beneath the man's workshirt and the overalls that skimmed her figure in a singularly feminine way.

She turned her head, then moved toward something across the way, her hand trailing slowly over the low credenza as she went.

Riley could watch her all day. Just watch and wonder what was going on in the complicated brain of hers. And wish—

"Foster Law Office, Mindy Nelson speaking. How may I help you?"

"Oh, hello, Mindy, this is Riley Walker. Is Carol there? I'm returning her call." He heard Carol's administrative assistant explaining something on the other end of the line but his attention stayed with Dixie.

She paused to look up at a dusty, stuffed pheasant perched on a glass shelf over the green-curtained windows.

"Sure, I'll hold." Riley lowered the mouthpiece. "What do you know, she's there, but she's on the other line. I'm holding."

"That's nice." Dixie sounded distracted, as if she could care less. Still, she did manage to meander over to stand and stare at the pictures hanging on the wall just to the right of the desk, the side nearest the phone.

Riley did not think for one moment she expected inspiration to spring from the pictures she must have all but memorized in her lifetime of coming to this office. He made a quick study of the rather eclectic display of work-related and family photos that looked to represent generations of relatives. "You know, since the reunion with Fulton seems iffy and writing Miss Lettie's life story isn't panning out, maybe you could do a scrapbook of some kind. Your family seems to have a lot of photographs."

"Yes, and Miss Lettie has seen them all so many times, too. I don't see how I could make that come as much of a surprise."

Riley nodded his head, even though Dixie wasn't looking at him. He sat back in the chair, his legs still up. His good mood had him jiggling one foot in rhythm to the cloyingly upbeat showtune of the "on hold" music. "Hey, what about something like that?"

Dixie turned first to him, then to face the large painting of the family home that dominated the paneled wall directly opposite the desk.

"Riley Walker, you are a genius!"

He leaned back further in the chair. He didn't even try to pretend her enthusiasm didn't please him. To be a hero in Dixie's eyes, even in some small way, just meant too much to him, made him feel too good. "Commissioning someone to do a painting of something meaningful for Miss Lettie is a good idea, I admit, but *genius?* I don't know about that."

"Forget the painting!" She rushed forward.

The song on the other end of the phone ended, then another one, every bit as annoyingly peppy, began. Riley didn't give a hoot, not about the wait, the music, or even that Dixie hadn't embraced his idea. Just being here with her, watching her light up and leap into action, lifted his spirits more than he'd ever imagined possible.

Up on her tiptoes, Dixie seized the painting with both hands and lifted it easily up then off the wall. "Behind this thing is Daddy's wall safe!"

"Wall safe? What—"

"It's where Daddy kept old family jewelry, military medals, a few old papers...I'm not sure what all, but there might just be something in here—something that belonged to my mom or my grandmother or even my great-grandfather—that Miss Lettie might just love to have for her own."

"Do you know the combination?" Riley squinted at her fingers nimbly working the large black-and-white dial.

"I should. It's my birthday. Ten."

The dial whirred and clicked into place.

"Twenty-eight." She flexed her fingers like some kind of safecracker, then glanced over her shoulder. "I think I'll keep the last number to myself, if you don't mind."

"I never figured you to be vain about your age, Princess."

"Vain? Ha! Look away, please." She waved her hands like someone shooing away a curious child. "It's enough you've moved into my house and taken over Daddy's office. I'd like to have one place that is designated Riley-free, even if it is just a tiny hole in the wall, thank you."

"You planning on crawling in there whenever you need a break from me?" He chuckled, but averted his eyes as she'd asked. "'Cause if you are, I think we're going to have some wallpaper left over after doing Wendy's room. You might want to use that to cozy up your new home away from home."

"Thank you, the Martha Stewart of wall-safe interior decorating. You're not peeking, are you?"

He heard a final spin, then the handle turning and Dixie wrenching the door open. "Can I look—?"

The music from the phone clicked off mid-note. "Mr. Walker, I can connect you now."

"Open Sesame! The Fulton family secret vault is now open for business!"

"Hold it a minute, Dixie, Carol's on the line." He tipped his chair back and played it up big for Dixie's sake alone. "Carol! Great to hear from you. I'm sorry we crossed wires before but you've got my undivided attention now. What can I do for you?"

"Riley, I had a phone call today that you need to know about."

He sat up. "That sounds serious. What—"

"Marcia called me."

His feet hit the floor with a thud. Suddenly the game was over. Reality had intruded, hard and unforgiving, into their lives. And it had brought with it the promise of reconciliation—either that, or the threat of tearing everything he truly cared about to shreds.

"Marcia? When? What did she say? Where is she?"

"Marcia?" Dixie turned, and the look on Riley's face confirmed she had heard what she thought she'd heard.

"Yes, I…Fulton Summers? When?"

She reigned in the impulse to rush over to him. If the shoe were on the other foot and this were about her family matters, she would want space and time to gather all the information she could and to deal with it as she saw fit. She held her breath and started for the door.

"Stay." The single whispered word riveted her in place.

She met his gaze.

"Dixie, please stay, I won't be long."

She nodded.

He returned to his phone conversation.

She let her breath out slowly to calm herself, saying a silent prayer that all would be well, whatever happened. *God, please keep your loving hand on every fragile heart involved.*

"I see." Riley's brow creased. His shoulders sagged. He rubbed his eyes. "Did she give any indication—"

Reluctantly, Dixie turned her back to him to grant him some privacy. She went through the motions of taking things out of the wall safe, though her excitement for the adventure had waned.

One by one, she removed each item, making a mental note of it as she did so. Three large flat boxes…those would be war medals for Grandpa, Daddy, and Young Bobby. All three had served their country with pride and valor. Next came a battered, accordion-style expanding file held with Daddy's trademark red rubber bands. Dixie knew it held Daddy's greatest earthly treasures: love letters from her mother and handmade cards and pictures drawn by Dixie as a child. She pulled out a cream-colored jewelry box with her mother's gold embossed monogram on it. Dixie inhaled deeply. The box still smelled of Mama's perfume…Dixie had spilled an entire bottle in the blue, satin lining. The last item was something she'd never seen before. Who knew how long it had languished in this safe. A memento, she supposed, a token bearing her great-grandfather's name that told anyone who saw it what her family truly valued most.

A family Bible. *That* she hugged to her chest.

"Yes, I understand. I know." Riley's voice was stretched so taut he sounded hoarse. "You did the right thing, Carol. Thank you for calling."

Dixie wondered how long she should wait before she faced him. She did not want to trespass on a moment of intimate reflection or exposed emotion, but she also did not want to seem insensitive to his pain, confusion, or even relief in finally hearing from his sister after so long.

"Guess you figured out that Carol heard from Marcia."

At the soft words, she turned, the newly discovered Bible still pressed tightly over her heart. "I thought so. Do you want to talk about it?"

"I wish I knew what to say. Apparently, Marcia saw one of the ads we ran and called the sawmill. Red Braden had the foresight to refer her to Carol and not give out any of my personal information."

"So your sister doesn't know how to reach you?"

"That's not because I don't want Marcia to find me or Momma or even Wendy. You know that, don't you?" He looked at her as if it mattered to him that she not think the worst of him. "I'm not hiding from her and I'm especially not hiding Wendy from her."

"You're *protecting* Wendy." Dixie stepped forward. "I know I'm not a parent, I may never be a parent, but having spent so much time with Wendy I can certainly understand the inherent need to shelter and protect her from things that could hurt her. Her mother just showing up unannounced on the doorstep— or worse yet at her school, where none of us is there to intervene—is one of those potentially harmful things."

"Marcia would never hurt Wendy." He put his hand in his head. "Of course, she *has* hurt Wendy by her absence, and my biggest worry is that she'd hurt Wendy by disappointing her, by coming into her life then running off again, that kind of thing. But Marcia would never try to kidnap her or turn her against Momma and me or do her physical harm."

"You're sure about that?"

"I'm sure. After all, what would be in that for Marcia? She doesn't waste her time and energy on things that don't produce direct and immediate gratification for her." He gave her a dead-on glare, but his expression and tone carried pain and weariness. "Just the same, I am thankful she has to go through Fulton before she finds me. At least that gives me some control over where and when she sees Wendy again."

"Fulton?" She stepped forward again, feeling a little like the participant in a grown-up game of "Mother May I?" She approached Riley with utmost caution, which she felt his mood and words warranted.

"Carol explained to Marcia that Fulton was the one to contact to get to me."

"Contact? By phone? Letter? In person?"

"I wish I knew." He put his head in his hands.

This time Dixie did not hold back. She went to him, laid

the Bible in the middle of her father's old desk, then put one hand on Riley's back and the other on his arm.

"What am I going to do, Dixie?" He looked up at her. "We were so close to having everything arranged. If she'd showed up next month, after the court had straightened out the legalities of who really had the right to be Wendy's parent, things would be so different."

"I know," she murmured. "Are you afraid that Marcia will try to take Wendy away from you?"

"Legally, we've never believed she'd be able to get anything more than visitation rights. Frankly, I don't think she'd try for even those. If she hasn't changed she wouldn't want the burden of taking care of a child even for a few days at a time. If she has changed, well, then she'd do what's best for Wendy, which is leave her with me, right?"

Dixie pressed her lips together.

"See, I wouldn't even have to worry about that if she had popped up after the court date had severed her parental rights. I'd be Wendy's father, and Marcia would be her aunt. Just that simple."

"It doesn't seem all that simple to me, Riley."

He exhaled hard, the sound something that hinted at but did not quite achieve a disheartened *ha*. "Maybe *simple* is the wrong word, but it gets pretty simple when you think that this is exactly how Wendy has seen things her whole life. She knows my sister gave birth to her, but she also knows beyond the shadow of a doubt that I am her daddy."

"You *are*."

"It means so much to me that you see it that way."

"I've seen you two together. I've heard how you talk about her and how you worry over her. Speaking as a former Daddy's Little Girl and proud of it, you are her true father. No doubt about it."

"Doubt?" He clenched his teeth and hissed an indistinguishable unintelligible word. "That's the emotion of the hour, isn't it? It's all about doubt, Dixie. One phone call and I'm doubting everything from my legal position to what kind of lasting effect Marcia's reappearance will have on Wendy. How much will it confuse her, especially if Marcia has come to fight to retain her parental rights? To have the dad Wendy's always known and the mother she's always longed to know at odds over her...that would be awful for Wendy, and worse for Momma, who, at some point, might have to choose sides."

"I guess that's why, if Marcia came back after everything was finalized, you wouldn't be so wary?"

"Wary? You'd better believe I'd be wary. But I don't think I'd have this gnawing in my gut. I could handle it, I could work with it. I'd feel like my feet were on solid ground instead of like I'm standing on the downward slope of an oil-slicked mountain."

"As long as your faith is on solid ground, Riley..." She touched the soft leather grain of the old Bible.

He raised his head and put his hand on hers. He let out a long, slow sigh.

"Riley, from what you've told me about Marcia, her greatest fault seems she's shallow and selfish. Is there something more you're worried about? Something she might involve Wendy in or—"

"Shallow and selfish is enough, Dixie, when you're talking about the welfare of a trusting, innocent child. My child." He rapped his fist against his chest once. "Marcia has lived a life of reckless self-indulgence. That's the kindest way I can put it. There are a lot of behaviors that probably go along with that, too many men, drugs, drinking, never taking responsibility for herself or her actions are but a few that come to mind. In the end, it's her focus on herself alone that has caused everyone, herself included, the most grief."

"How did she get to be that way?"

"For one thing, she was born stubborn."

"Hey! Some of my best friends were born stubborn." She tousled his hair, trying her best to lighten things so that he didn't suddenly decide he'd gone too far and withdraw into himself and not talk about what was obviously grieving him.

"You saying you're your own best friend?" He smiled, not a big smile, but enough to show his appreciation for her effort.

"I'm saying stubbornness alone is not an excuse for—"

"Whoa! I'm not making any excuses for Marcia's choices and actions. Been there, done that, got the T-shirt—and she stole it right off my back."

She slipped her hand in his.

"I've heard every excuse, made most of them myself at one time or another. She was too headstrong, she felt stifled by life in a mill town, she was rebellious, she fell in with the wrong crowd. She never listened, the rest of the family put all their spare time into making the sawmill viable and to make up for the lack of attention, we let her have her way too much, never made her have to work for anything, and just generally spoiled her." He looked up abruptly, gave her hand a squeeze, then winked. "Of course, we know that's not an excuse, either. Some of *my* best friends are totally spoiled."

"If I thought you really meant that…" she warned, her finger wagging.

"I do mean it, your family spoiled you—spoiled you with love, attention, kindness, a sense of history, home, and security… all the things I plan to *spoil* my own child with given the opportunity. God willing."

God willing. The simple phrase wrapped up his apprehensions and his convictions in one deceptively difficult principle: to let go of your fear and accept God's will, whatever came. Dixie gripped his shoulder.

He went on. "You said it best when you questioned my motivation for buying into the business. You told me I was trying to buy what I had failed to build, that I wanted the stability not found in my own home, a stability I feared I could not provide for Wendy."

"I didn't really know you then, Riley."

"But you knew the truth about me right from the start, Dix." He swiveled the chair slightly in her direction. "When I spoke with your father and decided to throw in with him, it wasn't just for the business deal. I liked what I heard from him about fairness and honor, about a company's social responsibility, and most of all about family."

A pang of sadness shot through Dixie. She missed her daddy so much! Riley's dilemma and having just gone through the treasures in the wall safe only intensified her sense of loss.

His smile was tender. "Outlandish as your family can be, they are all there for each other. They will give of themselves for the sake of the people they love, even for people who aren't related to them, like Wendy, Momma, and me."

"And Miss Lettie. She's not a blood relative but she's a part of our family, for sure."

Through it all, her family, such as it was, had always had one another, each person always ready to pitch in for the greater good. Thinking about it now chased away some of her blue mood over missing Daddy. She wasn't alone. She had people who loved her…and knowing that made her feel safe and satisfied.

Funny, she hadn't felt proud of the oddball collection of in-laws and borderline outlaws that made up her family in a long time. She'd regarded them for the most part as a burden, first to her father then to her, an inherited problem that she had to tend to, supervise, suffer. Now, seeing them collectively through another person's eyes made her feel blessed and grateful.

Riley was watching her as though he understood what she was feeling. "You see, you don't know how destructive a single person who thinks only of themselves can be to a desperate family that wants nothing more than to love and help that person." Riley sat back and raked his fingers through the thick waves of his black hair. "I've felt that hurt and seen the devastation in my mother's eyes. It's not something I ever want to see again, and yet Momma prays every day for Marcia's return. How can I hope for those prayers to go unanswered, even if only for a little while longer?"

"I just don't see how someone like Marcia can come out of a good, Christian family like yours, Riley."

"I believe some of the things I mentioned as her excuses were factors in the way she's led her life. But she's not a kid. She has the power to get her life in order and she knows who to turn to, to make the new beginning." He spread one hand over the Bible before him.

"Maybe she's done that, Riley. Maybe that's why she's made contact."

"She saw the ad. She told Carol that much." He shook his head. "If she'd gotten herself straightened out, if she'd put her heart right with God and wanted to heal things with us, it would not have taken a newspaper ad to urge her to reach out to us. That's what the voice of reason in my head keeps warning me."

"And?"

He drew his fingers down the length of the worn black

Bible, rubbing them very gently over the gold, stamped letters of her great-grandfather's name in the right-hand corner. "And then some part of me whispers, what if she *has* changed? We've certainly prayed for that long enough. Why can't I be excited about this, Dixie? Is something wrong with me? Am I the one who is now being shallow and selfish?"

"No. You said I knew the truth about you. Well, I'm not sure about that, but I do know that you are not putting your feelings first in this."

"Isn't that exactly what I'm doing? Putting how I feel about this ahead of everything else?" He picked the Bible up, ran his calloused thumb along the gilded edges of the thin paper, then set the weighty book down again. When he looked up at her, dampness washed his troubled eyes. "Is my faith so weak that it can't withstand an unexpected answer to a much-offered prayer?"

"Only you know the answer to that, but I don't see it that way at all, Riley. Your faith doesn't seem weak to me and it never has, but your resolution to put it into practice? Maybe that needs a little shoring up."

"Meaning?"

"What is that verse you're so fond of?" Pages slid over each other, rustling as she leafed through the find from the safe, noting as she did the many underlined verses, the passages set off with dark-penciled brackets. She passed the Old Testament, passed the pages of marriages, births, and deaths dutifully recorded on the prescribed pages, then flipped to the New Testament. "What book was it in?"

"James. James 2:17, but you don't need to bother to look it up. I have it memorized."

"'Even so faith, if it hath not works, is dead, being alone,'" she read from the yellowed pages of the King James version.

"So faith by itself, if it has no works, is dead," Riley repeated.

"It's one thing to apply that standard to a business deal that's financially sound, a good personal fit, and promises to deliver you everything you're hoping for and more. That kind of acting on faith just doesn't fall in the same category as surrendering your daughter's well-being to an unknown future, does it?"

"You got me there." He leaned back, his intense gaze fixed on her. "Guess I'm just one great, big, fat hypocrite."

"You're a *father,* Riley." She left the Bible opened to the page she had just read from. "You don't know if this new element is a wonderful blessing or a terrible threat to your child's happiness. You're right to proceed with caution, but you have to move forward in faith as well."

"You're right. Sitting here stewing isn't going to help matters any. Guess I'd better call Fulton to give him notice he may hear from Marcia, then go home and have a long talk with Momma." He blew out a long breath. "I don't look forward to that."

"Your mother is stronger than you think, Riley." Dixie stood and paced out a few feet away from the desk. "And where she isn't strong, she has God and you and Wendy and Sis and Grandpa and me and Miss Lettie to hold her up, physically, spiritually, and in whatever way she needs. The same goes for you and for Wendy…and for Marcia, if she comes back into the picture."

"You're saying that if Marcia comes back and wants to try to mend fences and be a part of our lives again, that you'd be there to help deal with it?"

She met his searching gaze without flinching and nodded. "Whatever way it goes."

"Thank you." He stood and reached his hand out to her. "For everything."

"Hey, don't thank me, thank the family that spoilt me." She hooked her thumb under the strap of her overalls.

He laughed. "I'll do that. You can count on it. Now, I'm going downstairs to get some coffee before I try to track down Fulton. Want to come down and shake things up in the showroom?"

"I've been shaken up enough for one day, thank you." The warm memory of the kiss they had shared washed over her. "I think I'll just stay here where things remain ever on an even keel, no shocks, no tremors, no surprises, and go through some of these old, familiar family things. You know, sort of remind myself of how boring and stable they really are down deep."

"*Way* down deep." She could hear the teasing in his voice as he headed for the door. "I'll be back in a minute."

"Okay." She watched him leave.

Her feelings still unsettled by the events of the day—their kiss, the promise to keep her heart unscathed by her attraction to Riley, the conflict of Marcia's possible return—Dixie turned to the one constant in her life. She sank into Daddy's old chair and opened up the old Bible to the stiff center pages. *Family Register,* it said across the top of the first page. Below the heading were lines for the name of the Bible's owner and spouse, and below those was the bold proclamation *were united in Holy Matrimony,* with a place for the date and place of the ceremony.

"Holy Matrimony," she read softly, glad that Riley had not been near to hear the wistful tone that she could not keep from her voice. Nestling down into the chair, she drew her feet up and pulled the Bible close. "'Samuel Prescott Fulton and Eugenia Anne Hamilton were united in Holy Matrimony on the fifteenth day of August, in the year of our Lord nineteen hundred eight in Fulton's Dominion, Mississippi.'"

She looked up at the stern-faced couple in the faded wedding photo on the wall and smiled. She knew little about them, really, only the small remembrances Lettie shared, which tended to focus more on Founder Fulton, whom the old woman revered, and his only surviving daughter, whom she'd all but raised.

Dixie sighed and turned the page to glance over the list of births. *Samuel Omar, Prescott Warren, Samantha Eugenia...*

She frowned. *Helen Bettina.*

Dixie blinked. Why on earth had her great-grandfather written down Lettie's daughter's name with his children? She looked to the next page, as though that might provide a clue. *Marriages*, the title stood out in boldest black on the stark white page. Two marriages were recorded there. One, she had fully expected to find. The other—

Dixie sat up. She blinked as though that might alter the names on the line beneath her grandparents'. They remained unchanged—and yet they changed everything she thought she knew about so many people she'd loved and trusted.

"I know you said you didn't want any but I brought you up some coffee anyway. Thought it might jolt the old system into—"

"My system has been jolted enough for one day, thank you."

"What?" He came to her, setting the two coffee mugs down on the desk as he did. "What is it? Dix, you look like you've seen a ghost."

"I *feel* like I've seen a ghost, or at least like something I can't fully explain has just come back to haunt me. And, truthfully, Riley, I have no idea what to think about it."

Fifteen

If anyone considers himself religious and
yet does not keep a tight rein on his tongue, he
deceives himself and his religion is worthless.

JAMES 1:26

"OH, NO YOU DON'T!" WITH THE WEATHERED, BLACK BIBLE IN HIS hand, Riley jumped up from his chair and took two thundering strides across the room.

"Oh, no I don't *what?*" Dixie started to shut the wall safe where she had just haphazardly replaced the boxes and file she'd pulled out earlier.

"Oh, no, you don't close that safe without this Bible in it, Princess."

She bristled at the nickname, just as he knew she would, but it accomplished his goal and stopped her dead. "I am keeping that Bible out, Riley. I need it."

"For what?" The direct approach had always worked with her before. In fact, that was one of the things he valued so much about this woman. Despite the delicate nature of this issue and the reality that both of them were running with their emotions cranked to full throttle, he decide not to change the way he dealt with Dixie now. "You want to keep that Bible out of the safe and do what with it? Take it home to confront your family and get them all lathered up over something that is none of your business?"

"None of my *business?*" She snatched the oversized book from his hand and let it fall open to the pages of the family register. "Did you not read the names listed here under the marriages?"

"'Samantha Eugenia Fulton married to George Robert Cunningham, July seventeenth, nineteen thirty-seven,'" he read, then raised his eyes to her.

"What about the one after that?"

"That's the one that's none of your business." He hit the last four words hard. If she'd have been a man, he'd have poked her in the chest with one finger to force the point home more fully.

"None of my…" She clenched her jaw, then lifted the Bible up and ran her finger along as she read, "'Samuel Prescott Fulton married to Letticia Sarafina Gautier, August first, nineteen thirty-seven.' That's Miss Lettie and Great-grandfather Fulton! This says she was his *wife,* and over here, listed under Samuel Fulton's children, Helen Bettina—that's her daughter, Helen Betty."

"Yeah, it didn't take a mathematical genius to put that two and two together, Dix. Now, let's move on to an English lesson—you said *his* wife, *her* daughter, personal possessive pronouns, neither of which indicate *you.*" He pointed at her, immediately saw how intimidating the gesture looked, then tried to smooth it over with a touch of humor that did not back away from his position. "Therefore, none of this is your business, Princess Snooty—"

"Don't you finish that."

"Why not? That's what you're acting like, isn't it? Like some princess who thinks she's got the right to go exposing something that many people have obviously gone to great lengths to keep private?"

"Don't you mean *secret*?" She put the open Bible to her chest and closed her eyes. "Family secrets, to be precise. The secrets may not be mine, but the family is and that makes it my obligation to—"

"To shut up and leave it be." He put his hand on her shoulder. "Dixie, if Lettie wanted you to know about this, she would have told you. She's certainly had plenty of opportunity, like your entire life, to do so. Not to mention most recently when you started trying to write her life's story. Maybe this is the reason she's been so evasive about that."

"Yes, but—"

"She is a very old woman, very dear and very revered. It's not your place to go against her wishes by bringing this into the open. There will be time enough to deal with this after she's gone. For heaven's sake, Dixie, she's one hundred years old. Let her finish her life with dignity."

"That's exactly what I want to do, Riley." Dixie glanced down at the painting, still propped against the credenza, of the house where they all now resided. "What kind of dignity has she had living most of her life posing as the maid, then having to rely upon the self-sanctioned benevolence of people living in the home that should have been hers?"

"Dixie, you are jumping to a lot of conclusions. You don't

know what was or wasn't willed or given to her by your family. Maybe your great-grandfather gave her something else besides the family home."

"We're getting sidetracked, here, Riley. This isn't an issue of property or inheritance." She turned to face him, shaking back her hair. "What about everything we just discussed regarding Marcia?"

"What about it?"

"You know about family and having the faith to do the right thing even when it challenged our comfort levels, threatened our own plans and expectation for the future?"

"Maybe the action your father took was the right thing to do, Dixie. He must have felt pretty strongly about defending Lettie's privacy on the matter. He did lock this Bible away and evidently took the story of Lettie's marriage and Helen Betty's parentage to his grave."

"Maybe he did that for all the wrong reasons, Riley. We can skirt around it all we want, but it's a little like trying to ignore an elephant in the parlor, isn't it?"

"I'm not sure—"

"Oh, c'mon. A racially mixed couple in Mississippi in nineteen thirty-seven? That one was still a tough row to hoe in nineteen *ninety-seven*. Did you ever think that all this secrecy, the lies, the cover-up might have been, well, *forced* on Miss Lettie? A condition my family put on her and she had no choice but to honor? To suffer in silence?"

Riley laughed. "Somehow that does not sound like our Miss Lettie."

"Allowing me to believe she was the retired family maid my whole life, living a lie…that doesn't sound like her either, does it?"

Having no ready answer to that, he just frowned.

"I wonder who else knew. Or knows."

"Do you suspect your grandfather or Aunt Sis have any idea?"

"They've never given any indication of it. But obviously Daddy knew. He was the one who had the Bible." She raised her head and the shadow of the safe's door fell across her face. "He had the Bible and kept it locked away in a place no one but he and I have gotten to without some drastic means like a court order or a short stick of dynamite."

Riley looked up at the bullet hole in the office ceiling. "You know, John Frederick might not have considered resorting to TNT all that drastic of a measure."

She glared at him.

He could see in her dispirited eyes, her slumped posture, her white-knuckled grip on the old Bible how her father's less-than-forthright treatment of this matter hurt Dixie. That made him think twice before offering yet another possibility, but he felt he had to say it, to make her look at this from more than just her own narrow angle. "Dixie, honey, you do understand that it's possible that you are the only member of your family that does not know about this big secret you think you've just uncovered? That maybe it's already been resolved by those directly involved?"

She drew a shuddering breath and nodded, then tipped her head to the side. "Do you think Fulton knows?"

"*Fulton?* His very name makes you suspect his mother must have shared the connection." Riley paused to glance around the room, recalling all the conversations he'd had with the man, the times they'd sat here and talked about raising their daughters, about business strategies, even about the Fulton family. Not once had Fulton given so much as a hint that he suspected he held any relationship to Dixie's family at all. He folded his arms over his chest and shook his head. "Actually, no, Dixie. In talking with him, I don't think he knows. But that doesn't mean it's your place to tell him."

"I think Fulton and his little girl, considering that they are heirs to a chunk of the family fortune, might argue with that, Riley."

"Heirs? How do you figure that?"

"It's family money, they are family. In fact, of all the people who have reaped the benefit of Samuel Fulton's fortune, which included most of the start-up money for the furniture businesses, there are only three survivors who are his true blood relations: me, Fulton, and Fulton's daughter." She reached up and shut the wall safe slowly, the Bible still clutched close with one hand. "If there is any *right* thing to do, in this case, Riley, it's to get to the truth in this matter and then see what I can do to make up for whatever wrongs have been done by my family."

"Did you get your phone call taken care of?"

Riley heard Aunt Sis's voice, but the sole creature he saw in the entryway was Peachie Too, just sitting there, her head cocked to one side.

"I, um…" Riley looked around. The house seemed hushed and deserted, like some old library. Dixie had pushed past him the second they came in the door to go find Miss Lettie and have a long talk with the elderly woman. Riley's heart was set on having a few words with Momma himself before he tried to contact Fulton and advise him on how to proceed should the lawyer hear from Marcia.

"Well?" Peachie Too sat up, her front paws in begging position. The dog blinked as though it were, indeed, awaiting some kind of response from Riley.

It seemed rude not to answer the question and even though he knew Peachie Too had not asked it, he leaned forward to inspect what the animal was up to as he said, "Yes, I did."

"Who are you talking to, son?" Momma came into the parlor just off the entryway, her gait hampered by the use of an aluminum walker.

"I, uh…" He pointed to Peachie Too, meaning to ask why the thing was acting so docile and beguiling.

Momma lowered herself onto "her" end of the large sofa, the one farthest from Miss Lettie's rocker.

In the weeks she'd been in the house, Momma and the others had established their own routines, complete with favorite seats, meals, television programs, and leisure activities. Sis and Momma had taken up opposite ends of the parlor sofa so that Peachie Too, who had taken a liking to Momma as intense and inexplicable as her seeming dislike for Aunt Sis, could lie between them. The Judge took the high-backed chair that faced the entryway and dominated the room, and Miss Lettie favored her carved, oak rocker. Wendy got the floor; Dixie, the footstool. Riley made himself at home pretty much wherever he could and that was fine with him because of that very thing: he was at home here.

"Stop fooling with that dog and come talk to me," Momma ordered. "Or better yet, bring that princess puppy-toes over here so I can visit with her."

Riley gave one last glance around for Sis, then reached cautiously toward the poodle.

"You don't have to tell me about the phone call, Riley, honey, but at least have the courtesy to acknowledge me."

Riley hesitated.

Peachie Too sneezed right into Riley's open palms, then darted off.

"Come back here you little—" He chose not to call the troublesome apricot-colored, dog-germ spritzer what he really wanted to call her. Momma was in the room and, injury or not, she could still nail his backside from forty paces with a sofa pillow. He glared at the dog. "I'll acknowledge *you*—" as opposed to the yet unseen Sis whom he knew he should be addressing "—all right. Acknowledge you as a good place to wipe this snout-goo off of my hands."

Bending down, he started after the beast, which ran under the rocker and around the footstool.

"Aha!" Riley caught a glimpse of pinkish fluff quivering behind the Judge's chair. He pounced.

"What are you doing, young man?" Aunt Sis rose from behind the chair and nearly gave Riley a heart attack.

"Nothing! I thought you were…your hair is the color of…" He put his hands behind his back like a ten-year-old with a slingshot caught standing outside a busted window. "Um, did Peachie Too run by here? Momma was wanting to hold her."

Dixie breezed into the room. "Miss Lettie is napping right now so I guess I'll have to wait to talk to her."

"Talk to her about what, honey?" Sis put her hands on her hips, her attitude suddenly as if she had appointed herself Miss Lettie's social secretary charged with screening who got through to the lady and what they discussed with her.

"Oh, never mind." Dixie took a side step and slid the Bible she'd kept cradled in her arms all the way from the office onto the end table beside a red, cloth-covered journal. "It can wait until she's rested and up and around. What are you doing crawling around on the floor, Aunt Sis?"

Riley gave her a thumbs-up nod of approval for the preemptive question. "Yes, what *are* you doing crawling around on the floor?"

"Oh! That's something you'll be glad to hear about!" Her face brightened but it still had a long way to go to rival the thousand-watt glow of her floral-patterned dress. "I have fixed Riley's precious little cellular phone."

"You *what?*" he managed to utter even as his jaw dropped.

"*Fixed* it?" Dixie threw him an apologetic grimace.

"Yes, I did. I took all the pieces and snapped them back inside and glued the cover back on good as new." Her hands flew as she reenacted the process of jamming the intricate parts of Riley's phone together. "It was sort of like putting together a jigsaw puzzle and you know how good I am at putting together jigsaw puzzles. Except that these pieces didn't quite fit right and there wasn't a picture on a box for me to follow, you know. So, I figured that I might have dropped a piece or two carrying it from the entryway to the kitchen. That's when I decided to retrace my steps on my hands and knees, combing the rug for any stray bits and pieces…"

Okay, Sis, come up for air. Riley was hoping against hope for a window of opportunity to speak.

Dixie did not wait for that window, she just barged right in, making her own door then sticking her verbal foot in to make sure Sis could not shut them out of the conversation again. "My! Isn't that ingenious of you Aunt Sis? Sounds like you've really worked hard while we were gone and you know what? You deserve a break!"

"Oh, it wasn't hard work, honey. Just trying to help Riley—"

"Gee, thanks," he muttered, his hand over his eyes.

"And who doesn't want to help Riley, Aunt Sis? He's done so much for all of us. And now we can do a little something just for him." Dixie took the older woman by the shoulders. "You do want to do something for him, don't you, Aunt Sis?"

"Well, I was—" She pointed in the direction of the kitchen

where Riley pictured his poor phone laid out on the counter like a victim in a mad scientist's experiment.

"Good! You know what Riley really needs right now?"

Sis opened her mouth to speak.

"What he needs right now is some privacy so he can have a long chat with his momma."

"I suspected as much." Momma patted the empty cushion on the sofa next to her. Out of nowhere, Peachie Too appeared to claim that spot.

"What say you and I muster the troops, Aunt Sis, and take Grandpa, Wendy, and ourselves down to the drugstore for a treat?"

"Drugstore? We going down to the drugstore?" The Judge flung open one of the glass doors to his office.

Sis glared at him, hands propped on her ample hips. "What were you doing, listening at the door?"

"Wendy, hurry yourself down here, child," the Judge called out, ignoring Sis with undisguised glee. "We're going to go get ourselves a treat!"

Wendy thundered down the steps, Baby Belle tucked under her arm.

Dixie leaned in Riley's direction. "You owe me. When it's time for me to have my talk with Miss Lettie, it's your turn to tend to the nut farm."

"Hey, you're referring to my child and my mother in that group."

"Where are we going, Grandpa Smilin' Bob?" Wendy marched right up and said it like she'd been born to the breed, Riley noted, like she'd lived here all her life. And when the Judge offered her his arm, she took it with her head high, just the way Riley imagined Dixie might have done when she was his daughter's age. Suddenly, it didn't seem so bad to find his family included with hers.

"The drugstore, that's where we're going!" The Judge grinned, then rubbed his hands together. "Now, isn't that just the thing to liven up a dull Saturday afternoon?"

Dixie nabbed Sis by the arm and prodded her across the room toward the old man. "Grandpa, if you're going into that drugstore with us, and you are, make no mistake about that, you have *got* to behave!"

"Oh, he'll behave all right, Dixie-sugar. He'll behave like a seventy-something-year-old juvenile delinquent!" Verdi called out with a laugh.

"Momma!" Riley folded his arms, ready to compare her rude outburst to something he might have done as a kid—the ultimate comeuppance for her, he thought, to be sure.

"Now don't you chide Miss Verdi, young man, she's only telling it the way it is." Sis shook her finger as she brought up the rear of the group heading out the door. "And I, for one, have got to just thank you for bringing her to be a part of our lives here. Heaven knows, I welcome one other voice of rationality and refinement around this place!"

The door slammed shut behind them.

"One *other?*" Riley gave his mother a skeptical look. "Meaning Aunt Sis believes that aside from you, she is the sole arbiter of rationality and refinement in this household?"

"No, arbitration is the Judge's bailiwick, dear." Verdi stroked the pink-tinged poodle now curled contentedly in her lap.

"The Judge?" Riley threw up his hands. "Momma, you know why Dixie has to warn him to behave himself when they go to the drugstore, don't you? He *shoplifts!*"

"Oh, that?" She batted away the very notion, rolling her eyes. "That's nothing."

"Noth—? Okay, Momma, I think you have been in this

household just a little too long if you think that some endearing little eccentric stealing from the drugstore is nothing."

"But he *doesn't* steal, son."

"What?"

"Oh, the whole thing goes way back. Seems ten years ago when Noni Philpot took over the town drugstore, she set everything up her way, which was all contrary to the way it had always been before. People, Smilin' Bob among 'em, complained they couldn't find things, that they liked it the old way. Noni responded by telling them if they didn't like it to go someplace else."

"There is no place else, not in Fulton's Dominion."

"Precisely. And Noni sure did take advantage of that fact—raised her prices right through the roof." Momma jerked her thumb upward.

"And this relates to the Judge's shoplifting how?"

"He never shoplifted a thing in his life. He just took it upon himself, as a pillar of the community, someone looked upon for guidance and to set a fine example—"

"Now there's a scary thought."

"He just took it upon himself—" she was using that stern don't-mess-with-Momma tone—"to start his own one-man protest committee. So every time he would go into the store, he'd move items back to their old places, one or two at a time. A box of razorblades here, a bottle of aspirin there. Smilin' Bob thought that after a few years of that he might just get the place back to its old way all on his own."

"This has been going on for ten years?"

"Oh no! Five years ago Noni got fed up with his tomfoolery and announced to everyone that things had started to disappear after Smilin' Bob's trips to the drugstore. She neglected to mention that they later reappeared someplace else in the store."

"Why, that old mischief maker." Riley walked to the sofa, laughing.

"Smilin' Bob challenged Noni to prove he'd ever taken anything. She answered by issuing the order that the Judge couldn't come into her store by himself except to go straight to the lunch counter."

"So it's true." He slumped into the sofa cushion shaped to the width and weight of Sis's behind.

"What's true, son?"

He leaned back and crossed his arms. "You *do* have some kind of inborn radar for getting all the good gossip."

"Yes, I do. God's radar." She raised both hands and tapped her ears with her fingers. "And it's not gossip. It's personal history, and the reason I know so much about it is not because I seek out dirt on people but because I *listen* when they talk to me about the things that matter to them."

"How Noni Philpot arranged her aspirin bottles is something that matters to the Judge?"

"No, standing up for what he thought was right mattered. Not backing down when someone who had the upper hand wanted to use it to bludgeon good people mattered. Making sure that as the newest member of this family, I understood that sometimes what one person called eccentricity another person might know was an ethical stand. That mattered."

"Whoa! As the newest member of *what* family, Momma?"

"You know what I meant."

"Momma, I'm not sure what I know anymore." He put his head in his hands.

"Love will do that to you."

"Love?" That went through him with a jolt.

"Yes, *love.*"

"Momma, you've got this all wrong. I do not love Dixie

Fulton-Leigh. That is, I am not in love with her. Sure I find her attractive, compelling, funny, exciting…but love?"

"Well, I wasn't thinking of you being in love with Dixie, son, but by that response I have to wonder—"

"Carol? Is that who you're talking about? Did you find out she called me today? Well, restarting that dead-end romance was about the farthest thing from—"

"I was thinking about your love for your little girl, Riley." She put her hand on his arm.

"For Wendy?" He wasn't sure he understood.

"And for your dear old mother…and even your…your sister."

"You know?"

"Not the details, but it's pretty obvious this has something to do with us. I can certainly see where your struggle to do right by all of us has worn you thinner than the sliced ham on a miser's smorgasbord."

Riley chuckled. "Is this another *listening* thing?"

"This is just plain horse sense. You're less than two weeks from the hearing to ask to sever Marcia's parental rights. You get a call from your ex-lawyer that you chose to go outside the home to return. When you come back all sullen faced, you're so distracted you try to converse with Peachie Too."

The dog lifted its head, looking at Riley quite indignantly and giving something between a woof and a growl.

"The next thing I know, you've allowed Dixie to empty out the house so you and I can talk. What else could that be about but Marcia?"

"Well, it could be about a number of things, but you're right, this time it is about Marcia."

"Yes, I thought so."

He dropped his hands to his lap and stared at them. For

most of his life he'd been able to help his family with these two hands…to work in the mill, to pay the bills, to carry the burdens for the people he loved. Now the rough and calloused fingers looked unsuitable for the tasks ahead of him—this would be a job too big for him to handle with mere hard work and determination. His chest tight, he bowed his head to hide the threat of tears that betrayed him, that proved him a man of small faith and overwhelming fear when it came to his child's future and happiness. He drew in a long breath.

"What, son?"

"She's back."

"Back?" Momma clutched at his arm. "Where?"

"I'm not sure yet." He dragged his knuckle under one eye then looked up. "She called the sawmill. They put her onto Carol, who referred her to my new lawyer."

"That mystery man you went clear to Jackson to get?"

"Yeah." Keeping Fulton's identity a secret from Momma had presented its own unique set of problems, but Riley had managed. "This being Saturday, it's not likely Marcia could get a hold of him today. I may have to do some fancy footwork to track him down myself. So, I wanted to make you aware of all this before I tell him what to do should he hear from her."

"Do? Riley, honey, you say that like he has choices."

"He does. He can tell her we'll see her in court or act as my representative and tell her what we want and what we expect of her and try to negotiate on my behalf, or…"

He could hardly force enough air through his vocal chords to make the sound. His head was spinning as he contemplated what he must propose. He swallowed hard.

Fear and personal pain had no place here. Faith not acted on was dead. His faith might seem small at times, but it was very much alive. Very much. "Or he can give her this address so she can come home to us, Momma."

"There's one other thing he can do, son. Something so obvious and simple, I can't believe you've worked yourself into such a state and overlooked it."

He lifted his gaze to find his mother watching him with a sobering mix of resignation and resolution shining in her eyes.

"He can ask her what she wants."

"What?" Riley shook his head.

"He can ask her what she wants, why she's made contact now. It's the most natural thing in the world for him to do and if he is a good lawyer, he'll know that. Until someone asks her what she wants, we really shouldn't rush to any conclusions or let ourselves assume the worst."

"What she wants? Momma, she got in touch because she saw one of those ads, the ones that we had to place to show we'd tried everything we could to reach her. Well, we've reached her." He pulled his shoulders up, presenting a far more in-control facade than his inner turmoil should have warranted. "She's coming back for Wendy, to make sure she doesn't lose her forever."

"You are a good man, Riley, my darling." She wrapped both her hands around one of his. "Maybe too good."

He snorted out a soft laugh. "Now those are words I never thought I'd hear from you, Momma. Me? Too good? I thought I was a troublement, someone you still might need to take to the woodshed."

"Don't think I won't if you do anything to risk Wendy's adoption, including inviting your own sister to waltz back into our lives pretty as you please at this stage of the game."

"Momma, I don't understand."

"Of course you don't, because you don't think like your sister does. You can't." She patted his hand. "You are trying to find a win/win situation where there just isn't one to be had. You're thinking there may still be some way this can work out so that everybody gets what he or she wants. But, son, Marcia, God bless her soul, does not deserve to get what she wants in this case. Not if what she wants hurts that precious little grand-daughter of mine."

"But it hurts Wendy not to see her mother, Momma, not to at least meet her and—"

"I'm not saying keep them apart forever. I am saying that if Marcia wants to stop you from adopting Wendy, from legaliz-ing the reality that you are the only parent that child knows and trusts and has ever had to rely upon, then Marcia will have to be disappointed."

He swallowed, which was hard to do around the lump in his throat. "That's the last thing I expected you to say. The way you pray all the time for Marcia to come back—"

"To be a part of all our lives, Riley. Not so she can stake some kind of claim on Wendy or use that child to make herself feel better by toying at motherhood until she gets bored with it and runs off again." The color had gone from Momma's lips. They had grown as thin and tight as her grip on Riley's hand. "I won't let it happen and I want your word here and now that you won't either."

Riley's stomach lurched. Suddenly he wondered if he should have taken Carol's advice and gathered whatever he could find to use against his sister. He met his mother's gaze. *You're a good man, Riley.* Her words rang again in his ears.

No, he'd followed the right course. Whatever the outcome he'd always be able to live with himself knowing that much remained true. *Whatever happened…Your will, Father. Your will be done.*

"I won't let that happen, Momma, I promise."

Sixteen

Blessed is the man who perseveres under trial, because
when he has stood the test, he will receive the crown of life that God
has promised to those who love him.

JAMES 1:12

RILEY SAT ON THE ELEVATED FRONT PORCH OF DIXIE'S HOUSE.
From the steps, he looked down the gentle sloping hill lined
with huge trees and grand old houses, none of which were half
as grand as the place he now called home. He could see where,
three blocks away, South Dominion intersected Main Street and
he realized that was the corner where Dixie had run the stop
sign...or had he run it?

Looking back now, he couldn't rightly say who'd been at
fault. What he did know was that it didn't really matter. What
did matter was that they'd made good of the situation...they'd
used it to build something solid, good, and lasting.

Of course, he wasn't thinking about the stop sign incident at all. He stretched his legs out and shut his eyes to let the late winter sun warm him. No, it wasn't the stop sign encounter on his mind. It was Dixie and how much she had come to mean to him. And he was thinking of Marcia.

Finding fault with Marcia now served no purpose but to feed his anger and justify his anxiety. He smiled. Leave it to Momma to be so right and so wise. He would just have to stay firm in his conviction to protect Wendy. And he would do that by waiting and seeing what Marcia wanted, all the while trusting and praying that God's will would prevail. On that basis, no matter what, all would be well.

He opened his eyes just as Dixie pulled the car into the long, slanted driveway. She gave him a wave and drove around to the back, presumably to let the older ones out nearest the back door—spry as Smilin' Bob might be, he walked down the steps of the big house much more easily than he could walk up them again.

Riley considered going inside to greet them but suddenly his legs felt too heavy to move, his seat on the cold stone steps too comfy to leave. Secretly, he hoped that if he lingered here long enough Dixie would come to him. Riley wanted a moment alone with Dixie before he took charge of everyone and gave her the privacy she needed to speak to Lettie about the findings in the family Bible.

A moment alone with Dixie. A new energy surged through him at the possibility of that small thing. His heart pounded, dull and hard, as he thought of her seeking him out. Now that he'd found a tentative peace, now that he knew he could and would handle whatever came his way, he felt as though he would see Dixie for the first time with his mind clear and his spirit sound. He leaned back and pictured her dark hair falling over her strong shoulders, a smile—or a double-edged remark—ever at the ready on her full lips.

Suddenly, his own words came back to haunt him: *Momma, you've got this all wrong. I do not love Dixie Fulton-Leigh. That is, I am not in love with her. Sure I find her attractive, compelling, funny, exciting, but love?*

"Yes, *love.*" Hearing himself murmur the word out loud made it all the more real. He couldn't deny it any longer. He loved Dixie. He'd known it for some time now. What was more, Riley suspected she loved him as well.

Even now, he could hear Dixie's reasoned response to their kiss as clear as day. *"We're living under the same roof. Our businesses are interdependent. Our families have come to care and count on one another. We can't lay all that on the line for some misplaced romantic notions…What if it didn't work out?"*

"And what if it does?" He planted his feet on one step, laid his forearms across his thighs, and leaned forward, his hands clasped. "What if it does?"

"What if what does, Daddy?" Wendy came tearing around the corner of the stairs and bounded up them. Baby Belle's cloth arms and legs bounced wildly in every direction with each step until his darling daughter reached him, and Riley gathered her close to kiss her on the cheek.

"What if…" He did not finish. He had no idea how to express this new, charged outlook to his child or if he should even try. When he heard a familiar humming growing closer, he grinned. "I thought you got something to eat at the drugstore."

"We did."

He lifted Baby Belle and put her to his ear. "Then I think your dolly must have come down with the stomach flu or something, sweetheart. I just heard the awfullest tummy grumbling!"

Dixie's humming grew louder.

Wendy stopped to listen to Baby Belle's stomach, her face a mask of motherly concern.

Completely unaware of Riley's joking, Dixie strode into view, still humming as she walked to the front of the house from the garage. Riley enjoyed the view, enjoyed the way she carried herself like she knew who she was and where she was headed at all times without seeming arrogant or conceited. Of course, now that he'd let himself acknowledge how much he truly cared for her—and how much he longed to know she felt the same way about him—he would not have minded if Dixie had forgone that ladylike comportment to come running straight into his open arms.

Instead, she strolled up the walk. The humming quieted.

"I don't hear anything." Wendy eyed him suspiciously.

"Hmm, I must have been mistaken."

"Then c'mon, Daddy, tell me what you were saying before," Wendy demanded again. *What if?*

"Yeah, what if…" He focused his gaze on Dixie as she started up the steps toward him.

"Oh, Daddy, you're acting all gooberfied!"

That snapped him back to reality—or what passed for reality around this place.

"I can't imagine where she heard that." Dixie looked skyward, striking a pose not unlike the chubby stone cherub that stood watch from the top of its tall pillar at the bottom of the wide, stone stairway.

Riley laughed and chucked his sweet child under the chin. "Yeah, well as long as you don't start calling me a rowboat or saying I'm oober-gay ied-fay, I guess I can live with it."

"Obber-what? Daddy, you're a big sillyhead!" She threw her arms around him.

"Ahhh, the wisdom of youth." Dixie whooshed out an exaggerated sigh. "Now, you were saying what if...something?"

"Um, yeah. What if..." Riley brushed Wendy's bangs out of her eyes, gave her another kiss, this time on the forehead, then propelled her around his feet and toward the front door. "What if Miss Wendy runs inside and picks out a jigsaw puzzle, preferably not one that's been made out of cell phone, and takes it into her grandma's room? Then she can round everybody up and we'll all work on putting that together for a while, okay?"

"Thanks." Dixie said the word softly, her gaze fixed in his.

"Jigsaw puzzle! Hooray!" Both of Wendy's hands shot up in the air. "First a treat at the drugstore now a jigsaw puzzle! This is turning out to be a great day!"

The slapping and scuffing of her small shoes as she scampered off echoed through the high-ceilinged porch. The front screen door creaked open.

Riley kept his eyes on Dixie, and she on him.

The screen door fell shut with a *whap*. The distinct sound of Wendy running toward them reached Riley's ears just seconds before she whisked past him.

"Thank you, Miss Dixie, for being so nice to me." Wendy stretched her arms toward Dixie, Baby Belle slung over her shoulder. Wendy went up on tiptoe, and even her fingers wriggled and strained to reach the woman standing at the foot of the steps. Her small body tensed as if singularly concentrated on getting her hands on something that she feared would always remain just beyond her grasp.

And just a moment before that thought and sight broke his heart, Dixie bent at the knees and wrapped his daughter up in a hug so all-encompassing that if he had not already admitted to himself that he loved the woman, he would have realized it on the spot and never been able to deny it again.

"You're welcome, sweetie-pie. I just wish I had more time to do things with you, but things have just been so hectic since you came to stay."

Wendy drew back. "Maybe when my bedroom is finished you can come in for a sleepover."

"I'd like that."

"Daddy, you can come too and it'll be like a slumber party." Wendy beamed at him in her exuberant innocence.

Dixie kept one hand on Wendy's back and put the other on her own hip. "If he so much as jokes about doing that, honey, he'll find himself sleeping in the doghouse."

"But Peachie Too doesn't *have* a doghouse. She sleeps under Grandpa Smilin' Bob's bed."

"All the better." Dixie winked at Riley.

He grinned.

"Now, you go on inside like your daddy asked." Dixie urged Wendy back up the stairs. "And pick out that puzzle—and not one of those easy hundred pieces, either. Get one with lots of sky and sea."

"But those are harder and take longer." Wendy trudged up the stairs this time, slowed, it seemed, by trying to process the logic of Dixie's request. "And sometimes Aunt Sis and Grandpa Smilin' Bob fight over which piece goes where."

"To quote a wise woman, 'all the better.'" Riley pretended to take a swat at Wendy's backside to hurry her along. "Now get a wiggle on and hop to it."

Wendy giggled, then she wiggled, and then she hopped right on up the stairs and through the front door.

"So, how did the talk go with your mom?" Dixie put her foot on the next step and leaned against the concrete handrail, the stone cherub looking down over her shoulder.

"Surprisingly well."

"Good."

"She gave me some sound advice about not borrowing trouble by worrying over what Marcia might want. I need to set my own goal, then deal with things as they arise."

"Not borrowing trouble is always a smart way to go." She bowed her head slightly and put her fingertips to her lips.

Riley wondered if she was thinking of their kiss. He knew he was. Unfortunately, that led to thinking about the promise they'd made to not get involved. He started to push up from the steps, to go to her and take her in his arms and tell her—or perhaps show her—how much he regretted sealing that bargain with her.

"Well, I need to go inside." Dixie ran her finger along the inside of her mother's necklace, straightened her back, and started up the stairs before Riley could say or do anything more. "Do you know if Lettie's up and around yet?"

"Yes, I helped her to her rocker just before I came outside."

"Her rocker? I left that Bible on the table right by there." She jogged to the top of the stairs, past Riley, and onto the porch. The screen door screeched in protest as she swung it wide.

Riley leapt to his feet, not ready to let her go so easily. "Dixie, wait!"

"What is it, Riley? I'm in kind of a hurry."

"I, uh…" What had he planned to do? Shout "I love you" from the front porch? He exhaled hard, gritted his teeth, then looked up and relaxed. He'd find another opportunity to talk to her soon. "I'm going over to Jackson Monday morning to see about getting a new cell phone."

"And?"

"And to meet with…" He stole a glance into the house

through the open door. The chances of anyone overhearing him were small but he chose to play it discreetly just the same. "To meet with our lawyer. Do you want to come?"

Dixie looked inside, then at him again, her actions brisk and agitated. "Can't we talk about this later? I'd like to come along but that may well depend on how things go with Lettie."

"I understand. Good luck."

"Luck? I can get along fine without luck right now. Courage, confidence, compassion—*those* I need in a big way."

"Then you are going to do just fine, Dix. You are going to do just fine."

"Not that one, this one." Grandpa's directive carried down the long hallway from the room at the back of the house.

"I want to do one of The Great Artists of the World series, Smilin' Bob." Aunt Sis's lamentful wail came wafting even more clearly through the house. "Isn't it bad enough I've relinquished my ties to the Every-Other-Thursday-Afternoon Arts and Culture Society and to most of my more aesthetic aspirings to stay here and run this household? Must I also be reduced to whiling away my leisure time fitting together ridiculous pictures of kittens with yarns balls or photographs of sailboat-littered harbors?"

Dixie tensed. She did not need this now. She wanted to approach Lettie with a clear head and a calm demeanor. She wanted to present this to the old woman in an atmosphere of love and kindness so Lettie could feel safe to talk and know that her disclosures would be taken seriously. A bunch of cater-wauling over the selection of jigsaw puzzles going on in the background was hardly conducive to that.

"I'll take care of it, Dix, don't fret." Riley had slipped in the door so quietly she had not realized he was there until he put his hands on her shoulders as he moved past her.

For a second she was tempted to grab his hand and ask him to stay, to help her do what she had to do, to be strong for her and perhaps, for Lettie, too. Funny, she thought as she watched him head down the hallway and out of sight, how quickly she had come to rely on the man, how deeply rooted her trust in him had become…how much she cared for him, despite her many protestations that she could never allow that to happen.

She sighed and whispered the words she'd heard him murmur as she met him on the steps this afternoon. "What if…"

The commotion in Verdi's room at the back of the house rose to a low rumble, then ebbed until Riley alone spoke softly, but firmly. She could not make out exactly what he told them but she recognized the tone and knew he had taken things in hand. Riley had done what he had set out to do, and now she must do the same.

"Miss Lettie?" She tiptoed to the sweeping archway that led to the parlor where the old gal loved to sit, soak up the sun, and still keep herself privy to every activity going on in the main floor of the home. "Miss Lettie, are you in there?"

"Come in, lamb. I've been waiting for you."

"You…you have?" Dixie stepped so carefully she could have walked across a field covered with wild birds feeding and never disturbed a feather. "That's good, I suppose, because we have to talk."

"Yes, child, we do." Lettie patted the black Bible lying in her narrow lap.

Dixie's stomach clenched and her throat went dry. For the last hour she'd rehearsed in her head every imaginable way to handle this—except one where Miss Lettie already knew what was coming. She didn't know why but this made her feel like a kid caught with her hand in the cookie jar. Having been in that actual situation a time or two with Miss Lettie doing the catching, Dixie had reason to feel uneasy.

"I guess it's really none of my business, Miss Lettie." Dixie sank onto the footstool next to Lettie's rocker. "But when I saw the names recorded in the family register there, well, I just have so many questions."

"Only way to get answers is to ask, lamb."

Dixie rounded her shoulders as she looped her arms over one upraised knee. "Where to start...I want to know why you kept it secret so long and who all you've kept it secret from? How'd you manage to get married in Mississippi and then stay married without anyone suspecting, especially when you had a child together—"

"Now that part is easy to answer, child. Let me start there. We did not marry in Mississippi. We never would have been permitted to, no matter how rich or powerful the Founder may have been." Lettie brushed her fingers over the gold-stamped name in the corner of the Bible. "We married up north while we accompanied young Samantha Eugenia and George Robert—your grandparents—on their extensive wedding trip."

"You...went with them on their honeymoon?"

"Different times, Dixie Belle, different times," she croaked out, her head shaking. "If you can't stop looking on this through modern eyes and try to see how it was back then, how it used to be so many years ago, then there ain't no sense even going on with the tellin' of it."

"I just...go on, please."

"You know, Founder Fulton hand-picked me to accompany him back to Fulton's Dominion from New Orleans in the summer of nineteen seventeen?"

"I know." She thought of trying to move Lettie along, to get to the marriage and the secrets and what needed to be done now concerning Fulton. But she held her tongue, knowing one wrong word might cause the woman with a century's-worth of history in her to withdraw and not speak of it again.

"He'd saw me standing on a balcony with my mother, who was much fairer than me." Lettie lifted her face as if she were watching it replay again before her age-clouded eyes. "I was brushing her long, black hair, ever-so gentle. She was a frail thing, my mother, prone to headaches and long bouts of taking to her bed. I loved her so and I loved to brush that long, silky hair of hers. I always took care not to tug or fight the tangles, but to stroke them out slow, over and over, until they got good and gone."

"I remember." Dixie smiled, recalling the times in her childhood when Lettie had combed through her snarled wet hair without so much as a snag.

"Founder Fulton thought I was my mother's serving girl and he came straightaway to the house to ask could he hire me off to come tend to his wife and the new baby they was expecting. My mother saw it as the answer to a prayer, seeing as she was so sickly and worried how I'd get on after she was gone." Lettie fell silent.

Dixie could see in the woman's ancient eyes how much she still loved and missed her mother. It was a sentiment Dixie knew well.

"Founder Fulton promised my mother that if I said yes and come along, he would look after me, look after my spiritual welfare, and that I'd always be treated like one of his own while in his home."

"But all those years, Miss Lettie, everyone thought you were the maid when you should have been the mistress of the household. That's not being treated as one of—"

"That was reality, child. I was the baby maid for a time,

until that baby grew up. Then not long after that, the baby come back to live here, and we had more babies to raise."

"One of them yours."

"Yes, one of them my Helen Betty."

"How did you keep who her father was a secret, Miss Lettie?"

She shrugged. "At the time, I figured ain't nobody cared what a little colored baby maid did, who her child was, or even who her child's father was. Looking back now, I reckon more folks knew, or at least suspected, than let on. But they never said a thing. They wouldn't, long as they thought we wasn't married and I was kept in my proper place."

"Why?"

"Marriage, now, that represented a threat to too many people. To say back then that a colored and a white could love one another like a husband and wife, to think that a little brown-skinned woman could be respected as a partner by the town's founder, it would have scared lots of folks—scared them silly. And when a thing like that happens, ain't no one safe."

Dixie's heart ached for all the wrongs she realized Miss Lettie had endured, for all the misunderstandings—many of them her own—that had affected how people had behaved toward the old woman. "But you loved and respected my great-grandfather no matter what people might have thought of it, I can hear it in your voice when you talk about him."

"Yes, I did, as he did me. I never once doubted Founder Fulton's affection for me, though he rarely showed any kind of emotion toward anyone. That's the way men acted back then."

"What about Helen Betty?"

"He loved her, too, dear, but you have to understand—"

"I know, it was a different time."

"And Founder Fulton was a man of his times, and his times

were even farther back than mine. He was over sixty when we married, you understand. I was nigh onto forty my own self."

"Oh." Dixie blinked. "I guess I didn't realize that."

"He acknowledged Helen Betty and provided a fine upbringing for her and remembered her generously in his will. For all the good *that* did her." Lettie looked away.

Dixie wanted to ask about the cryptic remark, but before she could find a way to phrase the delicate question, Lettie had started on her tale again.

"When Helen Betty was still quite young, her daddy passed over so that she never really knew him. But we went on living here, your grandfather running that fool automobile dealership of his that never earned a nickel and your grandmother and me raising our babies together. Strange as it may seem to you, we didn't stop to think what was fair or who deserved to inherit what. We were a family—one of our own making and not to everyone's taste, for sure, but a family all the same."

"A family that pretended to the world that you and your child were outsiders, Miss Lettie."

The old woman set the chair rocking and laid her head against the small, white pillow tied to the back of the seat. "I suppose that's so. And suppose days came I wasn't none too happy about that. But it's all so long ago, child. I've let go of any ill feelings I might have harbored and I ain't no outsider now, not in my heart, not in God's eyes."

"But—"

"Founder Fulton been dead half my lifetime ago, Miss Dixie Belle. That's a considerable long time." Lettie's mouth stretched into her broadest grin, revealing the pale gums where she'd been missing teeth since before Dixie was born. "Why you want to fuss over all this now? It don't make sense and it don't change nothing. It is what it is: the past."

"It's not entirely the past, Miss Lettie." She laid her hand on Lettie's bone-thin arm. "You say you feel like you're a part of this family and you are, just like Sis is, just like Grandpa."

"Now, you don't got no call to set to bad-mouthing me." Lettie held her hand up, coughing out her dry cackle.

Dixie shook her head. "What I mean is we all love each other, but because of this secret you've kept for so long, there's a part of our family that's missing."

"Ain't the secret that kept my grandson away, lamb."

"He knows about his lineage?"

"If he does it's because someone broke a promise."

"A promise?"

"My Helen Betty was hardly sixteen when she met that no-good Wallace Summers. I begged her not to see him. She ignored my advice. I warned her that if she ever told him about who her father was she might be placing herself and me in jeopardy."

"You actually feared for your lives?"

"It was the nineteen fifties by then, honey, turbulent times for colored and whites. Who knows what might have happened, and without Founder Fulton alive to protect us…"

Dixie cringed, her stomach tied in knots at the idea of what that must have been like for this sweet, dear soul. "Oh, Miss Lettie, I am so sorry. How many times you must have wanted to just—"

"Blessed is the man who endureth temptation: for when he is tried, he shall receive the crown of life which the Lord has promised them that love him." She quoted from the book of James without having to open so much as the cover of the Bible still resting in her lap.

"I have a feeling you've earned quite a crown in heaven," she whispered, even though she suspected the old woman could not hear her.

"Helen Betty never told Summers about who her daddy was, I'd swear that much is true." Lettie placed her hand on top of the Bible as if she were taking an oath in a court of law. "And she promised not to tell her son until he was full growed. Of course, you know she died before she saw that happen."

"Then don't you owe it to her, to yourself, to *our* family to correct that, Miss Lettie? To tell Fulton the truth?"

"Fulton." She gave a weak smile and her eyes closed. "You found him then."

"Found him? You mean you knew?"

"Well, I did tell you *and* Mr. Walker that I had a grandson who was a lawyer in Jackson at a time when you both said you needed a lawyer. Don't get much better of a rowboat than that, girl."

Dixie laughed. "Then you want to see him? Because he said you—"

"The question is, does he want to see me, lamb?" Lettie's usually rasping voice grew strong. "It's been his choice all this time. I ain't gone nowhere. He could have found me if he wanted."

"He said you told him he wasn't welcome."

"I never did no such of a thing. That Wallace Summers, now, he was not to set foot in this house. Onliest times he ever did come around he come asking after money because he'd spent my girl's inheritance and he figured to go through mine."

So Lettie *had* received some share of the family money. It gave Dixie some comfort to know Founder Fulton had taken care of his wife and child financially. She wished he had done more—much more—but as Lettie had told her, he was a man of different times.

"That weren't the worst of what that Wallace Summers done, you know that. After Helen Betty passed, Fulton was welcome in my home, but not if he come a-toting that man behind him. I don't think I have to tell you why that is so."

Dixie bowed her head. "No, ma'am."

"Now, if my grandson wants to be a part of this family, he has to take that first step."

"But you told him not to come back. Coming here makes him choose between his father, whom I'm sure he cares about, and you, whom he hardly knows." Dixie's pulse skipped as she realized she had never spoken so defiantly to Miss Lettie in her life. Still, she pressed on. "I don't think you're being fair!"

"I'm too old and too ornery to be fair, lamb." She rocked and laughed.

"Well, *I'm* not so old, but I can sure be ornery if I put my mind to it." Dixie stood and turned to leave, calling over her shoulder as she did, "Guess that means that I don't have to be fair, either."

"She only wants to know that her grandson has come back to her out of love, not because of some long-kept secret family connection, Dixie. Is that so wrong?"

"They are both so sure they are right. That's what gets me." Dixie shut the passenger door to Riley's truck, the solid *clunk* reverberating across the parking lot of Fulton's office building. "Too sure to even listen to the other side and each willing to fight like fools to defend their erroneous positions."

"Yeah, it's amazing I didn't catch on to that family resemblance earlier." Riley's sarcasm came without venom, more from frustration than anything else.

Yes, if one word could describe the time he and Dixie had spent together today, *frustration* would just about do it. He'd made such big plans for how he would use this time, how he'd dazzle Dixie, make her laugh, touch her heart, then finally confess his love for her.

"Oh…" She crinkled her nose up at him. A hint of amusement in her eyes mingled with the wariness she'd worn all morning long like some women wear a second layer of makeup. "Oh, go tell it to your cell phone."

Yup. Frustration. Pure and simple.

"Can't." He patted the new phone bulging in his jacket pocket. "I don't want to tie up the line in case your AWOL common sense tries to get in touch with you."

"My common sense is very much non-AWOL…like…um." She stopped just outside the door to the building, closed her eyes, cleared her throat, then held one hand up, looking for all the world like a soprano about to launch into an aria.

He watched her breathe in, saw the moods shift over her beautiful face, then her expression went still.

"I am in full possession of all my faculties," she told him. "Common sense included. Now, you have your goals—"

"To give Fulton some very basic instructions about dealing with Marcia, to hear any advice he has to offer, and to get a really good lunch." He held the door open for her.

"And I have mine, which is to convince Fulton to make up with Miss Lettie." She swiped her hands together to illustrate how smoothly she expected it to go.

He smiled and gave a quick, silent prayer that all would indeed go well for Dixie today. She'd handled her talk with Miss Lettie yesterday better than he'd hoped. Now what he offered on her behalf helped to focus him as well. His heart swelled. He wanted what was best for her, and right now that was having him in a positive frame of mind, strong and supportive, ready to help her in any way he could. "Then let's go pay a visit to Cousin Fulton."

"He does know we're coming, doesn't he?" She jabbed the elevator button.

"We have an appointment."

"Daddy never made appointments with the Greenhows. He'd just barge into their offices like John Wayne in a business suit and start barking out orders. Either that or he'd call over there and say 'Howard, get over here pronto!'" She bellowed it out in what he imagined was her best imitation of her father pulling rank on poor ol' Howard Greenhow.

It was just nervous chatter, Riley knew, but it seemed to help her relax, so he laughed and nodded to encourage her.

"Then he'd time it to see how long Howard took to get from his office to Daddy's. Daddy said it was his way of keeping Howard in shape, that if he didn't do it Howard would turn into a ball of blubber." She exhaled slowly, fiddled with her mother's pearls, then laughed. "The truth was, Daddy didn't like it very much when Mr. Greenhow Sr. let his son take over. He thought Howard was soft and spoiled and didn't appreciate how hard some people had to work to bring home a paycheck, so Daddy made sure the junior partner worked for his money."

"No wonder Greenhow longed for the day when he could take charge of your family businesses." He put his hand to her back and guided her onto the elevator and the doors rolled shut. "Think he's gotten over losing that yet?"

"Cashing your check as payment for his part in the sale of Fulton's Cartage went a long way toward assuaging his battered ego, I'm sure."

Riley nodded.

The buzzer blared to announce their arrival on Fulton's floor. A gentle backdraft blew over them as the door slid open. They stepped outside.

"This is it." Riley met her gaze. "You ready?"

"As ready as I'll ever be. You?"

"Hey, no problem. The hardest thing I'm facing here today is picking the place we eat lunch." Riley opened the door to Fulton's office. "As for the rest of it, I'm just going to leave it in God's hands and trust—"

"Riley?" A woman with hair as wavy as his and almost as dark stood up the second he walked through the door.

His heart stopped. Or that's what he supposed must have happened, otherwise he'd have felt something, thought something, done something except stand there, his entire body numb, and choke out, "Marcia?"

Seventeen

---◆---

But the wisdom that comes from heaven is first of all pure; then
peace-loving, considerate, submissive,
full of mercy and good fruit, impartial and sincere. Peacemakers
who sow in peace raise
a harvest of righteousness.

JAMES 3:17–18

"YOUR SISTER JUST SHOWED UP AT MY OFFICE THIS MORNING unannounced. I tried to call to warn you, but you'd already left town and your cell phone must not have been on." Fulton stood at the center of the room, his arms crossed like a sentinel keeping watch over Riley's best interests—and his openly hostile sister.

"His phone had a little, um, accident."

Riley felt Dixie slip into the room behind him. She edged in stiffly, standing near enough to seem supportive but not so close that her presence intruded on his reunion with his younger sibling.

The full weight of Riley's scrutiny was not with either his lawyer or with Dixie.

He remained riveted to the spot where he'd come to a dead halt when he'd seen Marcia sitting in the outer office. Now she sat perfectly still in the middle of a row of chairs. Though dressed sedately and thinner than he ever remembered her being before, that did not keep her outfit from looking too teenaged for her to pull it off with much style.

She wore her dark hair shaped close to her face, as if those wisps could hide the crows feet and the early beginnings of sagging cheeks, which gave her the appearance of someone aged by more than just the passing of time. The sight of a few coarse curls of gray near her temples and in her bangs took him back. How could his little sister, the girl he remembered more like Wendy looked now than as this grown woman, have gray in her hair? It spoke to him of how much time had gone by, how much they had lost together as a family, and it saddened him.

Despite how disappointed he was over Marcia's actions regarding Wendy, despite how angry he felt when he thought of how much Marcia had worried Momma, she was still his sister. Part of him wished he could tell her off but good for everything she'd done to those he loved, but another part wished he could just open his arms and wrap her in a reconciling hug.

"I'd jump up out of this chair and yell *surprise,* but then you might get the idea that my coming home was going to be some kind of party." Marcia crossed her legs, leaned forward, and gripped the arm of her chair. "When, big brother, it's going to be anything but."

Riley's jaw tightened, but he fought the impulse to grit his teeth. He fought every instinct, in fact, to seem defensive or antagonistic. Instead of folding his arms over his chest in a show of putting up boundaries and closing himself off to his sister after all these years, he pushed back his sport jacket and tucked his hands into the front pockets of his jeans.

Remembering his mother's advice and his own promise to not back down regarding Wendy's welfare, he steadied his breathing, swallowed to clear away any emotion from his tone, and looked his sister square in the eyes. "What do you want, Marcia? Why are you here?"

"Well, I couldn't exactly go *home,* now could I? Seeing as you've picked up and moved and didn't leave a forwarding address with anyone who would share it with me." Her chin trembled, but her eyes narrowed in cold defiance.

Riley wanted to believe the tremble, but he had to respond to the defiance, for Wendy's sake. "That's all happened in the last six weeks. Anytime in the last six years you could have returned home and found us right where we'd always been."

"Waiting with open arms, no doubt."

"Just waiting, Marcia. And hoping."

"Hoping what? That I'd fall off the face of the planet and make everything easy for you to take my child away from me forever?"

"You know better than that."

"I know that's what you're trying to do, take my baby away from me but good."

"She's not a baby anymore, Marcia. If you'd ever bothered to come around, you would see that. She's a little girl with a grandmother whose health is beginning to fail taking care of her." Was he wrong, or did the reference to Momma bring a flicker of emotion to his sister's hard, hateful gaze? "Wendy needs the psychological security of knowing she belongs to someone, that the man she has always looked to as her father is willing to make that a reality in every way."

Fulton spoke quietly at that. "Speaking as a father and as your brother's lawyer, it's his legal duty to pursue this avenue, Ms. Walker." Fulton did not move a muscle, and Riley felt he was an anchor of reason in the current of emotions prickling around them. "The child in question deserves the safety net that having a permanent, legal parent provides."

"Riley already has guardianship. He has legal custody," Marcia argued. "I'd say there is a certain amount of *psychological security*—" she threw Riley's own words back at him with a sneer—"in keeping a mother and daughter bond intact."

"There is so much wrong with that statement, I don't know where to start dealing with it." Riley held up his hands.

"Then deal with this. I left my baby with you and Momma because you were the only people on earth I knew I could trust *not* to do this very thing to me."

Riley stared at her, his own gaze hardening. "Oh, please, don't try to convince me that any forethought went into your abandonment of your baby. You didn't leave so much as a note behind when you packed up and left the hospital. Without Wendy."

"I didn't have to leave a note because I knew I had the world's most perfect big brother to step in and take charge of everything—"

"That's it, isn't it?" The whole thing began to make sense to him now. "Why didn't I see it before?"

You're a good man, Riley. Maybe too good. His mother's assessment echoed in his mind. *You don't think like Marcia. You can't.*

"Why didn't you see what?" Challenge colored Marcia's question, as though she doubted he really had an answer for her or, if he did, that he had the nerve to say it aloud.

"This isn't about you keeping your rights to Wendy because you so desperately want to preserve some bond you've romanticized exists between you two. This is about you keeping *me* from getting those rights. This is about punishing me for some grudge you hold against the family because we stopped making excuses for your behavior. You're using Wendy to get back at the family, aren't you?"

"Maybe I'm using Wendy to try to hang on to my family. Have you ever thought of that?"

"*Using* Wendy is never going to accomplish that."

No answer. Someone else might have taken that as disdain, but the fact that Marcia did not even try to refute Riley's point gave him a ray of hope that he might be able to reach her yet. "What is it you want to see happen here, Marcia? Do you envision some kind of joint custody arrangement where Wendy ping-pongs back and forth between us?"

"Riley, listen to me—" Fulton stepped forward—"don't say something here that might come back to kick you in the pants later."

"Is that legal consequence, counselor?" Riley couldn't hold back his amusement.

"That a judicious warning, my friend." Fulton was not laughing.

Clearly Fulton took this very seriously, and Riley appreciated that...but if he backed down now he might never get the chance to make his point like this again. He turned back to Marcia. "What do you say, little sister? Are you ready to petition for visitation rights? Will you make the big move to be near our new home so you can play a role in Wendy's day-to-day life?"

"Riley, be careful."

Riley loved Dixie even more for her whispered warning, but he wouldn't listen. He couldn't. *Careful*—in this instance—was for men of small faith, men who professed belief then held back. That was not who he was. He knew that now. So he asked the last question on his mind, the one he dreaded most but had to voice, trusting that God would deliver the answer best for all of them: "Or do you think that Wendy will come live with you? That you'll take over seeing to it that she has food, shelter, clothing, an education, spiritual guidance, and the million other things a child needs to grow into a healthy, self-sufficient adult?"

He sensed Dixie stiffening behind him, but he kept his gaze fixed on Marcia. She shifted, looking from him to Fulton, then back again. "I don't…that is, I can't…I'm in between jobs right now and I'm living with…a friend, so I can't…" She scowled at him, but for just a fleeting moment, Riley thought he saw tears in her eyes. She looked down and when she lifted her head, any trace of tears were gone. "But just because everything isn't sunshine and rainbows in my life right now does not mean it never will be. I'm working on myself all the time and some-day—"

"Someday will be too late. Wendy needs security right now."

"My retaining my parental rights is no threat to that."

"Pardon me for saying this, Ms. Walker, but allowing Riley to go through with this adoption is the only thing that guaran-tees that." Fulton patted his hand in the air like someone soothing an agitated animal. "Otherwise the *threat*—your words not mine—is very real, and Wendy and her father have to live with the *threat* that someday a woman Wendy wants to know better, but who is, in fact, a stranger to her, could come in and alter her entire way of life."

"More than that, Marcia." Riley searched her wary eyes for any sign that they were getting through to her. "Don't you understand that if anything would happen to me, with the way things are now, Wendy might have to go into foster care? At least temporarily, because Mom just can't take care of her? If I adopt her, I can name a guardian in my will, or—"

"Why would she need that?" Marcia came to her feet. "She has *me*."

"You've got to be kidding!" Riley glanced at Dixie in time to see her cover her mouth, her eyes wide with chagrin at her outburst.

Marcia glowered at her, and Riley could tell she wanted to say something cutting and cruel.

He stepped between the two women. He was prepared to take the full brunt of his sister's contempt, but he would not let her make this about anything other than the truth. All Marcia's life they'd made excuses for her, let her divert the blame, let her spew her own misery over her poor choices out onto anyone that got in her way. Not now. He would make no allowances for her today, not where Wendy was concerned—and certainly not if she made Dixie the target of her venom. "Even you can't believe what you're saying, Marcia."

She opened her mouth, her cheeks flushed, her lips so taut against her teeth that they had almost no color at all. She looked so filled with rage that her shoulders actually shook from it and her fingers coiled into white-knuckled fists. When she spoke, she seemed to force the words out, her breathing ragged and shallow. "What *I* can't believe is that you would do this to me, Riley. My own brother, taking my child away from me?"

"Like you've ever spent a day of that girl's life caring for her, teaching her, loving her—"

"I have spent every day of her life loving her, Riley!" Her eyes flashed. This time the tears did come, rolling down her cheeks unchecked as Marcia raised her chin and whispered, "Every day."

He believed her, but he wondered if that was because he just wanted to so badly.

No…as she stood there, so alone in her silent sorrow, he had to believe. Riley stepped forward and put his arm around her shoulders.

Marcia tensed under his embrace, looked up to meet his gaze, then shut her eyes and sighed, relaxing just enough to put her hand lightly on his back.

He fought the emotions sweeping over him, threatening to steal his voice, his resolve. He drew a deep, steadying breath and said what he knew he had to say. "Severing your rights does not mean we are cutting you out of our lives, Marcia. We love you." He paused to clear his throat so that he could go on. "We will always love you and there will always be a place for you in our family, it just can't be as Wendy's mother."

His sister's response came out small, muffled against his shirt front. "If I don't fight for Wendy, I'm afraid she will think that I don't love her."

"Then when you're ready you come to see her, and we'll all work through it, and she'll know differently." Riley knew Marcia didn't believe in God, didn't have a foundation of faith, but he also knew everyone had a point where they must act on their deepest convictions or confess themselves as frauds. Marcia had just come to that point. "If you truly love Wendy, Marcia, then you have to put your own fears and feelings aside and do what's best for her. Please, for your little girl's sake, relinquish your rights so she can have a real family."

Eighteen

---◆---

Is any one of you in trouble?
He should pray. Is anyone happy?
Let him sing songs of praise.
JAMES 5:13

"I AM OVERWHELMED. ABSOLUTELY OVERWHELMED." RILEY SPREAD his hands out over the legal documents on Fulton's desk like a man admiring a stockpile of pure gold.

Dixie couldn't help herself. She hugged him. "Who can blame you? I think anyone would feel that way if they suddenly had all their most fervent prayers answered."

"Not *all* my prayers, Dixie."

"Well, no, of course, you didn't get your sister to agree to make contact with your mother or even get a very firm commitment that she'd so much as send Wendy a birthday card,

313

but she did sign over her parental rights. Now you'll be recognized legally for what you've always been: Wendy's Daddy."

"Wendy's Daddy…" The dampness in his eyes was offset by the sheer, delightful, goofiness of his grin.

Dixie's heart soared to see that blend of humility and joy in the man she loved. *The man with whom you can't share your love. Yes, he's just had a tremendous personal breakthrough, but that doesn't change the things that stand between us.* She sighed. It was true. She and Riley could not jeopardize their professional relationship for something as unpredictable as romance. So she'd just have to pray for a different rowboat to come along and rescue her from her loneliness and answer her longing for children and marriage.

She brushed her fingers through the thick black waves of Riley's hair and smiled to hide her sadness, even though she knew he could not see it. "Sometimes God answers our prayers in ways we can't fully comprehend. Sometimes the answers come a little at a time."

"Or not at all," Fulton added as he straightened a picture of his late wife on the wall. "But that doesn't mean we shouldn't celebrate the good stuff." He touched the narrow, gold frame on his daughter's soccer photo. "In fact, it means we've got to grab onto God's goodness with both hands and shout out our gratitude."

"Light a candle, don't curse the darkness, right?" Dixie caught Riley's eye and winked. Talk about a perfect opening to deal with Fulton and Lettie!

"Got to do that." Fulton turned away from the photographs. "Otherwise it's awfully easy to lose yourself in that darkness until it gets to be so comfortable for you there that you're actually a little afraid of the light."

Dixie took a deep breath and plunged in. "Is that how it is with you and Miss Lettie?"

A scowl passed over his face. His mouth opened then shut. He adjusted his wire-rimmed glasses. He huffed out a sigh. "My, but you are direct, aren't you?"

"I learned it from my daddy." She held her hands up as if to imply she held no liability in the matter. "In fact, I fired my last lawyer for not dealing with me in kind."

"You saying you're going to fire me if I don't make up with my grandmother?"

"Oh, lands sake, no!" She folded her arms and raised her chin. "But I might just employ that legal tactic you warned Riley about earlier."

"What legal tactic?"

"I believe you called it a…kick in the pants?"

"Don't turn your back on her, man, she'll do it." Riley swiveled the chair around and shot her a cocky grin, his eyes dark and appreciative. "Now that our worries over Wendy are under control, you know our Dixie is going to turn her full attention to getting you to reconcile with Miss Lettie. Trust me, as a man with some experience in dealing with this woman when she's got her mind set on something, you have only got two choices."

"And those are?" Fulton's suspicion sounded remarkably good-natured.

"Do it now or do it later." Riley held his hands up.

"Except we don't *have* a later, Fulton." Dixie ignored the smart-aleck shading this conversation had taken on and went straight for her point. "Miss Lettie will be one hundred in June, if she lives *that* long. She is old and frail and at the end of a very long and faithful life. Now, you've had more than twenty years to make up your mind to try to repair this rift between you. That's enough time. You have got to do this now."

"Are you speaking as my highest paying client or as Miss

Lettie's little lamb, Dixie?" The soft quality of his voice had such a powerful, aching sincerity that it drove any hint of harshness from the question.

Dixie moved toward the man then stopped, her breath caught in the back of her throat. Fulton had her mother's eyes. She had not noticed it before, or if she did it had not registered completely. But his eyes were so like those that had looked on her with unconditional love and acceptance when she was little, and so like the eyes she'd seen in even the sternest photos of her great-grandfather. Those eyes confirmed to her that this man deserved to know his heritage even while her heart told her that news could only come from one source. "I am talking to you as someone who loves Miss Lettie as if she were my own grandmother and has come to think of you as a trusted friend."

He set his jaw, then put his hand to his forehead. "I just…*she's* the one who said never to come back."

"Right or wrong, and for what it's worth, she tells me that was meant only for your father. And there's no sense in either of us pretending we don't have some idea why that was."

"Yes, granted. There were a lot of reasons why she might turn my dad away, but she knew doing that would turn my mother and me away, too. Why would she do that?"

"You're asking the wrong person, Fulton." She shut her eyes. "Why don't you come over to the house and put that question to your grandmother in person?"

"Do it now or do it later," Riley mumbled, making great pretense of organizing the papers on Fulton's desk.

Dixie nodded. "And please bring your daughter. Out of respect for your feelings I haven't told Miss Lettie that she has a great-grandchild, but do you know how much it would mean to her to find that out? To see your little girl?"

"If she wanted to know how my life has gone, if I have children or not, she could have made more of an effort to find out from me personally."

"Fulton, hon." Dixie did go to him now and touched his arm lightly.

He glanced down at her pale hand.

She could feel the tension working through him, but she did not back away. "Miss Lettie is one hundred years old, Fulton. I don't know how better to get that point across to you. The last time you saw her she was already, what? Eighty? She spends most of her days in bed either sleeping or watching her stories on TV. Or she sits in a rocker in the front parlor keeping time to hymns neither you nor I can hear. Her biggest exertion comes from commenting on the eccentricities of my family—which does, I admit, tend to keep her quite occupied."

"Your point is?" He did not remove her hand, but his back stayed as rigid as his attitude toward his grandmother.

"My point is, what exactly did you expect that ancient, little old lady to do to put things right with you again? She can't *drive* over here, or even ride over here. Just taking her to the doctor is an all-day, three-ring circus."

"With clowns." Riley's grin was evident even as he kept his head bowed over the files. "Lots and lots of clowns."

Dixie ignored him. "Miss Lettie can't hold a pen to write a letter, and has no means of finding what address to send it to if she could. Fulton, as long as I have been alive I don't think she's heard well enough to use the telephone, even if she decided she wanted to try it."

"She could have asked someone else to write or phone. She could have sent someone to find me."

"Hello?" Dixie did raise her hand now and gave a quick wave. "We're heeere!"

"Gee, I guess that means I *am* a rowboat." Riley looked up at no one particular.

"A what?" Fulton pushed up his glasses.

"It's that story about the man on the roof who prays for help and God sends a rowboat—" Dixie made a circular motion with one hand to imply that the story went on in that vein rather than rehash the whole thing.

"Oh, yes, sure. I've heard that one." Fulton nodded.

"Miss Lettie thinks Riley came as a rowboat in answer to my prayer for help, and I think you've been one, too. For me."

"And for me." The chair creaked as Riley leaned back slowly in it.

"Seems the least we can do is return the favor." Dixie made the assertion as firm as she could manage.

Fulton met her gaze. "With your sights set to help me or my grandmother?"

This she could answer with all her heart. "Both, Fulton. Both."

Fulton had put three conditions on his meeting with Miss Lettie. First, he did not want to introduce his daughter into the situation until he saw for himself that all old hostilities had been resolved. Second, he did not want Dixie's family lurking about, trying to get a peek at him or even to make him feel welcome in their home. And last, he wanted Dixie to stay in the room, at least at the beginning, to act as a buffer for the possibly awkward situation.

They fulfilled the first prerequisite easily. The minute Fulton's daughter, Sarah, and Wendy met, they found an instant affinity for one another. Six-year-old Wendy squealed with delight at having her first guest in to show her new bedroom, and eight-year-old Sarah reveled in her status as the sophisticated second-grader. When they added Peachie Too into the mix, the girls had found pure bliss secreted away upstairs, dressing the surpassingly obliging poodle up in her extensive wardrobe.

The second criteria had proved a bit trickier, but once Dixie realized that the day Fulton had finally consented to come over was a Thursday, she knew just what to do. Aunt Sis had been in rare form today, dolled-up in layers of lavender chiffon over violet taffeta as she set off to the Every-Other-Thursday-Afternoon Arts and Culture Society meeting. She'd been intent on introducing her new bosom buddy, Verdi Walker, to all the dear and precious ladies of her circle. Riley and the Judge did the honors of driving the women to the meeting, then waiting to bring them home again. While they waited, they planned to loose themselves on the town, paying special attention, Grandpa had promised, to the antacid department of Noni Philpot's drugstore.

That left only Fulton's last request. Dixie took a deep breath, glanced around the front parlor to make sure the Founder's old Bible was tucked out of sight, then went to the rocker. Gently she worked her fingers over Miss Lettie's thin hair. She'd spent most of the morning trying to put it into two neat braids that hugged the old woman's head along the top, then met in an antique cherish clasp at the back.

"Do I look pretty?" Miss Lettie gave a toothless grin that didn't hide how anxious Lettie was over seeing her grandson after all this time.

"Yes, you do. You look—" Dixie put her hand under the skeletal chin. She held her breath and blinked away the beginning of tears. How she loved this old woman. Loved her as if they were the ones that shared a relative by blood and not just by marriage. The family secret that had taken Dixie by surprise before seemed incidental now, an interesting footnote that had not altered how Dixie felt toward her cherished Miss Lettie one bit. It didn't take a notation in a Bible register to make them family—their own hearts had done that long ago.

"You look gorgeous, Miss Lettie." She leaned down and kissed the dark-skinned temple.

Lettie made a dry, smacking sound in the air, like a baby who is first learning the act instinctively mimics the kiss of a loved one.

"Are you ready to see Fulton again, then?"

"I'm so nervous I'm all a-shakin'." Lettie lifted her gnarled hand, showing Dixie the balled up embroidered handkerchief she'd been clutching as if to offer proof. "But then, I'm always a-shakin', so don't reckon Fulton will know the difference." She lowered her hand to her lap, inched up her chin, and set her chair to rocking. "Show my baby in, lamb."

Dixie went to Grandpa's office and rapped on the door. "She's ready now, Fulton."

"Sorry to foil your plans, Dixie." The front door swung open and Riley walked in.

"What are you doing here? Is Grandpa with you?" She strained to look outside to see if the old man was waiting in the car.

"No, I'm alone. Seems Smilin' Bob took the Every-Other-Thursday-Afternoon Arts and Culture Society by storm. The ladies had a fit over him. Last I saw, he was seated at a table surrounded by women as he told some tale about owning the town's first automobile dealership."

"That's all well and good, but Fulton specifically asked—"

"Say, is your grandfather some kind of judge or something?" Fulton stepped through the office door, one of Grandpa's business cards in his hand.

"Smilin' Bob definitely falls in the *or something* category, friend." Riley gave Fulton a resounding pat on the back. "My plans changed. Do you mind if I hang around here while you…"

"No, that'd be fine." Fulton handed Riley the card, then squared his shoulders, looking professional and dapper in his impeccable charcoal-colored suit. "Good."

"You're ready, then?" Dixie was so excited she thought she'd burst. She couldn't believe it was about to happen.

"As I'll ever be." He pointed toward the parlor across the entryway.

Dixie nodded. "Right through here." She led the way, Riley on her heels and Fulton right behind him so that he was the last of them to come into Lettie's sight.

"Praise the Lord, it's my baby!" What might have been a shout of exhalation from a younger person came more as an anguished whisper from Miss Lettie. "It's my *baby*."

Fulton froze a few steps inside the doorway. "Granny Lett."

"Granny Lett!" She put both hands over her mouth. "I had forgotten that you called me that, sweet, sweet Fulton."

"I…" He turned toward Dixie, his eyes shinning with what must have been quite unexpected tears. "I had no idea she'd look so small and fragile."

"She's frail. Yes, she is." Dixie put her hand on the man's back, tempted to give him a little shove to get him headed in Lettie's direction. "But a hug wouldn't break her."

"A hug?" He more breathed the words than spoke them, his brow furrowed. He looked at Lettie, then Riley, then Dixie. "I came here filled with such hurt and anger…"

Dixie felt her own eyes tear up. "I understand, but it seems a little useless to hold onto those feelings now, doesn't it? Now when you see that dear, old face?"

He adjusted his glasses.

"Talk to her," Riley urged. "She's still sharp as a tack."

"She can answer all your questions, even some you may not yet know you have." Dixie touched her mother's necklace, and when Riley put his hand on her shoulder she sighed and went on. "Together the two of you can find your way to forgiveness."

Fulton looked down, sniffled, then nodded his head. Slowly, like a man carrying a heavy load, he approached his grandmother.

"Praise the Lord. Thank you, Jesus." Lettie rocked and sang softly over and over again.

Fulton came to a halt right in front of her.

She stopped her rocker and looked up, this time only mouthing the words, "Thank you, Jesus."

Fulton just stood there, looking at her.

She looked back.

"Granny Lett, I have been so mad at you for so long for choosing this white family over your own flesh and blood that I don't know if I have it in me to forgive you for turning us away."

"I never turned you away, baby. Never you or my Helen Betty. Never."

"When you turned away my father, you did."

"Your father—" Lettie shut her eyes. Her tiny hands curled into fists in her lap. Her mouth angled downward in a grim scowl. "Your father took away from me every child I ever brung up to full-growed or loved with all my heart. Every child 'cept my Dixie Belle."

Dixie reached for Riley's hand. After all these years, she had thought Lettie might have forgiven Wallace Summers. To see now how deep the scars still ran took her breath away.

"Granny Lett, it was an *accident.*" Fulton pronounced the

last word slow and hard, but Dixie breathed a sigh of relief that it was without anger.

She understood. Regardless of his feeling about his grandmother's treatment of his family, no one could fault the old woman for the almost unendurable pain she associated with Fulton's father.

"It was an accident," Fulton repeated. "My father had not been drinking that night. The weather was bad…that dirt road was a mess from the rain and all the cars that had driven down it that evening going to that party."

"Dixie, no." At Riley's hushed whisper, she turned to him. "He's not saying—" Riley looked her in the eye.

Dixie swallowed hard but the cold, tight lump in her chest remained. She pressed her lips together, then closed her eyes because she could not bear to see the all-too familiar horror reflected in the eyes of someone hearing this story for the first time. Even if that someone was Riley.

She didn't know how she managed it, but she spoke softly. "Fulton's father was driving the Fulton's Cartage truck that hit my mother and Young Bobby's car that night."

He said nothing, just pulled her close.

Her whole life she longed for someone to do that. Everyone around her in the days after the accident had been too crippled by their own grief to even try to comfort her. That's why Baby Belle had meant so much to Dixie. That was why she had clung to the little doll and why, when Miss Lettie pulled herself up out of her own devastation to see Dixie's pain and then did what she could to ease it, Dixie had been forever grateful.

"Helen Betty was riding with her husband in that truck." Dixie clutched at the soft cotton of Riley's pale blue shirt, then turned her face into his strong chest. "She was killed that night along with my mother and my uncle."

"And my sweet Samantha." Miss Lettie croaked out the words, referring to Dixie's grandmother. "That precious child that Founder Fulton came all the way to New Orleans to fetch me home to raise. She died of a broken heart just after. Samantha, Geneva, Young Bobby, my very own Helen Betty… and you, Fulton. That Wallace Summers took them *all* away from me that night."

Riley nodded slowly. He understood now. Dixie could see it in his eyes. "So that's why Miss Lettie never allowed Wallace Summers in the house again."

"Actually, Granny Lett turned us away before that, when my father came to ask for money. He had stopped drinking and wanted to make a fresh start someplace new." Fulton looked down at his grandmother, his face obscured by the angle of his head, his voice unreadable. "When John Frederick Fulton-Leigh found out, he offered my father a job at the Cartage, driving a truck."

Dixie let out a long sigh. "My father bore the guilt over that decision all the rest of his life. He did not blame Wallace for the accident. He knew that was what it was, but he never forgave himself for the role he played in putting those events in action."

The room fell silent except for the ticking of the antique mantle clock and the ceaseless creaking of Miss Lettie's rocker.

"Daddy never forgave himself. Miss Lettie never forgave Wallace. Fulton can't seem to forgive Miss Lettie…" Dixie felt her lips trembling and her cheeks were wet with tears. "What an awful, awful legacy to ascribe to these people we loved so much."

Dixie sank into Riley's embrace.

"It's not too late to fix this." Riley kissed Dixie's temple then turned his head toward the others. "Fulton, Miss Lettie, I know you both to be good Christians and I know you've heard these words from James before but they bear repeating now. 'So faith by itself, if it has no works, is dead.' Letting all these years go by, hanging on to hatred and keeping old wounds fresh…that is not the witness I think either of you really want to give. Is it?"

Miss Lettie set her jaw. Clearly, she did not like someone talking to her like this, challenging the way she lived her spiritual walk. And yet, it was almost as though Dixie could see Riley's counsel and the words of his favorite Scripture seeping under that decades-old veneer of pride and condemnation. Fulton's return had gone a long way toward breaking through, too. Seeing him again must have been powerful medicine for the years of wasted suffering.

Fulton seemed hesitant, but not resistant. Dixie had known that once he had made the commitment to come over to see his grandmother he would be well on his way to reconciliation.

Riley gave the two stern but thoughtful looks. "It seems to me that it's time for you two to breathe life into your faith and do the work of forgiveness."

Fulton's shoulders rose, then fell.

Tears stained Miss Lettie's rich brown face.

"He never meant to hurt them. It was an accident." Fulton's whispered words were full of sorrow.

"I know, baby. I know." Lettie held one tiny, trembling hand out to her grandson.

In no longer than a heartbeat, he was on his knees in front of her, his arms around her, gingerly at first then holding her close.

"I am so sorry, baby," she murmured into his neck. "So sorry."

"I should have come to see you sooner." He lifted the hankie from her hand and used it to wipe away the dampness beneath her deep-set eyes. "I was wrong to hold it against you for so long, not to come to see you. Not to let you get to know my family."

"Family?" Lettie caressed her grandson's face. "What family?"

"I have a little girl, Granny Lett. We lost her mother about a year ago, so she's all I have…besides you, now."

Dixie cleared her throat and took a sidestep toward the table where the Bible lay hidden under Lettie's birthday journal. "Actually, I think you might be surprised at just how much family you have, Fulton."

"Dixie Belle is right, baby."

In two quick strides, Dixie stood at Fulton's side, the Bible in her hands open to the family register. "I think you ought to have this."

Fulton took the Bible from her, gave her a wary, confused look, then re-settled his glasses on the bridge of his nose and began to read. His eyes widened. "Is this…true?" He looked to Lettie for an answer.

She nodded.

Dixie clutched her hands together. "Your mother was supposed to tell you this when you turned twenty-one. Sadly, she never got that chance."

Fulton stammered for a moment, apparently unable to speak.

Dixie gently touched his shoulder, then spoke quietly enough that Miss Lettie could not hear her. "While you take a minute to absorb all this, do you mind if I call the girls downstairs? Miss Lettie is beginning to wear out, and I know she'd love to meet her great-granddaughter before she's too tired."

Fulton glanced up from the Bible to Dixie. "How long have you known this?"

"Only a few days. May I call Sarah down?"

"I…I don't know. I'm not sure I'm ready to deal with any of this, especially not in front of my child. My mother always deferred any question about her father, and I always assumed… well, I never assumed *this*." He splayed his fingers over the open pages. "I have to confess I am stunned by this information."

"Not an altogether inappropriate response to finding out you are related to this family…Cousin." She patted his back. "Now, may I call the girls?"

"Do it now or do it later," Riley hastened to remind Fulton.

Dixie offered her most dazzling smile, and Fulton nodded.

"I'll go get them. I've been looking forward to this." Riley hit the stairs at an upbeat stride.

Watching Riley's unmasked satisfaction over the outcome of this meeting, it suddenly dawned on Dixie that he had probably unloaded Grandpa on the ladies' club on purpose. Like it or not, Riley Walker obviously felt like he belonged in the heart of this intensely personal family matter. He clearly felt he *was* family.

Dixie could not conceal her smile at that thought. *Maybe someday…*

"I just don't know what to think, Granny Lett. I don't understand why no one ever told me, why the years and years of secrecy."

"It was a different time, baby."

"That's about as much of an answer as you're going to get, Fulton," Dixie whispered. "And if I may be perfectly blunt, it's about all you need."

Their gazes met.

"I won't pretend I can possibly understand what it's like growing up in these parts as anything but a fair-skinned woman of rank and privilege. I won't insult you like that, but I have to assume that your own experiences tell you something of what Miss Lettie and your mother would have faced if the truth had been known."

Overhead the thunder of giggling girls made her pause and look up, then rush on to finish. "This was the nineteen thirties, forties, and fifties. Things have changed, I can see it, but not so much that you can't understand the motives behind all this."

He nodded, his mouth grim. "Sometimes I'm not really convinced they've changed all that much at all."

"Daddy, Daddy! Guess what, guess what?" Sarah Summers burst onto the scene her arms spread wide and her pigtails flying. "Wendy and I are *twins!*"

"You're what?" Fulton cupped his hand to the back of his child's head.

"We're twins!" The girls cried in unison as Wendy came skipping into the parlor, with Riley strolling along behind her.

"We both love chunky peanut butter, chocolate milk, and stuffed animals. We can't stand it when the gravy slops onto our vegetables and we both think having our daddies pick out our clothes for us is for babies!" Sarah beamed.

"I like for Miss Dixie to pick out my clothes," Wendy added, her face quite serious as though she were breaking important news to her father.

"And we're both doubles!" Sarah announced.

"Doubles?" Fulton shook his head.

"Yes, Sarah Summers, Wendy Walker." Sarah's hands flew in bigger and bigger gestures as she tried to make what seemed ridiculously obvious to her clear to her befuddled dad. "S.S., W.W.! Doubles."

"That makes us *twins!*" Wendy reached for her newfound friend. Sarah reciprocated, and the two girls locked in a big bear hug.

Dixie smiled at them, then met Fulton's gaze. "Well, maybe

things haven't changed all that much, but there's still hope, don't you think?"

Fulton laughed his wonderful laugh and that was answer enough.

Nineteen

◆

Every good and perfect gift is from above,
coming down from the Father of the heavenly lights, who
does not change like shifting shadows.
He chose to give us birth through the word of truth, that
we might be a kind of firstfruits of all he created.
JAMES 1:17–18

"HOW DOES THIS AFFECT YOUR FAMILY, DIXIE?" FULTON, SITTING ON
the couch nearest Miss Lettie, took a sip of the iced tea she'd
brought in for him on a silver platter.

"Makes it bigger?" Dixie put her arms around both girls,
who were seated on the floor beside the footstool, gazing up at
Miss Lettie in her rocker. Riley had gone off to gather up the
arts and culture set, or at least this household's contribution to
it, and left Dixie and the others to talk over some of the more
practical details of their new discovery. "But if I were you,

Fulton, I'd be asking myself how does this effect me?"

"Why?"

"Ask me that after you've met Aunt Sis and my Grandpa. You can call him Smilin' Bob." Dixie reached over and patted Miss Lettie's hand. "Seems to me we've got ourselves another rowboat to help out when things get really wild around here."

Lettie cackled.

Fulton tugged at his collar, then pushed up his glasses.

Sarah sat up straight. "What do you mean a rowboat, Miss Dixie?"

"Oh, my, you don't know about the rowboats?" Dixie slapped her hand to her thigh. "Well, you have got to ask your great-granny about that, sweetheart, she will be ever-so-pleased to tell you. Isn't that right, Miss Lettie? Now you've got a whole new generation of children who haven't ever heard your stories and songs or benefited from your sage advise!"

"I'm happy as a hog on ice, I tell you, Dixie Belle!" Her hands made no sound as she patted them together, but her broad grin spoke volumes.

"A hog on what?" Sarah cocked her head.

Her father laughed. "It means she's quite content."

"It's a good thing," Wendy assured her new friend, speaking with an air of expertise about Miss Lettie's expressions.

"Oh." Sarah looked downhearted. "I thought maybe they had ice-skating hogs out here in the country. That sounded like something I'd like to see."

"I wouldn't mind seeing that myself, Sarah sugar." Miss Lettie beamed at the child.

Dixie held up her hands. "Well, for heaven's sake, don't mention it to Grandpa, he might get ideas."

Immediately both girls' faces lit up.

Fulton winced.

From the back of the house Peachie Too began barking.

"They're back." Wendy leapt up. "C'mon, Sarah, you have *got* to meet Peachie Too's mama! You'll know which one is her on account of they have the same color hair. And Grandpa Smilin' Bob—he can do magic tricks and he don't act like any grown-up you ever seen!"

"Saw," Dixie called after the girls scampering toward the back door. "They really aren't that bad, I promise. They're just full of—"

"Beans!" Miss Lettie interjected at the top of her hoarse voice.

"I was going to say full of life."

"Beans and vinegar, that's what they're full of." Lettie rocked steadily. "And silliness. Lah, dressing dogs up like they ain't got no better sense than to do such a thing. Moving things around in the drugstore out a sheer stubbornness and mischief, jabbing one another on the hind parts when a body is minding they own business under the dinner table…"

Fulton cleared his throat.

Dixie muffled the laughter she felt building. "That's not what it sounds like—"

"But you got to love them." Lettie held her hand up as if giving her testimony. "Yes, you do. They's family, after all. We belong together. And you got to love your family."

"*What* have those children done to my princess puppytoes?" Aunt Sis's shriek carried through the house with enough dramatic flare to do even her proud.

Wendy and Sarah glanced at one another, eyes wide.

Fulton scooted forward on the couch. "Girls, you didn't do anything to hurt the little dog, did you?"

"Oh no, Daddy, no. We just dressed her up in her cutest outfit." Sarah's smile was pure joy.

Riley helped his mother into the parlor and onto the sofa. "Fulton, this is my mother, Verdi Walker. Momma, this is Fulton Summers, the man I've told you about."

They exchanged greetings while Peachie Too growled in the background.

"Let me help you. Come to Mama, precious puppy."

The clicking of claws scrambling over the kitchen floor gave Dixie visions of Aunt Sis stooped over in her new chiffon-covered dress, chasing around in circles after that poor animal.

Peachie Too snapped.

Aunt Sis yelped.

Lettie laughed.

Riley joined her.

Verdi sighed.

The girls huddled together.

Dixie smiled at Fulton like nothing unusual was going on.

And then in walked the Judge, his chest out, head high, a carnation clearly appropriated from the club centerpiece in his lapel and a telltale smudge of rose-red lipstick on his cheek.

"Grandpa, this is Fulton—"

"Yes, Miss Lettie's grandson." The older man grabbed Fulton's hand and gave it a hearty shake. "I'd give you one of my cards, but I'm fresh out." He made a show of searching the pockets in his jacket just the same, then leaned in, gave Fulton a wink and an elbow jab to the ribs. "Gave them all away to some female admirers, if you know what I mean."

"Yes, sir."

"Oh, no, none of that. Don't call me *sir,* call me Smilin' Bob. Or better yet, *Uncle* Smilin' Bob. Your dear mother, Helen Betty, was my late wife Samantha's half-sister."

"Actually, I'm not sure that I'm comfortable with that—"

"Ah, but this little gal is. Your daughter?" He pointed to

Sarah, made some motions with his hand, and produced another carnation out of thin air.

Sarah gasped.

He offered her the flower. "You'll call me Uncle Smilin' Bob, won't you?"

Sarah gave him a shy smile. "Thank you, yes. When are you going to teach the hog to ice-skate, Uncle Smilin' Bob?"

"The…" Grandpa's face scrunched up in confusion. "We don't have hogs, darling."

Both girls frowned.

"'Course, that don't mean we can't *get* some."

They brightened up again, and Dixie groaned. "I think one unpredictable poodle is quite enough, Grandpa."

"Gotcha!" Aunt Sis's triumphant cry made Fulton jump.

"Girls! Girls! I want you to please explain to me this unthinkable act you have perpetuated on my sweet Peachie Too." Sis stomped into the parlor holding Peachie Too around the midsection, an arm's length away. The poodle squirmed and wriggled and snarled, arching its back in an unmistakable effort to take a chunk out of Aunt Sis at all costs.

"Th-that dog! It was so docile before." Fulton looked down at the children clinging to each other on the floor like survivors in a life raft. "What did you girls do?"

"Nothing, Daddy. Honest."

"Nothing but dress her up." Wendy nodded.

"Nothing? Dress her up?" Sis's face flushed with her outrage.

"The dog is really very calm—" Verdi leaned in to whisper to Fulton—"with everyone but her owner."

"You dressed her up all right. In her *white* outfit, of all things. White!" She scanned the group as though she had just delivered the name of the real killer seconds before they condemned the wrong man.

"We think it's some kind of vibration she picks up from Sis that makes Peachie Too—"

"Don't you see it? *White*? Before Memorial Day!"

"High-strung," Verdi summed up.

"Crazy as a loon," Miss Lettie announced. "Like mother like dog, I always say."

The Judge hee-hawed at that.

Sis scowled.

Fulton looked like he needed some fresh air.

"If you don't like what the girls have Peachie Too wearing, just go change the outfit, Aunt Sis." Dixie stood, her smile plastered on.

"I can't leave. It would be rude, I have not been properly introduced to—" She stepped toward Fulton, the agitated dog still clasped in her hands.

Riley intervened, taking the dog and dropping it down to the girls. He made the introductions, then asked Wendy and Sarah to go put Peachie Too in a more suitable outfit as a favor to Aunt Sis's rattled nerves.

Dixie sighed. "If ya'll will excuse me, I'm going to go get some tea for the new arrivals."

She started toward the kitchen, feeling a little shaken, but all in all quite content with the way things had gone. Though not every bump in the new and the long-standing relationships had been smoothed out, this initial meeting had gone a long way toward mending fences and making new friendships.

Lord, you've certainly brought answers to many, many prayers. I know you'll continue to nurture the seeds that have been planted for things yet unresolved.

Riley hadn't been able to patch things up with Marcia, but he was going to adopt Wendy. Fulton and Miss Lettie hadn't worked out all their feelings or all the issues about their past and what they would do with their future, but Miss Lettie had her grandson back in her life. And a new great-granddaughter, too.

The businesses had a new boss in Riley, and Dixie knew he would keep things running well and move them ahead with confidence and character. Verdi was on the mend, and Grandpa had a veritable fan club. Everything had worked out so well for everyone.

Well, everyone but Dixie and Sis. Sis, because running the household still took her away from her more *creative* pursuits, as she might describe them, and Dixie…

Dixie glanced over her shoulder at the people gathered together. Her very being radiated with love for them all. And yet…

Despite her gratitude over everything God had blessed her with, she couldn't deny the sensation that washed over her then. Loneliness. Pure and simple.

"Isn't this lovely?" Aunt Sis cooed. "After all these years our family is complete."

Dixie lingered at the door a moment longer, then her eyes met Riley's.

"Not quite complete, Aunt Sis," Riley said, not taking his eyes from Dixie's. "Would you excuse me while I see if Dixie needs me for anything in the kitchen?"

He came toward her, his gaze intense, and suddenly she felt her pulse race and her mouth go dry. His mouth crooked with only the suggestion of that disarming grin that stole her breath away now just as it had the very first time she saw it.

He came to stand beside her, leaning close until his mouth was next to her ear. "Let's go in to the kitchen and see what we can stir up."

"Stir up?" she murmured, the words coming out almost

slurred thanks to her suddenly confused brain. How did he *do* that? How did he make her head spin just by standing close to her? Well, she just wouldn't let him see how he affected her.

"You know." He moved closer to her. "Like the tea."

"The—oh yes! The tea!" She giggled. Mortification swept over her. She had wanted to appear savvy and smart and clever and unaffected by his nearness—and here she'd gone and giggled! Immediately, she turned and led the way, unsure if her legs had the strength to carry her.

Beans. Beans and vinegar. Full of beans and vinegar…and silliness. The sobering thought left Dixie feeling depressed. How could she harbor any notion that Riley had changed his mind about the two of them getting involved? Why, she need only think about the scene they'd just watched in the parlor to know that wasn't so.

Beans and silliness, that's all her romantic ideas amounted to.

Who was she to think that Riley Walker would take a chance on loving her? On having her become the mother of his child? The mother of his children? Her heart thumped wildly at the idea of having a family with this man who now stood so close she felt his shirt sleeve chafe against her arm as he reached for the sugar jar.

"Dixie Belle Fulton-Leigh?" Riley set the sugar down and tugged her arm to get her turned to face him.

"Prescott," she whispered, losing herself in his wonderful eyes.

"What?"

"My middle name is Prescott. Belle is just a nickname that Miss Lettie gave me." She wet her lips. "Dixie Prescott Fulton-Leigh. *That's* who I am."

He inched closer still, and she backed up until her back

was against the counter. His eyes were on her mouth now. "That's a lot of names."

"I've heard of folks with more."

"Guess you'd be one of those folks."

She frowned. "I-I would?"

He nodded, a slow smile lifting his lips. "Uh-huh, if you had a married name."

She blinked. "Not if my husband took my maiden name instead of the other way around."

He put his knuckle under her chin and tipped it up to put her lips into perfect kissing position. "Don't count on that happening, Dixie Belle Prescott—Princess Snootie-Patootie—Fulton-Leigh."

"Don't call me—"

"How about I just settle for calling you...my wife?"

If he hadn't kissed her then, she'd have done something truly graceful and becoming of her upbringing, like leap with joy, hit her head on the cabinet, break open her skull, and have to be rushed to the emergency room. Where she'd probably get amnesia and forget Riley's proposal ever even happened.

And that was one thing she simply would *not* do!

She wrapped her arms around his neck and returned his kiss with all the joy and passion in her heart. Forget this? Never!

When he finally lifted his head, she stared at him, trying to make sense of it all. "I don't understand, though, Riley. I thought we said we'd just stay friends."

His smile was tender and amused. "We will stay friends, Dixie, for the rest of our lives. Because the thing is, I can't imagine the rest of today, let alone the rest of my life, without the best friend I've ever had sharing it with me. I want you to marry me, Dixie Belle. I love you with all my heart, and once I realized that, you know I had to act on it."

Love? The moment she heard the word her pulse picked up. Her thoughts whirled. Her cheeks went hot even as the sudden heaviness in the pit of her stomach felt cold as ice. She had not been looking for love, only help and guidance. And yet, when she looked into Riley's eyes, she could not deny what she saw there. She could not deny her own feelings. "I love you, too, Riley. I just can't believe this is happening."

"Did I ever tell you that the first time I saw you I knew I was in over my head?" Riley brushed her hair off her temple.

She didn't even try to stop the smile that eased over her features. "Did I ever tell you that the first time I saw you…"

"Yes?"

"I thought you were king of the great big Bubba-goobers?"

"King, huh?" He struck a cocky pose. "Well then, when you marry me, it'll be a step up, Princess—"

This time she kissed him before he could get the teasing title out.

"So can I take that as a yes?" He cradled her in his arms.

"Yes." She shut her eyes. Her heart sang with thanksgiving and she looked at the man God had brought into her life, the man who had helped her heal her family, hang on to her business, and now would be her life's companion. Her heart had wings as she laughed, threw her arms around Riley again, and sang out her response. "Yes. Oh, *yes,* I will marry you!"

Riley watched Dixie pick up the beautiful pen she'd had the day they'd first met. He smiled as she slowly inscribed on the first line of the family register in the brand-new family Bible they'd received as a wedding present from Fulton: *Riley Aaron*

Walker and Dixie Prescott Fulton-Leigh united in Holy Matrimony...

"Looks good." He took the heavy Bible from her, closed it, and laid it on the table with the rest of their gifts. "But the reception has been over for an hour. Don't you think we really ought to be going? I try to be a patient man—"

"Since when?" Dixie laughed, tossing back the shiny hair that Riley longed to run his hands through.

"I know you hate to say good-bye to the family, hon, but it's only for ten days. When we come back you'll get to see them all the time—considering you're now going to stay home and be a full-time Mom to Wendy so Sis can resume her...uh, *normal* lifestyle."

"Now there's a phrase I bet you don't hear too often—*Sis's normal lifestyle*." Fulton laughed as he came into the room. "Don't you two have a honeymoon to go on? What are you doing hanging around here?"

"There are just a few more things I need to make sure are taken care of." Dixie held up the pen. "Here, take this. I've been using it to write down Miss Lettie's life story. We're up to just after your mother was born, so I was thinking you might really enjoy jotting down anything she wants to share while we're away."

"Can do." Fulton took the pen.

"And then..."

"And then it's time for us to leave." Riley put his hands on her waist and guided her forward, loving the way she blushed. "Fulton has everything under control. He's familiar with the workings of the businesses, so if the people we've left in charge have a problem they know to call him."

"Be sure you run everything through Mavis Hornby, Fulton." Riley's sweet bride resisted his gentle urging just enough to slow them down, but not enough—he noted with a grin—to bring them to a halt. "She knows the whole story about the family and your position in it. I know we decided not to let the word out over town out of deference to Miss Lettie and until we had a better feeling for the response, but Mavis understands and she'll take up for you if there's any trouble."

"Got it. Mavis."

"And I know it's summer and that's why you're able to come over and keep watch on the loony bin while we go off on our honeymoon, but don't let Wendy stay up too late and—"

"And don't worry." Fulton held up his hand. "Everything will be fine."

Dixie stopped.

"Oh no." Riley sighed, fearing she'd had a total change of mind about going off and leaving the family and would suddenly insist they take their honeymoon in the attic or some such convenient yet out of the way place. "Dixie, *please*. Fulton can handle this."

"I know he can." She exhaled and stepped away from him. "Did I ever tell you, Fulton, that you have my mother's eyes?"

"Do I?" He smiled.

"Thank you for everything you've done for us." She reached out and gave him a hug, and for the first time Riley could remember, Fulton did not tense, but returned Dixie's affection with warmth and ease.

Yes, things were going to be just fine. On every front.

"Okay, now go, you two. Have fun and God bless."

Riley showed his beautiful wife to the door, smiling. He glanced around his new home…he could see them raising Wendy—and, God willing, other children as well—here in this place of love, laughter, and faith. He met the sparkling eyes of his beautiful bride, and his heart swelled with a peace and joy he'd never known before. "Yes, God has blessed us and I know he will continue to do so. It may take some time to see it come to fruition—" he grinned and gathered Dixie close—"but he blesses us. He truly does."